Understanding Teaching-Learning Practice

Series Editor

Peter Goodyear, University of Sydney
Sydney, VIC, Australia

This series publishes research on contemporary teaching-learning practices, and in particular, studies that provide evidence of the intertwined relationship between how practice informs research and how the outcomes of research can effectively inform practice. The series publishes studies that make use of diverse methodologies and conceptual framings that foreground real-world practice and trace the connections between teaching, learning activities and experiences, and learning outcomes. Focusing on research that goes beyond disciplinary, sectoral and national borders, the series reflects the following views on understanding teaching-learning practice:

- Student learning is central: one cannot understand effective teaching without understanding successful learning.
- Evidence of the quality and character of teaching-learning practice is best understood in context; the broader landscape in which it occurs must figure prominently in its analysis.
- A real-world application of research outcomes to improve teaching-learning is best informed by a real world analysis of its practice; the challenge lies in completing the circle.
- Innovations in learning and teaching practice, including those which involve new technologies, create quality, coherence and sustainability issues, which need to be addressed.

The series acknowledges the growing complexity of learning and teaching activities in context and studies the roles of digital and material tools and new spaces in teaching and learning. In doing so, it recognises the increasingly diverse nature of educational work and aims to publish studies combining multiple data sources to create richer, robust, more interpretable, more action-oriented evidence.

The ongoing goal of the series is to improve the scholarliness of practice - helping it to be better informed by research - and synergistically, to improve the practical applicability of research designs and outcomes.

For more information, or to submit a proposal, please email Grace Ma: grace.ma@springer.com

Yael Yondler • Nissim Avissar • Dovi Weiss
Editors

Cultivating Future-Oriented Learners

Polyphonic Education in a Changing World

Springer

Editors
Yael Yondler
Kibbutzim College of Education
Technology and Arts
Tel Aviv, Israel

Nissim Avissar
Kibbutzim College of Education
Technology and Arts
Tel Aviv, Israel

Dovi Weiss
Kibbutzim College of Education
Technology and Arts
Tel Aviv, Israel

ISSN 2522-0845 ISSN 2522-0853 (electronic)
Understanding Teaching-Learning Practice
ISBN 978-3-031-63255-6 ISBN 978-3-031-63253-2 (eBook)
https://doi.org/10.1007/978-3-031-63253-2

This Springer imprint is published by the registered company Springer Nature Switzerland AG
The registered company address is: Gewerbestrasse 11, 6330 Cham, Switzerland

Preface: Evolving Polyphonic Education in a Teacher Training College

In this book, we introduce an innovative humanizing educational paradigm. The paradigm aims to assist educators in designing a technology-rich learning environment that encourages learners to delve into real-life skills while nurturing humanistic inclusion, dialogue, and empathy values. We maintain that practical experience is a good way for learners to gain life skills and democratic values and turn them into an inseparable part of their personalities. Such a solid, value-based backbone will make them thriving members of a democratic society and help them contribute to their fellowmen.

A paradigm is born when new ideas reshape thinking fundamentals (Robinson, 2011). Various ongoing processes create favorable conditions for change: Technology has changed our approach to learning and thinking, and the COVID-19 pandemic has accelerated socio-cultural changes that introduce constant changes and uncertainty into our reality (the VUCA age—Volatility, Uncertainty, Complexity, and Ambiguity). Additionally, various threats in different areas characterize our time: democracy is under threat worldwide, and ecological, economic, and cultural crises shadow the world. We maintain that educational systems and processes are central to contending with these challenges and driving the change processes required to cope with them. Teacher education institutions must, therefore, prepare teachers-to-be to adapt to the volatile conditions and respond to the needs of their students and society in general.

These circumstances spurred the emergence of the proposed paradigm, given that changing rules and assumptions also change practices. We are increasingly aware of the central role of teachers in their capacity as educators, who are not merely "teaching technicians" but guide their students in shaping their identities, instilling in them values in response to burning issues. The proposed innovative, humanizing paradigm opens before teacher-educators ways to contend with the challenges they face. We have named it **the polyphonic paradigm.**

Polyphony in Education

Polyphony, originating in ancient Greek, means multiple voices. In the educational context, it represents a conceptual approach that allows for the simultaneous existence of two or more voices, where each voice is complete in itself, and no voice is secondary to the other voices (Naot-Ofarim & Solomonic, 2016). The educational concept deriving from this paradigm leans on a value-based worldview combining two educational approaches: humanizing and constructive-social. The response this combination offers enables learners to function successfully in the twenty-first-century global world, encouraging learner co-agency (OECD, 2017). We see this combination as beneficial as it enhances learners' well-being, individual mental and social welfare, and the communal welfare of society.

Technology has a significant role in the polyphonic paradigm. Consistent with the two combined educational approaches, technology assists educators in designing polyphonic, multi-spatial learning environments. Thus, the paradigm sets out from the understanding that nowadays, educators must be able to use technology in designing a learning environment that couples individual and collaborative learning spaces. In the individual knowledge spaces, teachers provide differential responses to the learners, encouraging them to build their knowledge independently, assert themselves, and actualize their potential. In collaborative spaces, teachers urge learners to communicate and collaborate toward creating products jointly while fostering collective knowledge for the community's common good. Hence, the polyphonic educational paradigm offers teachers a conceptual educational framework that functions as a "polyphonic lens," allowing them to scrutinize their approaches and practices in a changing reality. The paradigm aims to assist them in building "polyphonic wisdom" and putting together "a new whole," allowing for self-contemplation.

The polyphonic perspective was also the basis for setting up the community of the book's writers. In the context of teacher education, the polyphonic worldview facilitates in practice the emergence of pedagogical and technological innovation communities within a teacher training institute, applying the "knowledge-building community" methodology (Scardamalia & Bereiter, 1994, 2006). The purpose of these communities is professional development through learning or building a new body of knowledge. Such communities may be directed top-down and practice formal learning. However, more often than not, they actualize their unique learning potential (DuFour, 2004), directed bottom-up by the community members without a prior agenda or formal structuring (Vangrieken et al., 2017). A polyphonic worldview corresponds to the "knowledge-building community," as both maintain that diverse opinions are powerful and capable of building and expanding knowledge for the community's common good. In practice, both openly cultivate mutual relations between the personal and collective good in a structured manner. While encouraging individual learners to build personal knowledge and optimize their abilities and skills (Aloni, 2022), they also offer them interaction opportunities that contribute to building collective knowledge.

The process described below is an experience-based illustration of how a polyphonic worldview leaning on the knowledge-building community methodology gives birth to an innovative pedagogy in an educational institute in a spiral, bottom-up, and top-down movement. These two directions feed each other, generating growing knowledge. Such spiral processes embody the essence of a democratic polyphonic worldview attentive to the emergent needs of the field and the individuals functioning within it. It encourages individual proactiveness and considers group diversity a resource toward personal and collective knowledge building, where the whole exceeds the sum of its parts.

The Community's Story

The process began in 2017, when Kibbutzim College of Education, the largest teacher education college in Israel, opened two classrooms featuring innovative learning spaces. Another one followed a year later. At that time, Israel's Ministry of Education published a call for setting up 1500 innovative learning spaces that challenge the traditional classroom layout. The new learning spaces, titled Future Learning Spaces (FLS), were equipped with advanced digital and other means. Each of these spaces had the potential to illustrate various advanced pedagogical models combining technological and physical means. This top-down opening move represented the perception that a teachers' education institute is a change agent, should be attentive to the lecturers' needs and ongoing future-oriented changes, and must venture to innovate and rejuvenate. Thus, based on the assumption that a teacher is not a "sage on stage" but a partner in the learning process, the college decided to train future teachers in using innovative learning spaces and create opportunities for the students to experience knowledge building (Yondler & Blau, 2021).

To encourage using the FLSs in their first year, the teacher educators who were willing to use them received techno-pedagogical support from a member of the college digital pedagogy team. They were free to practice teaching-learning in any way they thought best. This exploratory process, where the teachers had complete freedom of action, made utilizing the FLSs a bottom-up experiment with unpredictable results. The teachers who used the FLSs that year expressed their professional satisfaction and noted the FLSs' contribution to the learning quality. In the second year, a knowledge-building professional teachers' body began to form, with a two-directional top-down and bottom-up nature. The top-down element involved research literature that indicated the need for FLS teaching practices and discussed the complex interrelations between space and the other mediators of learning (Kali et al., 2015). The complementary bottom-up direction emerged after the first exploratory year taught the participants they should join forces to build pedagogical and theoretical knowledge based on the FLS experience. Consequently, we became an active professional community intent on creating the collective knowledge required to conceptualize innovative teaching models in FLSs. The community functioned as a "collective brain" within a kind of innovative human laboratory, where the members experience each FLS teaching and contribute their experience to the community's collective knowledge. As such, the community explored, examined, shared, discussed, and documented new models, thus building knowledge. Throughout the process, it sought to find a response to the theoretical and practical challenge that emerged from the literature: How FLS teaching redefines teaching with regard to its three main components—pedagogy, space, and technology (Radcliff, 2009). The community also resolved to share the evolving knowledge with the college faculty members and colleagues from other academic institutions in various ways, such as workshops, conferences, and article writing. These prepared the ground for writing this book.

Writing the Book

The described chain of events motivated the community members to jointly launch an academic writing project to advance the theoretical conceptualization of the practical experiences under the guidance of this book's editors. We began by organizing the available information and formulating the unique characteristics of each teaching model. Initially, we asked the community members to complete each an identical table describing their model's elements and value, including title, abstract, background, theory-practice links, theoretical and practical contribution, conclusions and summary, and a paragraph dedicated to the writers' personal experience, titled "On a personal note." The table kept updating over the process, and following the polyphonic spirit, the chapters took on a similar structure while highlighting the uniqueness of each. We repeatedly asked the writers to highlight the synergy between space, technology, pedagogy, and content in each model, and its contribution to educational theory and practice. Having read the completed tables, we returned them to the authors for corrections, refinements, and expansions. We also invited expert community members to assist the writers in assimilating the essentials of the evolving conceptual framework—humanism and collectivity in physical and digital spaces.

The detailed tables were the basis for the next stage—writing the chapters. We read them, and after several rounds of revision, they underwent peer review and were re-emended. This elaborate process created a common language between the community members, elucidating the complex relations between theory and practice and between pedagogy, technology, space, and content. Like the community's knowledge building, we attached much importance to implementing the polyphonic approach in the book writing process, ensuring that the book's purpose, content, and writing were congruent. The main challenge was shaping work modes where the particulars converged into one polyphonic composition while the whole shaped the "how" and "what" of the particulars. With this in mind, the editors, in a top-down move, guided the writers in using a focused terminology to describe their polyphonic model. A complementary bottom-up move followed, where the writer had to describe their model's unique polyphonic combination of pedagogy, space, technology, and content. This dialogue-based process yielded an indicator that helped create a common lexicon and outline for all the chapters.

The Book's Structure

The book's structure follows the worldview underlying the polyphonic paradigm, highlighting the tension between unity and uniqueness. Its first two chapters—a foreword and an introduction—are the umbrella that brings together the other book chapters. The foreword, *A Polyphonic Humanizing View of Pedagogy and Technology*, written by Punya Mishra and Lok-Sze Wong, points out the book's added value in times of educational crisis. Punya Mishra, whose TPACK model (Mishra & Koehler, 2006; Mishra, 2019), is the basis for integrating technology into education and is a world authority in this field. The introductory chapter, *Technology, Values, Pedagogy, and Multiple Learning Spaces: Creating a "New Whole" in a Complex Reality* by Yael Yondler and Nissim Avissar describes the polyphonic approach principles, setting a theoretical basis for the book. It is followed by 13 chapters organized in four parts, each feeding the polyphonic composition. Each chapter introduces a specific teaching, learning, and assessment model responding to a particular socio-educational issue, illustrating an option for implementing the polyphonic approach in education and teacher training.

Below is a brief description of the book's four parts and their chapters by order of appearance.

The chapters of the Part I engage with issues of diversity and inclusion in education. They explore ways to contend with culturally diverse individuals and groups and their interrelations in educational frameworks. The first chapter by Miri Shonfeld introduces a teaching model that uses virtual platforms and tools to advance collective learning and intercultural skills. The model, which highlights gamification components leading to enjoyable experiential learning, paves the way for learning in 3D worlds. Students from two colleges participated in a competition styled after the television program *Race for a Million*, where teams competed in performing various tasks. The participants gained social experience in a varied learning space that allowed for interrelations and brought the groups closer while enhancing identity and belonging elements. In the second chapter, Miri Yochana's teaching model uses collaborative learning of English as a second language to introduce diverse identities. To achieve the model's goals, she assigned a learners' group to design a teaching unit engaging with issues of diversity and fairness and implement it in practice by teaching another group. Over the process, the students learn from each other and contend with social and cultural dilemmas using various digital teaching aids. They develop multicultural skills along with pedagogical proficiency and technological literacy. In the third and last chapter of Part 1, Tami Seifert connects two worlds that seem very far apart: social media in an intercultural virtual space context and body movement in various physical spaces. This type of learning generates numerous simultaneous events involving different social interactions. They spur the students to grow as learners capable of mediating knowledge resources, cultures, and diverse viewpoints to design learning environments. Combining physical movement with social media experiences expands the platform and, at the same time, enables the students to self-expand and express themselves.

The Part II comprises two chapters focusing on issues of sustainability and socio-environmental accountability in a glocal context and on implementing the eco-humanistic approach in education (Aloni & Veugelers, 2023). Chapter 4 by Dafna Gan and Adiv Gal engages with current eco-humanistic challenges, such as climate change, refugee immigration, invasive species, and decreased biodiversity. The authors propose a transformative education model that promotes personal and social change through active, collective, outdoor learning (on the beach, on a riverbank, and in the desert), applying various digital pedagogy tools. An enjoyable multi-channeled learning experience acquaints the students intimately with various natural resources and the threats they face. It develops their critical thinking and urges them to take action toward reducing the environmental crisis. In Chap. 5, Netta Baryosef-Paz and Dafna Gan introduce another facet of eco-humanistic education combining sustainability, literature, and art. Their model illustrates a holistic, interdisciplinary learning option that uses multiple pedagogical spaces in a non-hierarchical and non-chronological manner. The proposed learning mode challenges the traditional teaching and learning patterns, replacing them with a flow that creates a challenging uncertainty, requiring both teachers and students to re-adapt and be flexible. The contemplation accompanying these experiences gives rise to a comprehensive student experience and the realization that sustainability is omnipresent.

The Part III comprises three chapters engaging with dialogue between different, even opposing, approaches, namely, the ability to move between different viewpoints and explore reality through each. In Chap. 6, Efrat Harel introduces a teaching model whose purpose is to advance multicultural preschool education. The students form four groups (four homes with four mothers), representing different approaches to a predefined educational-linguistic issue. They engage in a debate that heightens the awareness of each group to the different rationale of the other groups' approaches. In the process, the participants develop listening and inclusion skills while re-exploring their own identities.

In the model introduced by Guy Moshe Pinku in Chap. 7, the students form four groups to discuss public matters based on Dewey's educational approach. The model confronts polarization trends and a shallow, harsh, public and educational discourse, offering an alternative pertinent, critical, fact-based discussion. Initially, the students determine their individual stands on the discussed issue. They then formulate with their group co-members arguments supporting a stand different than theirs, applying elements of contemplation and self-assessment. Following the experiential part, they learn its theoretical rationale and are introduced to Dewey's approach.

Chapter 8, the last in this part, aspires to cultivate dialogue skills through reading and role-playing. Lily Glasner aims to encourage teachers-to-be and their future students to read for pleasure, that is, regard reading as an activity that creates interest, enthusiasm, and involvement. To this end, they engage in a digital role-playing game revolving around a controversial topic or dilemma. Each participant assumes the role of a figure having a particular stand about the discussed topic. It is a dynamic, amusing game involving a lively real-time debate. After hearing each stand, the others react to it. In the process, the figures and stories come to life, offering collectively a sweeping interpersonal experience.

The last Part IV is dedicated to fostering self-direction and independent learning skills. Its chapters explore ways to develop independent, resilient learners with a sense of self-efficacy, capable of navigating their learning and life in our complex world. In Chap. 9, Efrat Kotzer addresses the challenge of differential learning, where students learn in individually tailored diverse ways, channels, and paces. The presented model follows the Universal Design Learning (UDL) approach. It helps develop various learning skills related to learned content using visual and auditory means to represent and express the knowledge acquired. This learning process can assist learners in identifying their strengths and discovering the learning method that best suits them, while creating an inclusive and equal educational and social environment.

Chapter 10 focuses on online learning, which currently occupies a significant place in educational systems and is predicted to expand further in the future. Adva Margaliot and Dvora Gorev describe a process of collaborative online learning. The process peaks with the students designing complex learning activities combining technology, pedagogy, and humanistic values. Special attention is given to promoting motivation, efficient learning, autonomy, creativity, and innovation. These elements advance all self-learning and self-direction (personal growth), yet none is self-evident in an asynchronous online course.

In Chap. 11, Ayelet Weizman introduces an innovative model of space education that helps contend with uncertain situations characterizing our time. Over the study period, the students face increasingly complex challenges combining content, technology, and pedagogy within a supportive, enabling environment. The learning combines advanced technologies with innovative pedagogies in contexts of education and space and boosts the ability to cope with complex challenges and improve self-efficacy and mental resilience. These are vital personal resources in an era characterized by volatility, uncertainty, complexity, and ambiguity.

Tal Shemer-Elkayam's model in Chap. 12 derives from the multiple-intelligence theory and project-based learning (PBL), creating a basis for teaching and learning processes that respond to learner diversity and enhance individual strengths. The learners' assignment is collectively producing an applicative digital product using the different individual strengths of the group members. It offers the students multiple choices and allows for considerable learner autonomy.

In Chap. 13, the last in Part 4, Miki Kritz introduces a teaching model using multiple screens displaying simultaneously different aspects of a learned topic to enable exploring the interaction between them. The model enables students to study and experience the perspectives of the teachers' trainer, the teacher, and the students in parallel. After learning how to use a particular techno-pedagogical tool, the students carry out activities related to the roles of schoolteachers and students. The activities include creating a product using the learned tool and presenting it to the group. This structure allows for learning in various channels while keeping aware of different perspectives and parallel processes.

Nimrod Aloni, a leader in humanizing education in Israel, concludes the book with an epilogue titled *Holding the Stick at Its Two Ends: Humanizing Empowerment and Technological Power in the Service of Education and Learning*. The chapter discusses the value of the polyphonic approach in the current ongoing educational crisis. Aloni suggests that collaborative humanizing pedagogy in hybrid learning spaces is vital for future education in a changing society. Such an approach will advance a more humanistic and less polarized society that allows for individual voice diversity, yielding a complex, broad-horizon collective composition.

Tel Aviv, Israel

Nissim Avissar
Yael Yondler
Dovi Weiss

References

Aloni, N. (2022). Empowering agency in the ethical, political, and the teaching/learning spheres of education: An integrative model of activist pedagogy. In D. Yitzhaki, T. Gallagher, N. Aloni, & Z. Gross (Eds.), *Activist pedagogy and shared education in divided societies: International perspectives and next practices*. Brill-Sense.

Aloni, N., & Veugelers, W. (2023). Ecohumanism, democratic culture, and activist pedagogy: Attending to what the known demands of us. *Educational Philosophy and Theory*, https://doi.org/10.1080/00131857.2023.2295216

DuFour, R. (2004). What is a "professional learning community?" *Educational Leadership, 61*(8), 6–11.

Kali, Y., Sagy, O., Kuflik, T., Mogilevsky, O., & Maayan-Fanar, E. (2015). Harnessing technology for promoting undergraduate art education: A novel model that streamlines learning between classroom, museum, and home. *IEEE Transactions on Learning Technologies, 8*(1), 5–17

Mishra, P. (2019). Considering contextual knowledge: The TPACK diagram gets an upgrade. *Journal of Digital Learning in Teacher Education, 35*(2), 76–78. https://doi.org/10.1080/21532974.2019.1588611

Mishra, P., & Koehler, M. J. (2006). Technological pedagogical content knowledge: A framework for teacher knowledge. *Teachers College Record, 108*(6), 1017.

Naot-Ofarim, Y., & Solomonic, S. (2016). Educational polyphony. *Studies in Philosophy and Education, 35*(4), 385–397. https://doi.org/10.1007/s11217-015-9491-2

OECD. (2017). *The future of education and skills: Education 2030 conceptual learning framework: Background papers*. Directorate for Education and Skills Education Policy Committee.

Radcliffe, D. (2009). A pedagogy-space-technology (PST) framework for designing and evaluating learning places. In D. Radcliffe, H. Wilson, D. Powell, & B. Tibbetts (Eds.), *Learning spaces in higher education: Positive outcomes by design* (pp. 11–16). The University of Queensland and the Australian Learning and Teaching Council.

Robinson, K., & Lee, J. R. (2011). *Out of our minds*. Tantor Media, Incorporated.

Scardamalia, M., & Bereiter, C. (1994). Computer support for knowledge building communities. *Journal of the Learning Sciences, 3*, 265–283.

Scardamalia, M., & Bereiter, C. (2006). Knowledge building: Theory, pedagogy, and technology. In K. Sawyer (Ed.), *Cambridge handbook of the learning sciences* (pp. 97–118). Cambridge University Press.

Vangrieken, K., Meredith, C., Packer, T., & Kyndt, E. (2017). Teacher communities as a context for professional development: A systematic review. *Teaching and Teacher Education, 61*, 47–59.

Yondler, Y., & Blau, I. (2021). What is the degree of teacher centrality in optimal teaching of digital literacy in a technology-enhanced environment? Typology of teacher prototypes. *Journal of Research on Technology in Education, 55*(2), 230–251. https://doi.org/10.1080/15391523.2021.1950084

Foreword: A Polyphonic Humanizing View of Pedagogy and Technology

I believe all schools, all theories can be useful in some place, at some time. But I have discovered that one can only live by a passionate, and absolute, identification with a point of view. ... For a point of view to be of any use at all, one must commit oneself totally to it, one must defend it to the very death. Yet, at the same time, there is an inner voice that murmurs; "Don't take it too seriously. Hold on tightly, let go lightly." Peter Brook, author, theater and film director

Polyphony, in music, is used to describe a texture consisting of two or more independent melodic voices. It is a style of composition in which each voice has its own melody, rhythm, and expressive qualities while harmonically interweaving with the other voices. Polyphonic music often results in a complex and rich sound, where multiple voices create both harmony and counterpoint, leading to depth and interaction in the composition, where the whole is greater than the sum of its parts. Polyphony is often contrasted with monophony where there is just one dominant melodic voice.

The Russian philosopher and literary critic, Mikhail Bakhtin, expanded the idea of polyphony from music to human discourse, describing it as a feature of texts or utterances that incorporate multiple voices or perspectives, without subordinating them to a single authoritative or dominant voice. Polyphony, according to him, allowed for diversity, complexity, and ambiguity in meaning, and challenged the idea of a single truth or interpretation. As he wrote, even "truth is not born nor is it to be found inside the head of an individual person, it is born between people collectively searching for truth, in the process of their dialogic interaction" (Bakhtin, 1984, p. 110). Bakhtin saw polyphony as a positive and creative force that enriched and transformed language and culture. He contrasted it with homophony which he described as the tendency to impose a single voice or perspective on others, a tendency that he saw as oppressive and limiting. As he wrote, "The essence of polyphony lies precisely in the fact that the voices remain independent and, as such, are combined in a unity of a higher order than in homophony" (Bakhtin, 1984, p. 17).

At the heart of polyphony and its respect for multiple voices is a deeply humanizing worldview. By reflecting the diversity and complexity of human experience, expression, and cultures, polyphony allows for multiple voices and perspectives to coexist and interact in non-reductive ways. By not imposing a hierarchy and valuing the uniqueness and autonomy of each voice, it fosters dialogue and understanding. By encouraging listening with openness and curiosity while questioning existing norms and inviting new possibilities and meanings, it stimulates creativity. It thus celebrates human dignity, freedom, plurality, and potential.

This contrast between multiple voices vs. a single voice becomes particularly relevant in educational contexts. Most traditional educational systems are more akin to monophonic music, where the voice of the teacher (or the broader educational system) is given primacy over others (learners for sure, but sometimes even teachers). As Bakhtin would argue, these structures and systems are limiting, dehumanizing, and oppressive. In contrast, polyphony in an educational context creates humanistic systems, where every individual, including learners, in a particular context is valued for what they bring to the educational conversation. It seeks to be multi-directional and non-hierarchical, valuing openness and creativity, recognizing multiplicity as being key to learning and education.

Polyphony helps prepare our learners in the globally interconnected, complex world we currently live in and for the indeterminate, emerging future as well. Learners are learning within the context of globalization; the ravages of the Covid-19 pandemic, imminent challenges of climate change, rapid technological change (particularly the expansion of internet and social media technologies and now AI), and the re-emergence of (post)colonial indigenous narratives. We have come to realize that a dominant monophonic approach to education only oppresses and does disservice to the complexity of current educational contexts, and the cultures and histories of learners and educators.

One of the critical drivers of change in the world and in education comes from technology and its evolution: from the invention of writing to the printing press and all the way to our social-media saturated present. Looking specifically at the invention of the printing press—arguably one of the most significant technological advances of human cultural evolution—it allowed for mass literacy, and in some ways, it can be argued that our educational system is built around the "book." Books facilitated the inscription and sharing of ideas, leading to the Renaissance, Reformation, and Scientific Revolution. They democratized information access, challenged authority, and popularized transformative ideas, with lasting effects. Today, because of the advent of the Internet and social media, we are seeing the next round of how changes in technology impact how we think, work, and socialize. In many ways, the culture of social media is more akin to an oral culture than one solely based on print (Leahy et al., 2022; Mishra et al., 1996). We can see the relative unraveling of the ways of thinking and being that were based on a print culture as we move into a social media dominated world. One can only guess how the rise of new AI technologies will influence how we live and work. These digital media, and their protean nature (Koehler & Mishra, 2008), can be seen as both a challenge and an opportunity for polyphonic humanizing pedagogy. Digital and networking media make possible new forms of communication, interaction, and expression—through online forums, digital storytelling, virtual reality, and artificial intelligence.

That said, technology also brings forward new risks, such as fragmentation, alienation, and manipulation.

These ideas of humanistic polyphony and the role of technology are key to understanding this book. Drawing on these themes, as well as on developmental psychology, learning theory, and humanizing pedagogy, this book presents a framework for designing and implementing educational experiences that foster dialogic and polyphonic learning. Learning in this context occurs through active participation in meaningful communication with others, where learners co-construct knowledge, challenge assumptions, explore alternatives, and reflect on their own thinking. The diversity of these voices and perspectives helps learners develop critical awareness, empathy, creativity, and intercultural competence.

In addition to offering learners humanizing polyphonic learning opportunities, this edited book humanizes teachers' current lived experiences. The vision offered by this book is exciting and yet ambitious, given the weight that teachers and administrators currently carry. The vision and frameworks describe a very different way of doing instruction and schooling, within very different systems than we currently have (Wong & Mishra, 2021). This book asks a great deal of educators during a time when the demands on them are greater than ever. In addition to helping their learners meet grade level standards and manage the stress of high-stakes tests, educators bear the burden of public expectations to catch their learners up because of a perceived "learning loss"; the very real responsibility of helping their learners, colleagues, and themselves heal from the multiple traumas caused by the COVID-19 pandemic; the current political and culture wars; the rise of tribalism across the geo-political sphere, the socio-emotional impact of social media, and more.

It is within this complex context that the chapters in this book offer a way forward, by providing examples that bring these ideas to life, illustrating what the vision could look like within educational contexts. The authors demonstrate that creating humanizing curricula and learning spaces where learners thrive is feasible in our current socio-historical, political, and economic contexts (Wong & Mishra, 2021). In fact, humanizing curricula and learning spaces can address some of these challenges by helping learners, educators, and families heal (Wong & Mishra, 2021).

Finally, this book itself is an example of humanizing polyphonic discourse, living by the ideals that it preaches. Though each chapter in this book is complete in and of itself, it is the way in which these different pieces speak to each other that give this book its intellectual heft.

Mary Lou Fulton Teachers College
Arizona State University
Tempe, AZ, USA

Punya Mishra

College of Education
University of North Texas
Denton, TX, USA

Lok-Sze Wong

References

Bakhtin, M. (1984). *Problems of dostoevsky's poetics.* University of Minnesota Press.

Koehler, M. J., & Mishra, P. (2008). Introducing technological pedagogical content knowledge. In AACTE Committee on Innovation and Technology (Eds.), *Handbook of technological pedagogical content knowledge (TPCK) for educators* (pp. 3–29). Routledge.

Leahy, S., Scragg, B., & Mishra, P. (2022). Creatively confronting the adjacent possible: Educational leadership and the Fourth Industrial Revolution. In R. Beghetto & G. J. Gaeger (Eds.) *Uncertainty: A catalyst for creativity, learning and development.* Springer.

Mishra, P., Spiro, R. J., & Feltovich, P. J. (1996). Technology, representation, and cognition: The prefiguring of knowledge in cognitive flexibility hypertexts. In H. van Oostendorp & A. de Mul (Eds.), *Cognitive aspects of electronic text processing* (pp. 287–305). Ablex

Wong, L., & Mishra, P. (2021). Reforming our school systems around a humanizing curriculum: schooling during and after COVID-19. *ECNU Review of Education*, *4*(4), 890–898. https://doi.org/10.1177/2096531120980750

Acknowledgments

We would not have succeeded in completing this book without the generous help of many people we wish to thank. We are deeply grateful to the members of our community who wrote the book's chapters, accompanied us hand in hand, and contributed their professional experience, knowledge, and creativity to the community and to building the collective knowledge that made this book possible.

Our thanks go to Kibbutzim College of Education, our academic home, where our project was conceived and developed. We are grateful for the trust, resources, and infrastructures that facilitated rethinking education and teacher training.

Special thanks go to the Institute for Advanced Education, headed by Prof. Nimrod Aloni, for guiding the community's work. Prof. Aloni has inspired us with his advice and generous assistance that went far beyond the scope of his duties.

We thank Dr. Rinat Arbiv-Elyashiv, Head of the College Research Authority, who has devoted herself from the start to supporting our community and has been a close partner in preparing the ground and managing the publication processes. Thanks go to Tova Shany for her willing cooperation and professional advice on terminology and style issues in English and to Yossi Arza for his willing assistance in the book's graphic design.

Contents

About the Contributors

The Editors

Yael Yondler is an educator and researcher. She leads the Learning Design path of the Master's program in Technology in Education at Kibbutzim College of Education. An educational assessment specialist, she trains assessment coordinators. She trains and leads academic and other learning teams and communities in knowledge-building and learning design in hybrid spaces. Dr. Yondler's post-doctoral research on digital literacy was conducted at the Learning Technologies and Learning Systems Program of the Open University of Israel.

Nissim Avissar is a clinical-social psychologist, teacher educator, and qualitative researcher. He heads the teaching-advancement units at Kibbutzim College of Education and trains educators and therapists. His expertise covers cultural sensitivity, social-emotional learning (SEL), resilience building, and coping with trauma and crisis. His current academic research and writings focus on ethnic and class gaps in education and resilience building in a complicated violent reality.

Dovi Weiss is Head of Digital Learning and Training Development Specialization (B.A) at Ono Academic College. He also consults various organizations on effective and innovative learning, particularly in educational technology. Until 2021, he headed the digital pedagogy unit and management team at Kibbutzim College for 7 years. He was the pedagogical founder of *Et Hada'at* (www.timetoknow.co.il) and its chief scientist during 2005–2019. In 2010, Dr. Weiss was declared one of Israel's 50 most influential people in education. In 2012, he received an Honorable Mention from Israel's Prime Minister in the Initiatives and Innovation Award Competition for his pioneering work in Educational Technology.

Guest Writers

Nimrod Aloni is a senior lecturer in Philosophy of Education at Kibbutzim College of Education. He currently holds the UNESCO Chair in Humanistic Education. Prof. Aloni has published several books and articles on humanistic education, ethics in education, and proactive education for ecohumanism and democratic culture. In 2004, the Movement for Quality Government in Israel declared him "Knight of Quality Government." In 2021, he received the Distinguished Alumni Award from the Teachers College—Columbia University.

Punya Mishra (punyamishra.com) is associate dean of Scholarship and Innovation at Mary Lou Fulton Teachers College, Arizona State University, where he leads multiple initiatives, providing a future-forward, equity-driven, collaborative approach to educational research. He is internationally recognized for his work in educational technology, creativity, and the application of design to educational innovation. With over $11 million in grants, 200+ published articles, and 5 books, he is ranked in the top 2% of scientists worldwide and the top 50 scholars (top 10 in psychology) with the biggest influence on educational practice and policy. He is an award-winning instructor, engaging public-speaker and an accomplished visual artist.

Lok-Sze Wong studies system reform policies as attempts to address systemic inequities. Drawing on education, sociocultural, and organization theories and mixed methods, her research unpacks how systems (re)produce inequities and how to humanely reform schools and districts as complex social systems. She focuses on professional learning opportunities that support teachers and administrators as they shift their practices while redesigning the very organizations in which they work. Dr. Wong began her career in education as an elementary school teacher in Los Angeles and has a Ph.D. in Educational Administration and Policy from the University of Michigan.

The Writers

Netta Baryosef-Paz teaches literature and mindfulness at Kibbutzim College of Education. Her research and teaching fields include an ecocritical approach to contemporary American and Hebrew fiction, representations of the environment in art and literature, environmental education, and contemplative pedagogy. She co-edited with Lilach Naishtat–Bornstein the book *Practicing Equanimity: Contemplation and Mindfulness in Israeli Education* (2022, in Hebrew).

Tal Shemer Elkayam is a faculty member at Kibbutzim College of Education. Her main research fields are social emotional earning (SEL), pedagogical innovation, the effects of parents' divorce, and LGBTQs in the educational system. She leads SEL at Kibbutzim College of Education and coaches schools on matters of social-emotional pedagogy.

Adiv Gal is dean of the Science Faculty, senior lecturer, and co-founder of the Center of Education for Environmental Sustainability at Kibbutzim College of Education. Dr. Gal teaches varied undergraduate and master's courses on environment and sustainability issues at Kibbutzim College of Education. He has led environmental education programs in Israel for over twenty years and has been teaching in elementary schools since 2004. His current research interests include studies of climate change education, ecohumanism, sustainability, and environmental education (empowerment, self-efficacy, experiential learning, and outdoor learning).

Dafna Gan is an environmental and sustainability education researcher. She completed her post-doctoral program at the Israeli MOFET Institute. Gan is a lecturer and the head of the Environmental Education Master's program at Kibbutzim College of Education Technology and the Arts. Her research interests include environmental education, multicultural education, transformative learning, leadership in higher education, and non-governmental sustainability organizations. Her academic practices are devoted to sustainability implementation in the college sector and Israel's educational system in general. She is the founder of the "Center for Sustainability Education."

Lily Glasner teaches literature at Kibbutzim College of Education and at the Department of Comparative Literature at Bar Ilan University. Her research and publications mainly engage with children's literature and comics. She is a member of the Literature Committee of the Israeli National Program, *Sal Tarbut Artzi.*

Dvora Gorev is a senior lecturer (emerita) in mathematics education, researcher, and supervisor of bachelor's and master's degree students. Her main expertise areas are integrating technology in mathematics teaching, the required overall knowledgebase of mathematics' teachers, and advancing struggling mathematics students. Over the last decade, her research focused on teaching, learning, and assessment in online and hybrid planned and unplanned courses. She co-authored several mathematics books and co-edited the book *Classroom Management.*

Efrat Harel is a researcher of language development among bilingual children. Her research focuses on the typical linguistic profile of English-Hebrew speakers in preschool years and on the development of linguistic norms for bilingual children. She trains pre-service teachers at Kibbutzim College of Education in handling issues of multiculturalism, aiming to cultivate educators sensitive to diverse linguistic and cultural perceptions. Dr. Harel collaborates with education universities in Germany in exploring cross-cultural awareness among future English teachers in Germany and in Israel.

Efrat Kotzer is a lecturer in the Department of Special Education at Kibbutzim College of Education, a countrywide instructor in the MOE supervision of elementary Hebrew language studies department, and researcher at the Attention Lab of Tel

Aviv University. She specializes in the diagnosis and treatment of attention and learning disorders, the development of printed and online learning materials, and in the integration of technological tools in teaching and learning as a response to student diversity. Dr. Kotzer holds a bachelor's degree in educational counseling, a master's degree and a teaching certificate in special education, and a PhD in education from Tel Aviv University.

Miki Kritz is a senior faculty member at Kibbutzim College of Education and the Post Graduate Design Program at the University of Haifa. He has written three books related to the Internet, published by Kineret, Zemora, Bitan publishers. His over a hundred published articles and research papers engage with progressive education and teaching in online and collaborative multicultural environments. He teaches multi-participant online courses on educational technology and digital pedagogy. He is a member and an instructor in the development and management team of the near non-profit organization for cooperation between students of varied cultures in Israel and worldwide.

Adva Margaliot is a senior lecturer, the head of the Science Department at Achva Academic College and Former Dean of the Science Faculty at the Kibbutzim College of Education. Her areas of expertise are (in research and teaching): creative thinking, pedagogical innovation, and motivation for online learning. She has an extensive experience in academic management in times of crisis. Dr. Margaliot develops STEAM courses and holds seminars in creative thinking and sustainability. She trains teachers for the gifted in Israel and abroad; she implements pedagogicalinnovationwhilepromotingself-motivationandcultivatingself-managementskills.

Guy Pinku is a senior lecturer at Kibbutzim College of Education and at Academic College Levinsky-Wingate Academic College. Pinku's research focuses on care ethics and empathy in education, and moral education. He studies Dewey's educational theory, Nodding's educational theory, and Buber's approach to education and meaning in life. He received his MA in Psychology from Ben Gurion University and a PhD in Philosophy from the University of Haifa.

Tami Seifert is a senior lecturer at the Kibbutzim College of Education. She specializes in research and implementation of innovative learning environments, educational initiatives, and groundbreaking teaching pedagogies. In 2005, she was a postdoctoral fellow at Tel Aviv University Knowledge Technologies Laboratory. Prof. Seifert also holds an MA in Movement Therapy from Haifa University.Her career highlights in Kibbutzim College of Education are head of the computer teaching applications unit, head of the unit for postgraduate conversion to education, and ICT unit head. Her research interests are educational contexts of social media, implementation of mobile technologies in teaching, self-assessment, and online peer assessment. Currently, she combines movement and technology in her teaching and research.

Miri Shonfeld is Secretary General of the International Association of Intercultural Education (IAIE) and head of the TEC Center at MOFET Institute. She heads the thesis program for a master's degree in Technology in Education at Kibbutzim College of Education. Her research focuses on cultural diversity, online learning environments, collaborative work, and faculty development. In recognition of her outstanding work, Prof. Shonfeld was granted several awards: an award for an outstanding educational project promoting tolerance (2010), an MOE acknowledgment of her contribution (2013), and the Unity Award from the president of Israel (2018).

Ayelet Weizman is an expert in space education and physical-digital technology. She leads the path "Technologies of Tomorrow," a part of the MEd in EdTech program at Kibbutzim College of Education. She hold a PhD in Planetary Sciences from Tel Aviv University and a postdoctorate in Science and Technology Teaching from Michigan State University. She is a lecturer and researcher in Computational Thinking and Space Education and guides students in action research as part of their final theses. Active in national and international space education organizations, she was the VP of Education at SpaceIL and a techno-pedagogy developer at the Israeli MOE.

Miri Yochanna is Head of the English Department at Kibbutzim College of Education. She is a linguist and has been a TESOL (Teaching English to Speakers of Other Languages) teacher trainer for over thirty years. Her fields of expertise are applied linguistics, ESL methodology, material development, and language assessment and evaluation. Her research focuses on bilingualism and bilingual identity, preservice ESL teachers, self-efficacy and the enhancement of preservice teacher ability, self-perception, and self-confidence. In addition, Dr. Yochanna develops, edits, and evaluates teaching materials for English language education for schools in the Israeli education system.

Conceptual Framework: Technology, Values, Pedagogy, and Multiple Learning Spaces: Creating a "New Whole" in a Complex Reality

Yael Yondler and Nissim Avissar

> *Our duty as educators is "to facilitate youth to lead worthy and flourishing lives: an autonomous and full life in which one realizes one's inner powers and participates meaningfully and justly in the natural, social, and cultural realms of life". (Aloni, 2023, p. 26).*

Introduction

The birth of this book coincides with historical moments evolving before our eyes that dramatically change our life reality and our approach to learning. The traditional approach that sees learning as a linear process has been shifting due to accelerated technological developments, particularly virtual communications, alongside the deepening establishment of social media. Change patterns gradually tend towards community learning, where the community members choose their fields of interest and create and structure knowledge based on shared principles (Hoadley & Kali, 2019).

The digital revolution has melted the boundaries of the traditional classroom. Learning is changing, occurring in various interactive knowledge spaces, including social media and virtual spaces, next to technology-enhanced physical spaces (Goodyear, 2020). Developing research on Future Learning Spaces (FLS's) assists in conceptualizing future innovative technology-enhanced learning spaces (see Ellis & Goodyear, 2016; Hod, 2017). The generative AI revolution that has burst into our lives over the past year also challenges conceptualizing this subject and the learning process in general (Mishra et al., 2023). The changing learning process encourages learners to discover a wide range of new content worlds. It exposes them to central

Y. Yondler (✉) · N. Avissar
Kibbutzim College of Education, Technology and Arts, Tel-Aviv, Israel
e-mail: yael.yondler@smkb.ac.il; Nissim.Avissar@smkb.ac.il

Y. Yondler et al. (eds.), *Cultivating Future-Oriented Learners*, Understanding Teaching-Learning Practice, https://doi.org/10.1007/978-3-031-63253-2_1

issues and controversies in our complex reality, including social and multicultural divisions, economic crises, and political conflicts.

In 2022, the Collins English Dictionary chose permacrisis as its word of the year. Permacrisis, defined as "An extended period of instability and insecurity," comprehends all the effects, ongoing changes, inherent disruption, and uncertainties that have become our daily life reality. The COVID-19 crisis underscored the value of online learning in times of crisis while exacerbating human sensations of loneliness, anxiety, and existential uncertainty. It brought to the surface the need for interpersonal interaction and belonging to a community (Schleicher, 2020). These combined challenging circumstances resulted in a life-changing, chaotic reality that faces educators, particularly teacher educators, with adjusting the training approaches and practices to the twenty-first-century reality, bearing in mind the complexity and frequency of the occurring changes. In response to the described challenges, this book proposes educators, particularly teacher educators, a humanizing, inclusive educational paradigm titled **The Polyphonic Paradigm**.

Definition and Goals of the Polyphonic Paradigm

The ancient Greek term polyphony stands for multiple voices. In the educational context, it is a conceptual standpoint endorsing the simultaneous existence of two or more voices where each voice is complete of itself and none is secondary to the others (Naot-Ofarim & Solomonic, 2016; Schwarz-Franco, 2019).

The polyphony-inspired educational approach underlying the proposed paradigm is anchored in a value-based worldview combining a humanizing, educational approach with a socio-constructive one. At the heart of this combination are two interacting axes feeding on each other: One regards cultivating the strengths and interpretive capacities of individual learners (Aloni, 2011a, b) and the other highlights the importance of a community culture that promotes social ways of personal knowledge building while bolstering collaboration in building collective communal knowledge (Scardamalia & Bereiter, 2014). The reciprocal relations of the two axes encourage student co-agency, meeting learners' needs to function successfully in the dynamic twenty-first-century world (OECD, 2017). Moreover, combining these two educational approaches enhances learners' mental and social well-being and the well-being of society as a community. We believe that this achievement has significant benefits.

Based on the assumption that a complex reality and learning environment closely interrelate, the book proposes a paradigm representing space multiplicity, polyphony, and diversity that characterize our life in this constantly changing and fast-evolving era. The paradigm comprises three inter-feeding components: (1) **Glocal democratic values**, especially promoting human dignity and liberty and commitment to the community in the spirit of "Love your neighbor as yourself," which embodies mutual accountability. (2) **Inclusive humanizing pedagogy** with dialogue at its center, encouraging learners to assert themselves and their inner world, while offering them an opportunity to be attentive to varied stands and opinions. (3) **Technology as a transformative force** that melts the boundaries of familiar worlds and exposes the learners to new contents in different glocal interdisciplinary arenas.

Combining these core components of the polyphonic paradigm reveals the broader context of educational work as "a polyphonic system with many instruments and tones. [...] Human polyphony has an active meaning. Based on a dialogue and mutual attentiveness, it allows for multiple meanings and interpretations, and stands at the core of learning" (Inbar & Inbar, 2020, p. 41). Hence, being open, diverse, inclusive, and flexible, the polyphonic paradigm has high potential as a futuristic, sustainable paradigm with constantly updating flexible components capable, by nature, of predicting uncertain conditions (Hadar et al., 2020).

In general, one might describe the polyphonic educational paradigm as a conceptual-educational framework for teachers, a "polyphonic lens," allowing them steady contemplation of their approach and practice in a changing reality. The paradigm also aims to assist teachers in shaping a personal "polyphonic wisdom" and putting together "a new whole," enabling self-contemplation of their approach and practice. Ultimately, it aspires to assist educators in coaching future citizens and teachers in value-based, successful, and productive functioning in a democratic society.

From a **functional perspective**, the proposed paradigm aims to assist educators in processing the multiple-spaced, polyphonic, and diversified reality to shape a broad, solid, yet flexible outlook to help them understand the need to offer learners varied options for becoming digitally literate and critical knowledge producers. Such capabilities would enable them to actively build their knowledge through teamwork and be partners to building collective knowledge for the community's wellbeing and growth. From the **perspective of values**, the proposed paradigm aims to boost educators' proficiency in using pedagogy to design a humanizing learning environment that mirrors our multiple-spaced, polyphonic, and diversified reality. This value-based lens would enable educators to design an inclusive, pluralistic learning environment that would open ways to experience knowledge-building in different content fields. Such knowledge would derive from democratic cultural values that allow space for each individual voice and a broad range of viewpoints that put human dignity at their center and interact to foster the personal and collective good.

The Learning Environment as a Polyphonic Hub

According to the polyphonic paradigm, the optimal learning environment agrees with Dewey's approach that education is life itself. It is an approach that understands the value of mutual relations between the education system—from schools to teacher-education institutes—and the complex reality, and the central role of technology in them, which keeps gathering momentum. In this spirit, we propose regarding the learning environment as a polyphonic hub that mirrors our complex, mobile reality. Contemplating the learning environment through the lens of a polyphonic hub highlights the connection between the perception of the learners' role and the concept of knowledge in a changing reality. This connection stands at the heart of the polyphonic paradigm, linking a humanizing approach with a constructivist social one. Both advocate active learner knowledge building, individually and independently and through socio-cultural mediation (Bransford et al., 2000).

The three mentioned components of the polyphonic paradigm feed the link between the learners' role and the concept of knowledge in our changing reality, highlighting three of this link's characteristic features:

(a) Knowledge is **multi-spatial rather than linear**. It dissolves all the existing dichotomies, creating learner **agency** that enables roaming knowledge-rich spaces and building knowledge independently.
(b) Knowledge is **rhizomatic** (cf. Deleuze & Guattari, 1988). It encourages learners to be **productive** and generate knowledge and new ideas in an unfixed multidirectional way that is not pre-structured.
(c) Knowledge is **fluid**: Being dynamic, changing, and ever-renewing, it allows learners to be **reflective**, navigate their learning through changing contexts, and assess it in ways that enable them to progress and improve.

The link between the learners' role and the concept of knowledge in a dynamic reality, as manifested in the polyphonic setting, is anchored in theoretical literature engaging with the design of hybrid learning spaces in higher education (Hilli et al., 2019). The literature indicates that we may regard hybridity as polyphony since the mentioned connection between the learners' role and the concept of knowledge makes the hybrid learning space multifaceted and heterogeneous (Hartcourt-Rorabaugh & Stommel, 2012). Such a perspective could assist educators in observing the learning environment through the polyphonic lens to broaden their field of vision. That is to say, it acquires a deeper view of the learning environment, and appreciates its multi-dimensionality of its being multi-spatial, multidirectional, and polyphonic—all at the same time. This observation suggests that educators should perceive the learning environment as a microcosmic image of the ever-changing complex reality. Scrutinizing it as an aerial photo, educators would get a correct picture of reality and design the learning environment as a Polyphonic Hub. This would pave the way for observing reality from a humanizing and equal glocal perspective that puts human dignity at its center, advocating diversity and change, varied perspectives, risk taking, empathy, dialogue, and creativity (Köppe et al., 2017). At the same time, the polyphonic lens allows for designing educational processes that encourage learners to experience social interactions and a culture of mutual commitment, respect, and collaboration to cultivate collective knowledge in a shared world (Aaen & Nørgård, 2015; Nørgård et al., 2019).

Instruction, Learning, and Assessment for Learning

The evolving tendency to switch from traditional learning spaces, where instruction, learning, and assessment for learning (ILA) are preset and predetermined to ones where ILA is flexible, processive, and varied (Birenbaum, 2003, 2018) is an outcome of observing the learning environment through the polyphonic lens. It follows the alternative assessment culture (Birenbaum, 2014, 2016), based on open interpretive processes that keep feeding each other. Educators may lean on such processes in designing a learning environment as a polyphonic paradigm, offering students learning and assessment choices where knowledge is not fixed, structured, or predicted. Such options encourage learners—individually and collectively—to build and generate knowledge in ever-changing contexts through dialogue in dynamic ways.

Below is a brief description of ILA advantages in establishing the learners' and teachers' roles in a polyphonic hub:

- **Nature of the learning**: The polyphonic paradigm, anchored in educational humanizing and socio-constructive foundations, regards learning as a significance-building process based on the learners' unique experiences (Vygotsky, 1989). It envisions learners as complex entities that have agency and affect the polyphonic environment while building personal and collective knowledge proactively and reflectively in different contexts through communicative feedback and peer collaboration. The polyphonic paradigm can be a prism that assists educators in observing the learning environments as mirrored by reality. On this basis, they can design ILA processes that encourage learners not to be content as mere knowledge consumers but evolve as knowledge producers and active partners to navigating their learning within the Polyphonic Hub. Consequently, the learners have the following characteristics:
  - **Autonomic learners with agency**, building knowledge by navigating non-dichotomous knowledge spaces (Cohen & Ezra, 2018; Ellis & Goodyear, 2016), associating knowledge items, and creating their own interpretations around them in diverse contexts.
  - **Proactive learners** who explore and produce knowledge, contents, and new ideas in rhizomatic, multidirectional (Bennett et al., 2020; Gardner, 1995; Hilli et al., 2019), not predetermined ways opted for by choice and preference.
  - **Reflective learners,** aware of their learning processes, navigate and regulate them in the personal and collective knowledge spaces within the polyphonic hub and act to assess the learning processes (Blaschke, 2012). Applying their reflective assessment capacities, they create a personal compass of strengths, points that need strengthening, and proposed improvements, which they can use to navigate fluid knowledge in frequently changing and renewing contexts, and regulate themselves accordingly.
  - **Critical learners**, trained in critical thinking and applying discretion. Learners taught to doubt the information they encounter even if it appears self-evident.

  - **Learners endowed with communicative and social capacities** and keep a constant dialogue with themselves and their peers while creating and structuring knowledge. Educators can thus take advantage of the polyphonic paradigm in planning ILA processes that expand knowledge sharing through social configurations that encourage dialogue, empathy, and respect for others (Gershon et al., 2020). In these configurations, learners express their opinions, listen to varied voices and opinions, raise ideas, and develop them while navigating between their thoughts and those of their peers. Expressing and discussing different learners' ideas advance personal and group knowledge, thus expanding shared collective knowledge (Scardamalia & Bereiter, 2014).

- **Nature of the Instruction:** The described connection between the perceived role of the learners and the concept of knowledge in a Polyphonic Hub further clarifies the purpose of polyphonic instruction: Encouraging learners to produce and mold significant knowledge while expanding their conceptual understanding via individual experience as independent learners and partners to social interactions. Hence, in a Polyphonic Hub, teachers are not the "sage on stage" (Kramer, 2017), pouring knowledge into the learners' heads, providing both the information and the rules, or defining the learning environment. In encouraging multidirectional learning, teachers are partners in the learners' knowledge-building processes through dialogue and collaborative thinking (Yondler & Blau, 2021). Moreover, as partners in knowledge-building, teachers plan open-ended ILA processes that are not predetermined. These strategies allow the learners to pick the content they think is most relevant, study and interpret information from various perspectives, share the information with their peers, and build knowledge in unique, creative ways.

In a Polyphonic Hub, the teachers' role is not limited to being knowledgeable in technology-rich instruction, learning, and assessment for learning, namely, professional craftsmen. In a polyphonic learning environment, they have to be artistic. As artists, they must have broad, flexible horizons in a wide range of contexts and possess the intelligence and discretion skills required to provide a functional and value-based response that would enable learners to develop the skills they need in the twenty-first century (Cf. Whitehead, 2005). Artist-teachers can offer their students learning and assessment opportunities to break the familiar school boundaries and challenge basic, seemingly self-evident assumptions. While doing this, teachers also assist the learners in shaping their worldview through a dialogue with reality. They encourage them to acquire much-needed functional skills and experience processes that help them build a value-based backbone and assert themselves while remaining attentive and tolerating other voices guided by equality, ethical and empathic awareness of the other.

- **Nature of the assessment**: The polyphonic paradigm is anchored in the Assessment for Learning (AFL) culture (Birenbaum, 2016), which integrates it into the instruction and learning processes and navigates it (William, 2011). The teachers display their role as artists by integrating assessment processes into the

Polyphonic Hub, cultivating learners who are active partners in setting the assessment criteria (Blau et al., 2020), and embracing self-reflection thinking patterns (Tishman et al., 1993).

Over these assessment processes, teachers offer each learner the opportunity to experience various alternative assessment assignments, which evolve, similar to reality, around authentic issues related to the learners' worlds. Due to the complexity of these assignments, they do not call for simplistic responses, requiring understanding performances (Perkins & Blythe, 1994) and inspiring rich original products (Olsher et al., 2016). Such assignments also highlight the teachers' artistic capacity, requiring them to formulate several responses to the question of how to shape a culture that stimulates learners to propose various ideas of their own while building collective knowledge, assuming that any idea renders itself to improvement (Scardamalia & Bereiter, 2014). The teachers' role as artists also manifests in designing the educational process and in their capacity to encourage individual learners to deepen their knowledge through dialogue and collaboration.

Polyphonic Wisdom: An Applicative Knowledge Model

Behind the polyphonic paradigm stands the understanding that a Polyphonic Hub must be compatible with the teacher's practice. In other words, teachers must own ready-to-apply practical knowledge to scrutinize their daily practices through a polyphonic lens. The lens should reflect reality and help them translate the polyphonic worldview or paradigm into practical tools. To meet this need, we propose the **polyphonic wisdom model**—an applicative knowledge model that leans on four components: Pedagogy, space, technology, content (Fig. 1), deriving from the TPACK (Mishra & Koehler, 2006; Mishra, 2019) and the TPeCS (Kali et al., 2019) models. TPACK defines the links between pedagogy, technology, and content, indicating what educators must know to integrate technology optimally into their teaching. TPeCS expands TPACK, adding to it the space component, explaining that "TPeCS contends that good teaching nowadays requires not only 'an understanding of how technology relates to the pedagogy and content' (as in Mishra & Kohler's TPACK, 2006, p. 1026), but also an understanding and skill to adapt existing physical spaces, take advantage of alternative spaces, or design new ones." (Kali et al., 2019, p. 2163). The applicative polyphonic model is also in line with the developing research on technology-enhanced learning spaces (Hod, 2017; Tissenbaum & Slotta, 2019) that views space as linked and interdependent with the other three components, similar to a dynamic ecology (Radcliffe, 2009).

We assume that viewing this applicative model through a polyphonic lens may assist teachers striving to gain polyphonic wisdom. Such wisdom not only requires understanding the complexity of technology integration in teaching but also knowing how to use technology in designing a polyphonic learning hub, whose multiple spaces, voices, and directions urge learners to apply global humanizing values. To

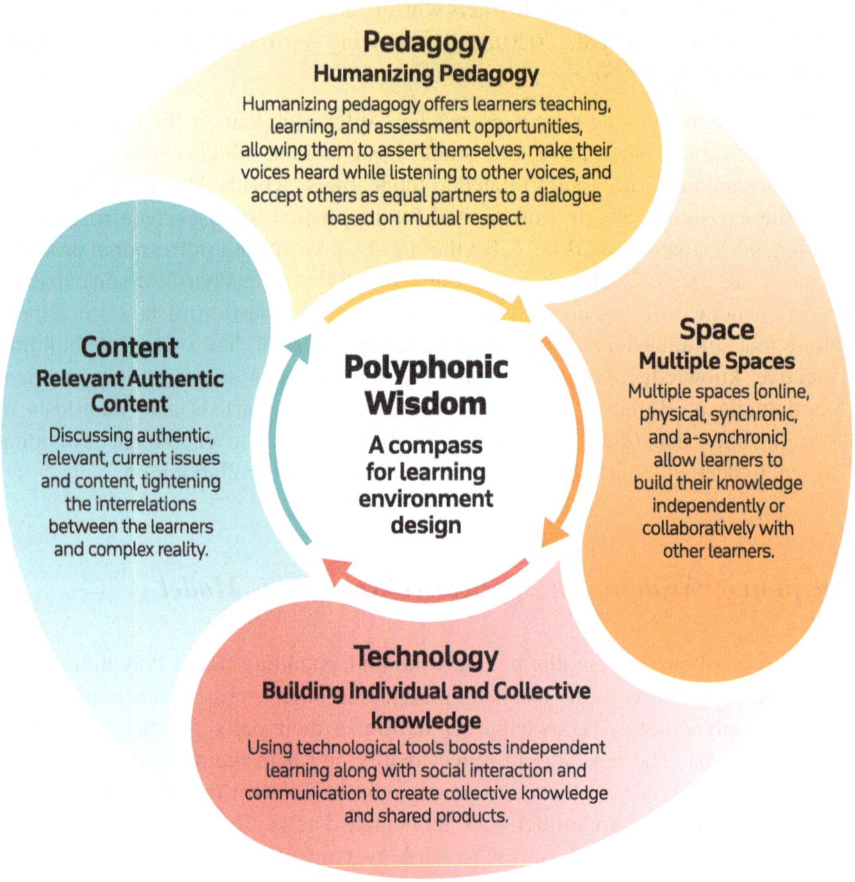

Fig. 1 The polyphonic wisdom model

discern the specific and general aspects of the applicative model's four components –technology, pedagogy, content, and space—it would be best to zoom in and out on them. Zooming in would allow the teacher to characterize the polyphonic features of each component, to enable analyzing it and determine how to integrate it into the polyphonic hub compatibly with the other three. Zooming out would help the teacher understand how to synergize the four components in the polyphonic hub.

Zoom-in: The Individual Components

Pedagogy Polyphonic pedagogy is the primary generator of learner experience in the proposed model. It produces educational significance and illustrates the combined humanizing educational approach and the socio-constructivist one at its base.

By its very nature, polyphonic pedagogy is humanizing, characterized by being processive, tolerant, dialogue-based, and formative (Cf. Aloni, 2011a, b). Moreover, it springs from the understanding that learning processes are not made of isolated events but are iterative, consistent, and continuous, aiming to create a significant educational learner experience. The pedagogical component assists teachers in translating the polyphonic approach into mental, educational, and value-based tools to cultivate learners sensitive to others and the environment who are glocally aware citizens with personal and social accountability in a democratic twenty-first-century society.

Space Observed through the polyphonic lens and given the growing understanding of learning design in higher education, space is no longer a merely physical notion but a conceptual one (Stommel, 2012). The current space concept derives from academic literature about designing and developing hybrid learning spaces (Cohen et al., 2020; Hilli et al., 2019). Hybrid learning spaces dissolve the still-existent traditional dichotomies in high education, such as between digital and analogue concepts. They create new interlinking space formations, such as physical and digital learning spaces, informal and formal learning contexts, frontal and online classrooms, academic and real-life learning, and other creative configurations (Stommel, 2012). Hybrid learning spaces offer new combinations of complex hybrid breeds (Cf. Hilli et al., 2019, p. 67), broadening and refreshing the observation of learning spaces in high education and teacher training.

Viewing the hybrid space concept through the polyphonic lens enriches it with deep educational multidimensionality whose perspectives focus on global humanistic values of equality, brotherhood, and friendship, revealing its prospective potential for teacher training.

Like the hybrid space concept, the polyphonic multi-spatial, multi-directional, and multiple-voiced hub corresponds to the current reality. The learning process no longer relies on a single knowledge space but several co-existing ones, including social media, blogs, and various virtual and physical places such as relevant off-classroom or off-educational institute sites. The resulting multi-spatial hub comprises various dynamic interactive spaces encouraging multiple voices by being both individual and collective. The teachers must design those spaces so as to allow learners to move between them, assert themselves, make their voices heard, build personal knowledge, and sometimes create knowledge spaces of their own. At the same time, teachers should urge the learners to be attentive to their peers and actively participate in building collective knowledge through dialogue, with mutual and interactive involvement and mutual respect.

Technology The perceived role of technology corresponds to the polyphonic view that technology possesses transformative and cultural powers (Clark, 1994; Collins & Halverson, 2009). The teachers' polyphonic wisdom mirrors this in harnessing technology's "superpowers" to integrate ILA processes into the polyphonic hub design. Thus, teachers can apply their polyphonic wisdom by using technology to promote democratic culture, be intellectual partners (Ashburn & Floden, 2006) of the learners, and support autonomic learning and complex critical thinking. They may be the force that dissolves the limits of the traditional classroom and assists the learners in building knowledge in multidirectional, fluid glocal contexts. Technology can be the toolkit that enables teachers to create an illustrative and experience-oriented learning experience focused on and adjusted to the learners and their personal needs while offering communication and social interaction channels (Harasim, 2012).

However, technology's power and added value should not be alone in shaping polyphonic wisdom. To own it, teachers must also be aware of the origins of this power and the challenges and dangers involved in using technology-based networks. For example, students must be taught to doubt any information that comes their way and mold their own tools to cope with fake news. They should know that various technological means, particularly algorithms, are designed to influence the consumers' consciousness, choices, preferences, and attention. Teachers must possess the polyphonic wisdom required to guide them in using technology as a constructive force, generating AFL processes that offer learners the means to navigate and regulate technology and apply them to promote a democratic culture. Such processes may simultaneously gain teachers insights about the challenges of technology by contemplating it critically and consciously and harnessing it to the cause of education rather than the other way around (Mishra et al., 2023).

Contents Two central insights underlie the approach to contents in the proposed model. One regards the close interrelations between a complex reality and a polyphonic learning environment. The other underscores that the content of the education system curricula should be detached from the national and international social, political, and cultural contexts (Cf. Pelletier et al., 2022). It would appear, therefore, that the foundations of teachers' polyphonic wisdom should include extensive knowledge to allow for informed discretion in approaching such contexts sensitively and inclusively. In line with Dewey's approach, we maintain that the starting point in content contemplation within a polyphonic model should prefer content related to resolving authentic, real-life issues while applying integrative observation that crosses the boundaries of different knowledge fields (Dewey, 1956). Accordingly, teachers should select content related to major local and global issues, phenomena, and socio-political, educational, and cultural processes that simulate reality. This way, they would assist learners to understand that resolving problems requires complex, interdisciplinary global contemplation, which a single knowledge field cannot enable. (Cf. U.S. Department OF Education, 2016).

Zoom-Out: The Model as a System

Pedagogy, Space, Technology, and Content Affinity Understanding and synergizing these four components assist teachers in designing the learning environment as a polyphonic hub. They make an inseparable part of teachers' polyphonic wisdom while productively engaging with two aspects of knowledge building in a polyphonic paradigm: (1) Amplifying the unique individual voices. (2) Applying various social interaction configurations that advance and cultivate the community's collective knowledge.

Polyphonic wisdom combines the three paradigm components: (1) Glocal democratic values, (2) Inclusive humanizing pedagogy, and (3) Technology as a transformative power. Combining these three components enables teachers to design the learning environment as an information- and technology-rich multiple-space hub. It is a hub that generates rich blends of physical and online information sources, digital tools, and resources that synthesize individual learner-focused knowledge sources with technology-rich collective ones (Ellis & Goodyear, 2016; Hod & Katz, 2020).

Similar to real life, polyphonic wisdom thus helps teachers create various knowledge and learning spaces that avoid the artificial distinction between personal and collective knowledge building. It also advises teachers on how to use technology as a transformative force in designing the learning environment as a network of personal and collective spaces based on collaboration, empathy, mutual respect, and peer learning (Blau et al., 2020; Cohen et al., 2020).

Significantly, another advantage of polyphonic wisdom is being an educational-cultural force that allows learners to experience global humanistic values by applying inclusive humanizing pedagogy. The technology-enhanced and content-rich learning space presents teachers and learners with a wide range of humanistic experiences that encourage free thinking and choice (Cf. Rogers, 1980). Teachers can thus enable learners to connect to their inner values and passions and choose the learning mode that suits them best and a knowledge field that interests them. In the process, they instill in the learners the value of each community member's personal and social responsibility and their role in cultivating the community's collective knowledge (Scardamalia & Bereiter, 2006, 2014).

In summary, polyphonic wisdom helps teachers focus on humanizing pedagogy practices that build an infrastructure of democratic culture values: (1) Encourage a social climate advancing a sense of safety, interpersonal trust and respect, collaboration, mutual assistance, and transparency and integrity norms, (2) Allow learners to experience fundamental humanistic values: love of humankind, tolerance, caring attentiveness, and sensitivity to the needs, wishes, and difficulties of others, and (3) Introduce learners to multiple perspectives, empathizing with others, creative thinking, performing research studies, formulating questions, and starting a discussion (Aloni & Veugelers, 2023; Birenbaum, 2018; Hilli et al., 2019).

Polyphonic Wisdom Context of the Book

Behind this book stands a pragmatic approach. It derives from the understanding that a theory cannot be declared successful before being tried and proven in practice (Dewey, 1916). With this in mind, the book demonstrates how polyphonic training can function in "real life" once translated into a concrete teacher training method. Each of the book's 13 chapters proposes and ILA model that illustrates the polyphonic paradigm worldview.

True to academic writing, each chapter begins with a theoretical introduction that describes theories and theoretic models specific to the proposed model's field of knowledge. From the practical angle, each chapter provides a detailed description of the model's makeup and stages, specifying how it yields polyphonic wisdom that assists in designing the learning environment as a polyphonic hub.

In line with the book's polyphonic wisdom perspective, each chapter describes an already implemented ILA model, illustrating that it is possible to acquire polyphonic wisdom through synergy between the pedagogy, space, technology, and content components (Mishra & Koehler, 2006; Kali et al., 2019). The individual chapters and the book as a whole invite the readers to independently form a polyphonic wisdom of their own and examine how they might devise such synergy between the four model components. Listed below are questions relevant to each model component to assist readers in developing and implementing polyphonic wisdom in their respective specialization fields.

1. **The pedagogical component**: How can we use pedagogy to offer learners optional ILA processes that enable them to assert themselves and make their voices heard while being attentive and embracing other voices as equal through partnership, dialogue, and mutual respect?
2. **The space component**: Given that space, in addition to being physical, is also conceptual, how can we design a multi-spatial humanizing educational learning environment that synthesizes individual and collective technology-enhanced learning spaces?
3. **The technological component**: What are the best ways to promote informed technology use as a power that directs, constructs, and produces personal and collective knowledge? At the same time, how can we harness it to cultivate the socio-cultural skills required in our world and channel it to serve education rather than the other way around?
4. **The content component**: How can we create close mutual relations between the complex reality and a polyphonic learning environment design? How should we select content to assist learning, considering the importance of engaging with the varied, complex issues reality imposes?

By contemplating each chapter through the polyphonic lens, the readers understand how the polyphonic wisdom model helped the writers leave a personal mark while designing a unique polyphonic learning environment adjusted to the specific model they discuss. We strongly believe that contemplating each chapter through the polyphonic lens would assist the readers in optimally designing a pluralistic, inclusive and technology- enhanced learning environment where students can experience knowledge-building in varied content worlds. Such knowledge will rely on democratic values, primarily human dignity and interrelations between the individual and collective good.

Accordingly, each chapter proposes ways to design and implement a polyphonic hub in real-life teacher training to produce learners who are partners in processing and building knowledge independently and as a social process within personal and collective knowledge spaces. In each chapter, knowledge-building occurs around relevant content and current burning issues through a dialogue with reality. Among the issues dealt with are natural resources in an era of environmental crisis, the ability to understand and respect other viewpoints and worldviews, acknowledging the value of cultural diversity, individually tailored learning, and project-based learning (PBL) in hybrid learning spaces. The learners get the opportunity to apply and experience global humanistic values encouraging personal, social, and the glocal environmental responsibility, understanding and tolerating the viewpoints of others, openness and empathy towards members of other cultures, and independent learning directed consistently and methodically at achieving the learners' goals (OECD, 2020).

The book contributes by expanding on the theoretical aspect of educational literature and the applicative facet in teacher training institutes. Theory-wise, it proposes a terminology and a conceptual framework that educators engaged in teacher training could use as a democratic, value-oriented theoretical compass to understand the multidimensionality and dynamicity of the current complex reality. From a practical perspective, the book is a handbook of instruction, learning, and assessment models, that help design a polyphonic learning environment in the current and future teacher training. It aims to make the essentials of polyphonic wisdom accessible to teachers and assist them in creating an optimal synergy between its components.

In the broader teacher training context, the book may pave the way for basing teacher training on an educationally humanizing and socially constructive agenda, an ever-updating, flexible agenda with broad horizons. Educators endowed with rich polyphonic wisdom who are digitally literate and use technology in an educated manner can design a polyphonic learning environment that is inclusive, value- and dialogue-based. Such broad-minded educators would apply their well-developed human sensitivity to offer learners significant educational experiences that provide functional and value-based responses toward coping successfully with the complex challenges of the twenty-first century.

References

Aaen, J. H., & Nørgård, R. T. (2015). Participatory academic communities: A transdisciplinary perspective on participation in education beyond the institution. *Conjunctions: Transdisciplinary Journal of Cultural Participation, 2*(2), 1. https://doi.org/10.7146/tjcp.v2i2.22920

Aloni, N. (2011a). Humanistic education: From theory to practice. In W. Veugelers (Ed.), *Education and humanism: Linking autonomy and humanity* (pp. 35–46). Sense Publishers.

Aloni, N. (2011b). Empowering dialogues in humanistic education. *Educational Philosophy and Theory, 45*(10), 1067–1081. https://doi.org/10.1111/j.1469-5812.2011.00789.x

Aloni, N. (2023). *Virtues worth attaining: challenges toward full humanity and sustainable futures*. HaKibbutz HaMe'uchad. In Hebrew.

Aloni, N., & Veugelers, W. (2023). Ecohumanism, democratic culture, and activist pedagogy: Attending to what the known demands of us. *Educational Philosophy and Theory*. https://doi.org/10.1080/00131857.2023.2295216

Ashburn, E. A., & Floden, R. E. (2006). *Meaningful learning using technology: What educators need to know and do*. Teachers College Press.

Bennett, D., Knight, E., & Rowley, J. (2020). The role of hybrid learning spaces in enhancing higher education students' employability. *British Journal of Educational Technology*. https://doi.org/10.1111/bjet.12931

Birenbaum, M. (2003). New insights into learning and teaching and their implications for assessment. In M. Segers, F. Dochy, & E. Cascallar (Eds.), *Optimizing new methods of assessment: In search of qualities and standards* (pp. 13–36). Kluwer.

Birenbaum, M. (2014). Conceptualizing assessment culture in school. In C. Wyatt-Smith, V. Klenowski, & P. Colbert (Eds.), *Designing assessment for quality learning. The enabling power of assessment* (Vol. 1, pp. 285–302). Springer.

Birenbaum, M. (2016). Assessment culture vs. testing culture: The impact on assessment for learning. In D. Laveault & L. Allal (Eds.), *Assessment for learning: Meeting the challenge of implementation* (pp. 275–292). Springer.

Birenbaum, M. (2018). Tarbuyot habhina veha'aracha vehashpa'oteihen al yisum ha'aracha leshem lemida [Testing and assessment cultures and their effect on implementing Assessment for Learning]. In M. Birenbaum (Ed.) *Mehkar veyisum ha'aracha leshem lemida (HLL) of students and teachers in Israel* [Research and implementation of Assessment for Learning (AFL) of students and teachers in Israel] (pp. 220–240). Mofet Institute. In Hebrew.

Blaschke, L. M. (2012). Heutagogy and lifelong learning: A review of heutagogical practice and self-determined learning. *The International Review of Research in Open and Distributed Learning, 13*, 56–71.

Blau, I., Shamir-Inbal, T., & Avdiel, O. (2020). How does the pedagogical design of a technology-enhanced collaborative academic course promote digital literacies, self-regulation, and perceived learning of students? *The Internet and Higher Education, 45*, 100722. https://doi.org/10.1016/j.iheduc.2019.100722

Bransford, J. D., Brown, A. L., & Cocking, R. R. (2000). *How people learn: Brain, mind, experience, and school* (Expanded ed.). National Academy Press.

Clark, R. E. (1994). Media will never influence learning. *Educational Technology Research and Development, 42*, 21–29.

Cohen, A., & Ezra, O. (2018). Development of a contextualised MALL research framework based on L2 Chinese empirical study. *Computer Assisted Language Learning, 31*, 764–789. https://doi.org/10.1080/09588221.2018.1449756

Cohen, A., Nørgård, R. T., & Mor, Y. (2020). Hybrid learning spaces: Design, data, didactics. *British Journal of Educational Technology, 51*(4), 1039–1044. https://doi.org/10.1111/bjet.12964

Colins, A., & Halverson, R. (2009). *Rethinking education in the age of technology: The digital revolution and schooling in America*. Teachers College Press.

Deleuze, G., & Guattari, F. (1988). *A thousand plateaus: Capitalism and schizophrenia*. Athlone Press.

Dewey, J. (1916). *Democracy and education*. Macmillan.

Dewey, J. (1956). *The child and the curriculum: The school and society*. University of Chicago Press.

Ellis, R. A., & Goodyear, P. (2016). Models of learning space: Integrating research on space, place, and learning in higher education. *Review of Education, 4*, 149–191.

Gardner, H. (1995). Reflections on multiple intelligences: Myths and messages. *PHI Delta Kappa, 77*(3), 200–209.

Gershon, W. S., Appelbaum, P., & Schwarz-Franco, O. (2020). *Polyphonic teaching: The ability to facilitate multiple voices as a crucial teaching skill* (pp. 87–108). Routledge/Sonic Studies in Educational Foundations.

Goodyear, P. (2020). Design and co-configuration for hybrid learning: Theorising the practices of learning space design. *British Journal of Educational Technology, 51/4*. https://doi.org/10.1111/bjet.12925

Hadar, L. L., Ergas, O., Alpert, B., & Ariav, T. (2020). Rethinking teacher education in a VUCA world: Student teachers' social-emotional competencies during the Covid-19 crisis. *European Journal of Teacher Education, 43*(4), 573–586.

Harasim, L. (2012). *Learning theory and online technologies*. Routledge.

Harcourt-Rorabaugh, P., & Stommel, J. (2012). Hybridity, pt. 3: What does hybrid pedagogy do? *Hybrid Pedagogy*. https://hybridpedagogy.org/hybridity-pt-3-what-does-hybrid-pedagogy-do/

Hilli, C., Nørgård, R. T., & Aaen, J. H. (2019). Designing hybrid learning spaces in higher education. *Dansk Universitetspædagogisk Tidsskrift, 15*, 66–82.

Hoadley, C., & Kali, Y. (2019). Five waves of conceptualizing knowledge and learning for our future in a networked society. In Y. Kali, A. Baram-Tsabary, & A. Schejter (Eds.), *Learning in a networked society: Spontaneous and designed technology enhanced learning communities* (pp. 1–21). Springer.

Hod, Y. (2017). Future learning spaces in schools: Concepts and designs from the learning sciences. *Journal of Formative Design in Learning, 1*(2), 99–109.

Hod, Y., & Katz, S. (2020). Fostering highly engaged knowledge building communities in socioemotional and socio-cognitive hybrid learning spaces. *British Journal of Educational Technology, 51*(4). https://doi.org/10.1111/bjet.12910

Inbar, D., & Inbar E. (2020). Al ha'yesh veha'ein, al hagalui vehasamui bema'arechet hahinuch [On what is and what is not, on the overt and covert in the education system]. In Y. Harpaz & A. Hurwitz (Eds.), *Hinuch bezomet: Si'ur mohot al atid ha'hinuch beIsrael* [Education at a crossroad: Brainstorming on the future of education in Israel] (pp. 33–45). Dvir. In Hebrew.

Kali, Y., Sagy, O., Benichou, M., Atias, O., & Levin-Peled, R. (2019). Teaching expertise reconsidered: The technology, pedagogy, content and space (TPeCS) knowledge framework. *British Journal of Educational Technology, 50*(5), 2162–2177. https://doi.org/10.1111/bjet.12847

Köppe, C., Nørgård, R. T., & Pedersen, A. Y. (2017). *Towards a pattern language for hybrid education*. In Proceedings of the VikingPLoP 2017 conference (pp. 1–18). https://doi.org/10.1145/3158491.3158504.

Kramer, M. (2017). Sage on the stage or bore at the board? *Communication Education, 66*(2), 245–247. https://doi.org/10.1080/03634523.2016.1272129

Mishra, P. (2019). Considering contextual knowledge: The TPACK diagram gets an upgrade. *Journal of Digital Learning in Teacher Education, 35*(2), 76–78. https://doi.org/10.1080/21532974.2019.1588611

Mishra, P., & Koehler, M. J. (2006). Technological pedagogical content knowledge: A framework for teacher knowledge. *Teachers College Record, 108*(6), 1017.

Mishra, P., Warr, M., & Islam, R. (2023). TPACK in the age of ChatGPT and generative AI. *Journal of Digital Learning in Teacher Education*. https://doi.org/10.1080/21532974.2023.2247480

Naot-Ofarim, Y., & Solomonic, S. (2016). Educational polyphony. *Studies in Philosophy and Education, 35*(4), 385–397. https://doi.org/10.1007/s11217-015-9491-2

Nørgård, R. T., Mor, Y., & Bengtsen, S. S. (2019). Networked learning in, for, and with the world. In *Networked professional learning: Emerging and equitable discourses for professional development* (Research in networked learning) (pp. 71–88). Springer. https://doi.org/10.1007/978-3-030-18030-0_5

OECD. (2017). *The future of education and skills: Education 2030 conceptual learning framework: Background papers*. Directorate for Education and Skills Education Policy Committee.

OECD (2020). *PISA 2018 results (volume VI): Are students ready to thrive in an interconnected world?* PISA, OECD Publishing. https://doi.org/10.1787/d5f68679-en.

Olsher, S., Yerushalmy, M., & Chazan, D. (2016). How might the use of technology in formative assessment support changes in mathematics teaching? *For the Learning of Mathematics, 36*(3), 11–18.

Pelletier, K., McCormack, M., Reeves, J., Robert, J., Arbino, N., Al-Freih, W.M., Dickson-Deane, C., Guevara, C., Koster, L., Sanchez-Mendiola, M., Skallerup Bessette, L., & Stine, J. (2022). *EDUCAUSE horizon report teaching and learning edition*. EDUC22. Retrieved February 27, 2024, from https://www.learntechlib.org/p/221033/

Perkins, D. N., & Blythe, T. (1994). Putting understanding up front. *Educational Leadership, 51*(5), 11–13.

Radcliffe, D. (2009). A pedagogy-space-technology (PST) framework for designing and evaluating learning places. In D. Radcliffe, H. Wilson, D. Powell, & B. Tibbetts (Eds.), *Learning spaces in higher education: Positive outcomes by design* (pp. 11–16). The University of Queensland and the Australian Learning and Teaching Council.

Rogers, C. R. (1980). *A way of being*. Houghton Mifflin.

Scardamalia, M., & Bereiter, C. (2006). Knowledge building: Theory, pedagogy, and technology. In K. Sawyer (Ed.), *The Cambridge handbook of the learning sciences* (pp. 97–118). Cambridge University Press.

Scardamalia, M., & Bereiter, C. (2014). Knowledge building and knowledge creation: Theory, pedagogy, and technology. In R. K. Sawyer (Ed.), *The Cambridge handbook of the learning sciences* (2nd ed., pp. 397–417). Cambridge University Press.

Schleicher, A. (2020). *The impact of COVID-19 on education insights from education at a glance 2020*. OECD. https://eric.ed.gov/?id=ED616315

Schwarz-Franco, O. (2019). Polyphonic teaching: The ability to facilitate multiple voices as a crucial teaching skill. In W. Gershon & P. Appelbaum (Eds.), *Sonic studies in educational foundations* (pp. 87–108). Routledge.

Stommel, J. (2012). Hybridity, pt. 2: What is hybrid pedagogy? *Hybrid Pedagogy*.

Tishman, S., Jay, E., & Perkins, D. N. (1993). Teaching thinking dispositions: From transmission to enculturation. *Theory Into Practice, 32*(3), 147–153. https://doi.org/10.1080/00405849309543590

Tissenbaum, M., & Slotta, J. D. (2019). Developing a smart classroom infrastructure to support real-time student collaboration and inquiry: A 4-year design study. *Instructional Science, 47*, 423–462. https://doi.org/10.1007/s11251-019-09486-1

U.S. Department of Education, Office of Educational Technology (2016). *Future ready learning: Reimagining the role of technology in education*. 2016 National Education Technology Plan. http://goo.gl/2GPxJD

Vygotsky, L. S. (1989). *Thought and language*. MIT Press.

Whitehead, A. N. (2005). *Hahinuch hahumanisti kehadracha beomanut hahayim* [Humanistic education as instruction of the arts of living]. In N. Aloni (Ed.), *kol shetzarich adam: masa befilosofial hinuchit* [Everything a person needs: A Journey in educational philosophy], (pp. 430–431). Mofet Institute and Hakibbutz Hameuchad. (in Hebrew).

Wiliam, D. (2011). What is assessment for learning? *Studies in Educational Evaluation, 37*(1), 3–14.

Yondler, Y., & Blau, I. (2021). What is the degree of teacher centrality in optimal teaching of digital literacy in a technology-enhanced environment? Typology of teacher prototypes. *Journal of Research on Technology in Education, 55*(2), 230–251. https://doi.org/10.1080/15391523.2021.1950084

Part I
Towards Inclusion: Acknowledging Cultural Differences

Amazing Race: Collaborative Learning, Gamification, and the Virtual World

Miri Shonfeld

Introduction

Learning in a game-like and collaborative virtual world is more relevant today than in the past, because students now spend many hours in social and gamified 3D environments using digital devices, including mobile phones. Accordingly, significant technological companies such as Facebook and Microsoft have begun to develop virtual worlds for social uses (the metaverse), thus making virtual worlds accessible to education as well. Although these worlds are attractive to children, they have not yet penetrated the educational sphere, and teaching staff are not trained in their use. Therefore, teacher training programs should enable preservice teachers (PSTs) to practice teaching in virtual worlds to better prepare them for twenty-first-century classrooms (Badiee & Kaufman, 2014; Rayner & Fluck, 2014).

In this environment, it is possible to address the challenges that arise in learning in a multicultural setting. Multicultural online learning raises difficulties related to the discourse between cultures, identity, language, social codes, and learning styles (Ganayem et al., 2020). Asynchronous collaborative learning reveals language and style gaps, while synchronous Zoom learning stigmatizes appearance. However, in the virtual world, students can change the appearance of their representative avatar according to the group of belonging, thus eroding cultural differences. In addition, collaborative work in the virtual world takes place in the same space shared by everyone with the same pool of materials.

The activity in the virtual world allows the learners a unique encounter in which they feel they are in a shared learning space. This feeling is created because their avatars sit side by side in the auditorium, travel together, move together from one place to another and even create together a new world that enables collaborative

M. Shonfeld (✉)
Kibbutzim College of Education, Technology and Arts, Tel-Aviv, Israel
e-mail: mirish@macam.ac.il

Y. Yondler et al. (eds.), *Cultivating Future-Oriented Learners*, Understanding Teaching-Learning Practice, https://doi.org/10.1007/978-3-031-63253-2_2

Fig. 1 Sailing together—Prof. Paul Resta from the University of Texas and Prof. Miri Shonfeld from the Kibbutzim College of Education

learning. Collaborative learning provides learners with experience in teamwork and sensitivity to group needs (Abinun, 2013; Slavin, 2014), and it provides a variety of personal, social, emotional, and creative activities.

Since 2010. Experience in gamified collaborative learning in a virtual world has concluded with a final workshop at the Kibbutzim College of Education as part of the master's degree studies in technology in education. In the first decade, this type of learning was conducted in cooperation with the University of Texas at Austin, and since 2020, activity with other colleges of education in Israel has continued. During these years, a learning model has developed that began as virtual collaborative learning for which the collaborative product was the goal where the PSTs developed an educational video. Over the years, the rules of gamification were introduced into the virtual-pedagogical space, and the final product became a learning tool. The collaborative online learning environments used in the workshop (MOODLE, Zoom and Virtual World) bridge geographic and cultural gaps and enable learning in an international environment as shown in Fig. 1 below.

The virtual world is rich, providing opportunities for multi-sensory learning that challenges the imagination. In this chapter, we will discover the magic of combining collaborative learning with gamification and a virtual learning space.

Theoretical Anchors

Learning in Virtual Worlds

Virtual worlds, such as Second Life (SL), provide new opportunities for learning, including experiential, immersive, collaborative, and game-based learning activities (Warburton, 2009), which are often not available in asynchronous and synchronous learning environments offered by traditional learning management systems (Shonfeld et al., 2011). In a virtual world environment, learners can see and hear their friends' representations, teleport or meet the group somewhere, creating a sense of being together. SL is an open virtual world built by an extremely large international community. It contains many sites—historical, scientific, cultural and political—that facilitate learning, research, creation and interaction with others. Despite its educational value as a rich learning environment, SL is not safe for children due to the asocial behavior of some participants or inappropriate content, however, educators should be aware of SL's educational values and the challenges involved in adopting it for teaching. It should be noted that there are closed virtual worlds based on SL technology, such as Eureka's Open Sim, where the world of TEC (Technology, Education and Cultural diversity) takes place. The TEC Island is used by students from different sectors and schools as a meeting place and collaborative creation to build trust and break stigmas and prejudices (Ganayem et al., 2020). This chapter describes an Open World Academy activity in SL, designed to prepare PSTs for the future use of teaching in 3D environments.

The use of 3D virtual worlds (VWs) evolved rapidly in the first decade of the twenty-first century, not only for entertainment but also for education, practice, research, commerce and socialization. VWs are learning platforms that present digital simulations of people, environments, content, and activities. Participants are represented by avatars who can write, talk, walk and fly (Shonfeld & Kritz, 2013). The virtual world provides a sense of presence for collaborative learning (Warburton, 2009), it gives participants a protected environment in sensitive situations, and therefore has the potential to improve intercultural interaction. It has also been shown to provide more practice time and opportunities for a variety of ways of learning that are not available in other learning environments (Carrington et al., 2011). The VW offers many benefits, such as increased learner motivation and engagement, and facilitates collaborations (Resta & Shonfeld, 2016), because synchronous communication and the spatial dimension contribute to the sense of interactivity (Gallego et al., 2016; Hoter et al., 2018; Merchant et al., 2014). The VW has unique characteristics that increase the sense of self as a learner and as a creator, it stimulates a sense of social presence and encourages self-presentation, exposure, involvement and immersion in what is happening (Ghanbarzadeh & Ghapanchi, 2018). This environment also acts as a powerful communication channel, raising awareness of others, increasing the sense of belonging to the community and providing an opportunity to learn and explore cultures in a multicultural environment (Resta & Shonfeld, 2016). Using exhibits in the VW creates a stimulating and close-knit learning environment where learners can feel free to discuss sensitive topics (Shonfeld & Kritz, 2013).

Collaborative Learning

The model described in this chapter is based on the social constructivist pedagogy that advocates collaborative learning. Collaborative learning involves ongoing dialogue among the learning partners; between the teacher and the learners, and among the learners themselves, so that everyone learns and teaches at the same time. The emphasis in collaborative learning is on the reflective process through which learners construct their personal knowledge. The learning process includes gaining insights from mistakes made while learning, and it leads learners to take responsibility for the entire process, from organizing the learning to its actual implementation (Abinun, 2013). In collaborative inquiry, each learner must plan how they will learn, formulate questions on the topic under study, search for relevant answers, and thereby help construct the group's knowledge (Sharan, 2015). Collaborative learning promotes cognitive and social skills such as the ability to manage conflicts, share ideas and opinions, creative thinking, and higher-order thinking (Shonfeld & Weinberger, 2019). Moreover, collaborative learning facilitates a wide range of, personal and social activities that can be both emotional and creative, so that they learn from each other, and develop trusting relationships that contribute to increased self-esteem, which, in turn, leads them to successful learning. This method of learning also enhances twenty-first-century skills (Shonfeld, 2017; Shaw, 2021).

In order to maintain optimal collaborative learning, groups must be as heterogeneous as possible in every respect, such as gender, achievement level and ethnicity, so that the group will be composed of learners who differ in their strengths and can lean on each other during the learning process (Slavin, 2014). The shared discourse, which includes expressing diverse opinions, asking questions, and providing mutual feedback, leads to learners' support for each other and a sense of group belonging, which may increase the desire to collaborate and invest efforts towards the common goal (Peacock et al., 2020).

Moreover, collaborative work invites learners to experience teamwork, causes them to develop awareness of the emotional aspects of learning, and in the process, learn to be sensitive to others (Abinun, 2013). Group members must ensure that everyone achieves the goal of collaborative learning: either understanding the material learned or developing specific skills (Slavin, 2014). In the reflective process that takes place at the end of the group learning, among other things, members relate to the forms of cooperation that occurred and to the possibilities for improving their teamwork in the future (Sharan, 2015). Sharing emotions during collaborative learning, including harsh feelings, contributes to the alleviation of personal tensions, and leads to the resolution of learning difficulties (Peacock et al., 2020). For the most part, students prefer to collaborate remotely online rather than face-to-face in class. Online learning makes it possible to establish quick social connections between group members (Romero-Hall & Vicentini, 2017).

First and foremost among the challenges of collaborative learning is the variation between learners' work habits. Therefore, the division of tasks should be adapted but equal. However, sometimes the division of tasks is unequal and leads to idleness and the phenomenon of "hitchhikers", those who do not contribute to the group (Zhampeissova et al., 2020). The main challenge is organizing a collaborative process: planning the work, time management, group management, division of roles and joint evaluation. In addition, the planning of activities raises a real need to take into account the heterogeneity and size of the community, and there may be difficulties in logistics and coordination of the quality of learning (Shonfeld, 2020).

Hence the importance of a facilitator who is proficient in collaborative methodology and knows how to manage it properly. To this end, the teacher has to agree to become a facilitator, and then is required to learn how to do it properly. Online collaborative learning also entails challenges related to time coordination and availability of communication (computer, internet, etc.) and of an appropriate teacher. A technologically literate teacher who knows how to operate synchronous and asynchronous learning groups may increase learning motivation, learner autonomy and responsibility, and learning success (Lane, 2017).

Methods of collaborative teaching and learning and appropriate tools for such learning are emerging at an accelerated pace that exceeds the ability of institutions of higher education to adopt and implement them, so that they lag behind in their use for teaching. Nevertheless, teachers must supplement this essential knowledge on their own in order to be able to teach collaborative skills (Shonfeld & Gibson, 2019). Recommended tools for collaborative learning are blogs, LMS tools such as forums, collaborative databases, wikis, Google tools and virtual worlds, which are gaining momentum following the development of the metaverse by Microsoft and Facebook.

The assimilation and integration of collaborative learning in education requires a change in pedagogical perceptions on the part of both students and teachers. Students move from passive to active learners and must display responsibility for learning and participate in peer learning, while teachers must organize the environment and conditions, structure knowledge and encourage students in active learning. Preparation and practice in teacher training assists teachers in their work at school (Shonfeld, 2017).

Gamification

Gamification is not a game, but it is a product of the characteristics of the game and the culture of gaming. The terminology was invented in 2003 by Nick Pellling, a British game developer, and was introduced in 2010 as the use of computers for learning evolved (Burke, 2016). In the broadest sense, gamification is the introduction of gaming elements such as points, prizes and game boards, leading to content worlds unrelated to the game, in order to increase motivation to act among the target audience. Gamified learning focuses on the end user and the design of the learning experience and has become a common concept used by instructional designers. Designing a learning experience has become an evolving field in its own right, adding to the focus on the "end user" the scholastic and educational dimension. Today, learner enjoyment is positioned as one of the goals of developing units of study (Bergin, 2019; Chou, 2015).

Gamification makes it possible to have a reality-like experience, but in a protected environment that allows trial and error. Gamification measures integrated into a highly immersive virtual environment and collaborative work have shown good learning outcomes and high satisfaction (Resta & Shonfeld, 2016). Gamification enables learners to role-play and go beyond the boundaries of the familiar and fixed, thereby developing their imagination and stimulating intrinsic motivation to continue learning. The experience also enables specialization over time and a sense of power and independence. Gamification has eight core drivers: meaning, development and achievement, empowerment, ownership, social impact, desirability, vigilance, avoidance of losing. All these drivers increase motivation to learn (Chou, 2015). However, the results of gamification do not always lead to positive learning, and there can sometimes be anxiety about competition and fear of losing, and later a decrease in scholastic outcomes. Consequently, gamification mechanisms must be adapted to a heterogeneous and multicultural population. Competitive play is usually played between individuals, but it is advisable to integrate competition between groups and thus reduce tensions and increase motivation. Hence, the effect of gamification depends on additional factors. Hence one must understand the complexity of gamified learning within the ensemble of the components of the learning environment.

Learning Model: Online COllaborative Learning and Gamified Virtual Worlds (OCOGAV)

The learning model described in this chapter expresses polyphonic intelligence in the synergy it creates between space, technology, pedagogy and content. The virtual world is the interactive learning space that corresponds with pedagogy built on a combination of collaborative online learning (OCL), gamification in teaching and learning (gamification) and virtual worlds (VW). The content of the missions, which also corresponds with all of these, encourages familiarity with multicultural places and experimentation with humanistic values. Thus, the learning environment becomes a social space in which the members are located and the environment is not foreign to them. This social space encourages the two main aspects of the polyphonic paradigm: learners move in the learning space independently and build their own knowledge, while at the same time communicating among themselves, collaborating and building collective products. The Model in Fig. 2 below demonstrates the components of polyphonic intelligence.

Learning in the proposed model takes place within a space that combines collaborative learning pedagogy, a VW, and gamification rules. The content is non-specific, selectable and depends on learners and what is available within the virtual world. The technology tools are used for group communication and collaborative

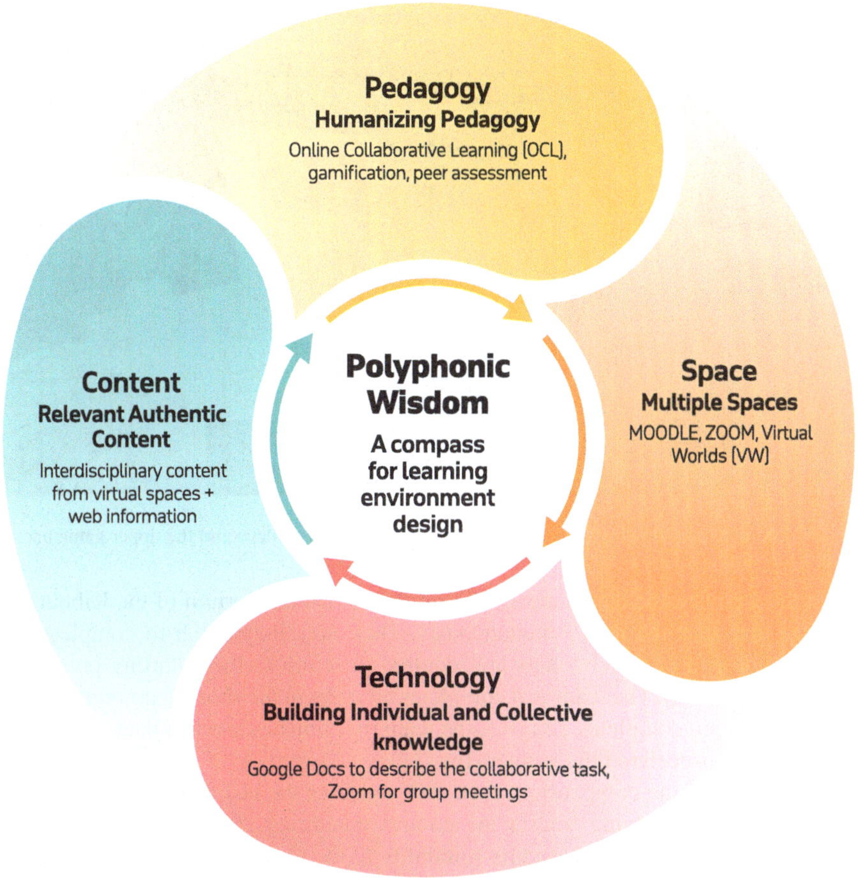

Fig. 2 Model of gamified OCL in VW spaces

writing of the game. The goals of the learning model are to expose PSTs to a VW, and to develop insights into the pedagogical potential of this environment, its advantages and the challenges involved; enable them to experience immersed learning; be involved in collaborative learning and reflect on it; and propose new practices for teaching in school. The model is based on a competition between teams, in which each team is required to build a learning assignment for each other on one of the SL islands. The PSTs study in small groups of four or five who are in different places and study in different institutions, so the meetings are held remotely. They design learning tasks based on visits to historical, cultural or scientific locations reconstructed in the virtual world. After 1–2 months of collaborative learning in the VW, an experiential climax event is held based on the format of the television program Race for a Million, in which teams compete to perform the tasks already built by the other groups.

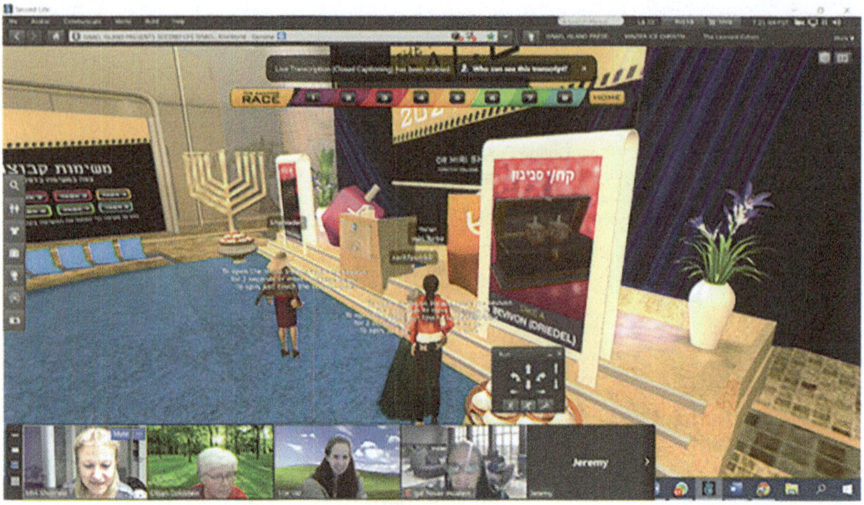

Fig. 3 Zoom screen showing the auditorium at the Kibbutzim College and the upper game bar

In this activity, the teams meet in SL in the virtual auditorium of the Kibbutzim College and start the race simultaneously. They are allotted 1 h to complete the tasks, at the end of which teams are required to return to their starting point (the virtual auditorium). The team that completes all tasks in the shortest amount of time wins. If no team completes all tasks, the team that finishes most of them at the end of game time is declared the winner (Fig. 3).

At the end of the competition, each PST assesses the tasks of the other groups according to the following criteria: the amount of learning, clarity of the task, enjoyment of performing the task and its suitability to the time required to complete the task. Following the PSTs' scores, the team that came in first, second and third for each criterion is selected. The competition helps team building and team identity. This breaks down the barriers of culture and institutional identity. As a result, the level of enjoyment increases and active cooperation between students improves. These affect the motivation to achieve academic goals in the course.

Instructions to the PSTs contain the following steps:

- Step 1. Individual activity with examples of products designed by PSTs from previous years: Arriving at the Kibbutzim College teleport in SL, including technological preparation and practice on the island. This involves self-learning, coping with technological difficulties and an unfamiliar world.
- Step 2. Group activity: discussion in groups and choice of the learning task topic. Exploration of the VW and locating a suitable place to construct the learning task agreed upon by the group members. Here learners encounter teamwork, collaborative learning and a multicultural environment.
- Step 3. Group activity: writing a task to be performed in the VW. The task is co-written on a collaborative screen on GoogleDocs. The rules of gamification are

learned and applied to the task. The assignment should be clearly written and detailed so that colleagues in other groups can execute it without further clarification.

- Step 4. Group activity: trying out the group's task before posting it for other groups. After finishing the writing, the group experiments with the task it has written and optimizes it. Students work collaboratively to fine-tune the assignment and understand the benefits of working in a diverse team that can adapt the assignment to different learners.
- Step 5. Group activity: participation in peer tasks and competition between groups. All teams play in the team game—Amazing Race. Each group tries to reach a greater number of points and perform all the tasks in cooperation with all the group members who are in different places in Israel and around the world. During the competition, intensive communication takes place via WhatsApp and via a group Zoom.
- Step 6. Evaluation of tasks by the groups. The competition checks for rapid arrival in the virtual group to all places and execution of tasks in a limited time (90 min). In addition, there is competition for the quality of the task in various dimensions: task, task enjoyment, learning from the task, and adapting it to the time allotted in the race. The assessment for each dimension is given by each PST using a questionnaire on the Google form.
- Step 7. The discussion of the competition results and of the various dimensions takes place in the post-race lesson. The ensuing reflective discussion leads to a discussion of the experiences of the model and the educational value of each of its components, the learning method and theories that reinforce learning in this model. Similarly, the challenges of this process and the ways to solve them are also addressed.

The tasks below demonstrate their heterogeneity and diverse content areas. They combine the rules of gamification, social constructivist learning and a group product. The vast world of SL challenges the imagination and allows teams to roam the world together and create a learning mission based on human development. The possibilities for roaming the VW are diverse and allow multicultural teams to relate to learning in an interdisciplinary context.

In light of all this, it can be said that the polyphonic intelligence model reflects how the interactive virtual learning environment invites learners to have practical experiences with global humanistic values that encourage personal responsibility, social and environmental responsibility, responsibility and caring for the glocal environment, understanding the other and accepting their point of view, openness and empathy towards people from other cultures, and independent learning that is consistently and systematically channeled to achieve the goals that learners have set for themselves and to create collective products.

The learning possibilities and content are many and tangible, but the great challenge is teamwork and collaborative learning that is not easy to carry out due to its complexity and the interdependence dependence of the learners, and this requires accountability and frequent and proper communication (Shonfeld, 2017). In addition, activity in the VW is based on advanced computers (bandwidth, memory, etc.) and is not easy for the user. In order to promote the project and facilitate the students' activities in the VW, a pilot study was conducted based on the students' reflections written during and after the experience. The study examined the challenges and the contribution of the model to learning.

Challenges to Executing the Model and its Drivers

The PSTs encountered many challenges during the activity. Following is the division into subcategories in the category of challenges:

Technology The challenge noted by almost all the PSTs concerned technical problems such as the software requirements for operating SL (mainly the screen's graphics card) and the quality of the Internet connection. These problems delayed task performance and caused frustration among participants:

> The most significant disadvantage in my opinion and according to my experience is the technical difficulties—lack of connection and inability to enter Second Life. It frustrated me a lot on a personal level and created a sense of helplessness.

Some students had trouble managing the avatars in SL: "*Sometimes it is difficult to move the avatar, which requires patience and openness.*" Many students complained about the complexity of the new learning environment: "*Sometimes it's hard to get around. It requires practice and is frustrating. In all the missions we were busy most of the time getting to know the new environment.*" Some students had trouble using multiple environments at once, such as SL, ZOOM, MOODLE, and Google Docs.

Time Additional challenges related to task execution. Some PSTs reported that the time allotted to each activity (10 min) was too short, and recommended allocating more time to tasks in the competitive game. They also noted the difficulty in finding time for collaborative work.

Adaptation to Students With regard to the use of SL in their teaching work, the PSTs felt that the environment was not suitable for their students because it was "*too open*". They found strange behavior in some of the avatars, such as characters in immodest clothing or harassing messages from strangers: "*The obvious disadvantage is that there is exposure to educational and immodest figures. Sometimes there is a sense of bullying when messages and requests from outsiders arrive by chance.*" These encounters appeared at the beginning of the work. However, after a while, the students learned to ignore these figures and flew to other islands where there were no outsiders.

The Contribution of the Model

The reflections indicate that the activity helped the participants understand the educational value of the model. Examination of the reflections yielded the following categories:

A Diverse Environment for Teaching and Learning The students discovered rich content that can be used for teaching: "*a learning environment that definitely creates interest and provides a tremendous experience*." In their opinion, SL offers a variety of possibilities for exposing students to historical, geographical, scientific and other topics, and to different cultures and world knowledge. In the words of one participant:

> At Second Life there are very interesting places, where you can learn and find information that cannot be seen in reality, especially during the difficult period of the coronavirus. That's definitely one of the advantages of software, the fact that a person can travel around the world without leaving home.

Social Experience The PSTs cited as an advantage the possibility of meeting people in SL and using it as a social platform. They perceived learning in the model as active, creative, fun, interesting, intriguing, stimulating and able to give children meaningful experiences: "*It's a very enjoyable experience, without a doubt*."

> The environment allows you to visit realistic places and also the world of stories and fairy tales. We have seen through the tasks that it is possible to learn history, such as Kristallnacht, connect objects and proverbs, enjoy snow battles and more.

The PSTs also shared their sense of belonging to the group when their avatars were together, describing it as "*being present*." The presence of the various avatars in a shared virtual space is what created a sense of actual reality.

The students emphasized that the group work contributed to their friendship: "*I think it was an opportunity to socialize while working on the task, and it was significant during this time of COVID-19*". Group work also contributed to academic achievements: "*Working together contributed to the connection and familiarity between us, as well as to the shared sense of success*."

Collaborative Learning in a VW High satisfaction with learning in this way was evident. Almost all participants (98%) said it was their first encounter with SL, and almost all (95%) enjoyed the activity: "*We had fun and laughed together on tasks*," "*It was great to work in SL with my group*." They perceived group work as an essential factor in the success of the project. They noted the mutual help in their groups: "*At first it was hard for us to get along, but we supported each other and helped each other*." The mutual help led to a sense of group belonging:

> My team was great! During the race, when I encountered technical problems and couldn't stay connected to the virtual world, I told my team to continue without me. When I managed to connect, they sent me the teleport and waited until I got to the right place.

Mutuality Group members developed empathy and caring: "*I must say that I had the privilege of being part of an active, caring and considerate* [group]."

> We took care of all the members of the group, helped each other, were able to share places and teleport for those who couldn't make it—and saved a lot of time. It brought us closer, the fact that we talked, shared, laughed and played together. It was an amazing experience.

The sense of belonging—the PSTs also recognized the power of belonging to a group:

> The collaborative work process allowed me to learn many things about myself and my teammates, and to use the strengths of the group members in a way that made it possible to both enjoy the learning process and succeed in meaningful learning.

They assessed their ability to contribute equally to the work together:

> Working together on the project was excellent—each contributed her share equally. To succeed, we also opened Zoom at the same time. I read the missions, one of us started searching the world, while another wrote the findings in our joint document. And so the whole group functioned, and each played an active role.

We can summarize by saying that the group was a motivating factor in supporting learning and also in the sense of belonging that encouraged learning. When there is a sense of belonging, the desire for cooperation and investment of effort to the success of the group increases (Peacock et al., 2020). It seems that the combination of the game in which the teams competed increased the sense of belonging and the motivation to learn, as found in previous studies (Resta & Shonfeld, 2016).

The analysis of the reflections shows that the experience in the VW combined with collaborative pedagogy and gamification led to enjoyment and strong motivation to learn. It was also found that the discussion following the SL activity enabled the participants to gain insights about the educational value of the model and the possibilities for its integration into education. The peer evaluation was in accordance with the rubrics given to the PSTs in advance, which also helped them structure the task. However, questions were also raised about the dangers of roaming in SL. In light of this, a review was conducted on VW environments aimed at educational goals, based on avatars in a 3D world. A VW that was extensively presented and demonstrated was the virtual island of TEC (Ganayem et al., 2020), which is built on SL's technology, but can be used to build a closed environment (OpenSim).

In summation, this chapter discusses a project conducted in SL's virtual learning spaces in collaborative work between two colleges, so all learning was conducted online. The project was based on competition between groups, with the intention of promoting group cohesion and improving collaborative learning. A collaborative learning activity that includes gamification in SL allows participants to explore the SL environment, discover the human treasure built in this environment by a global community, and enjoy its inherent content and artistic richness. This is because the avatar environment raises awareness of others and strengthens the sense of belonging to the community (Resta & Shonfeld, 2016).

Alongside the advantages presented here, it is also important to note the limitations of using the SL environment in education, due to its being open to outsiders and due to the danger of exposure to inappropriate content. We therefore recommend that at school PSTs use a closed VW such as the "Island of TEC" in the WORLD EUREKA environment, Mindcraft for Education, and other closed environments that allow entry only to registered students.

The other challenge is organizing a collaborative process, hence the importance of a teacher-facilitator skilled in collaborative learning management, who must be familiar with methods for collaborative learning and appropriate tools for such learning, including the VWs, which rivet students to their screens in their free time. By bringing the contemporary playground to the school world, teachers can enter the children's world and challenge them with socially constructivist learning, which will influence them even after they leave school.

In conclusion, the virtual world serves as a rich learning space replete with opportunities for development and creation. The combination of collaborative pedagogy and gamification in this space has led to enjoyable learning, increased motivation and the promotion of social skills. The PSTs who graduated from the course are trained in online collaborative learning, VWs and gamification as a model to be assimilated into their future teaching in schools. Some of the PSTs who took this course are now leading learning in this model in schools, in training at the Ministry of Education and in informal education spaces.

References

Abinun, Y. (2013). Collaborative learning. *Hed Hachinuch, 86*(5), 92–93 [in Hebrew].

Badiee, F., & Kaufman, D. (2014). Effectiveness of an online simulation for teacher education. *Journal of Technology and Teacher Education, 22*(2), 167–186.

Bergin, J. (2019). LXD: Ten critical differences between LX and UX. The emerging learning. *Design Journal, 6*(1), 4.

Burke, B. (2016). *Gamify: How gamification motivates people to do extraordinary things*. Routledge.

Carrington, L., Kervin, L., & Ferry, B. (2011). Enhancing the development of pre-service teacher professional identity via an online classroom simulation. *Journal of Technology and Teacher Education, 19*(3), 351–368.

Chou, Y. (2015). *Actionable gamification: Beyond points. Badges, and leaderboards* (Kindle ed.). Octalysis Media.

Gallego, M. D., Bueno, S., & Noyes, J. (2016). Second life adoption in education: A motivational model based on uses and gratifications theory. *Computers & Education, 100*, 81–93.

Ganayem, A., Hoter, E., & Shonfeld, M. (2020). In W. J. Hunter & R. S. P. Austin (Eds.), *Blended and online learning for global citizenship: New technologies and opportunities for intercultural education* (pp. 32–50). Routledge.

Ghanbarzadeh, R., & Ghapanchi, A. H. (2018). Investigating various application areas of three-dimensional virtual worlds for higher education. *British Journal of Educational Technology, 49*, 370–384.

Hoter, E., & Yazbak Abu Ahmad, M. (2018). Designing pedagogy for virtual worlds in multicultural environments. In *Designing for the user experience in learning systems* (pp. 65–80). Springer.

Lane, L. (2017). Introduction. In S. Dent, L. Lane, & T. Strike (Eds.), *Collaboration, communities and competition*. Sense Publishers.

Merchant, Z., Goetz, E. T., Cifuentes, L., Kenney-Kennicutt, W., & Davis, T. J. (2014). Effectiveness of virtual reality-based instruction on students' learning outcomes in K-12 and higher education: A meta-analysis. *Computers and Education, 70*, 29–40.

Peacock, S., Cowan, J., Irvine, L., & Williams, J. (2020). An exploration into the importance of a sense of belonging for online learners. *The International Review of Research in Open and Distance Learning, 21*(2), 18–35.

Rayner, C., & Fluck, A. (2014). Pre-service teachers' perceptions of simSchool as preparation for inclusive education: A pilot study. *Asia-Pacific Journal of Teacher Education, 42*(3), 212–227.

Resta, P., & Shonfeld, M. (2016). Challenges and strategies in designing cross-national learning team projects in virtual worlds. In T. Anderson (Ed.), *Virtual worlds in online and distance education* (pp. 262–275). Athabasca University Press.

Romero-Hall, E., & Vicentini, C. R. (2017). Examining distance learners in hybrid synchronous instruction: Successes and challenges. *Online Learning Journal, 21*(4).

Sharan, Y. (2015). Meaningful learning in the cooperative classroom. *Education 3–13, 43*(1), 83–94.

Shaw, A. (2021). Teaching or cheating? Using collaboration and technology to support student learning. *International Journal on E-Learning, 20*(1), 47–58.

Shonfeld, M. (2017). Online collaborative learning in academia. *Hora'a B'Akademia, 7*, 8–11 [in Hebrew].

Shonfeld, M. (2020). International online writing community. *Dapim, 73*, 227–259.

Shonfeld, M., & Gibson, D. (Eds.). (2019). *Collaborative learning in a global world*. Information Age Publishing.

Shonfeld, M., & Kritz, M. (2013). Virtual representations in 3D learning environments. *Interdisciplinary Journal of E-Learning and Learning Objects, 9*, 249–266.

Shonfeld, M., & Weinberger, Y. (2019). What influences teacher educators' use of collaborative learning? In M. Shonfeld & D. Gibson (Eds.), *Collaborative learning in a global world* (pp. 155–174). Information Age Publishing.

Shonfeld, M., Resta, P., & Yaniv, H. (2011). Engagement and social presence in a virtual worlds (second life) learning environment. In M. Koehler & P. Mishra (Eds.), *Proceedings of the society for information technology & teacher education international conference 2011* (pp. 740–745). Association for the Advancement of Computing in Education (AACE).

Slavin, R. E. (2014). Making cooperative learning powerful. *Educational Leadership, 72*(2), 22–26.

Warburton, S. (2009). Second life in higher education: Assessing the potential for and the barriers to deploying virtual worlds in learning and teaching. *British Journal of Educational Technology, 40*(3), 414–426.

Zhampeissova, K., Kosareva, I., & Borisova, U. (2020). Collaborative mobile learning with smartphones in higher education. *International Association of Online Engineering, 4*(21), 4–18.

Creating Collaborative Multicultural and Multidimensional Teaching Tasks from Non-teaching Specific Materials

Miri Yochanna

Introduction

Engaging, meaningful, culturally diverse, and authentic classroom activities are an essential part of education in today's school system. The learners in the classrooms should be exposed to real life multicultural situations that will aid in preparing them for life in the future. Thus, a polyphonic classroom, 'into which multiple voices are invited … to engage each other in dialogue' (Depalma, 2010, p. 437) is called for, as the learners need to learn about each other, how to collaborate with others, to think critically about what they are learning and encountering and to be exposed to a vast number of varied materials, topics, situations and issues. This is of high importance in order to prepare the future generation.

Experience in a multicultural setting, learning together, planning for and developing teaching materials based on multicultural points of view, and a polyphonic dialogue offers the preservice teachers an opportunity to cultivate a 'mindset of social consciousness and social action' (Senyshyn & Martinelli, 2021, p. 21). Today's classrooms are made up of learners from diverse multicultural and ethnic backgrounds, at different levels of ability and knowledge. 'Each of the participants may be considered a distinct voice…, which utters new subjects by introducing new themes in the discourse, or reiterates an already uttered theme, using his/her own "voice"' (Trausan-Matu et al., 2007). With this in mind, the use of a variety of materials opens many possibilities for teachers to create lessons that are multiculturally inclusive and diverse, supporting the makeup of students in the classroom. The planning process is highly benefited by working together to create the teaching materials as this enables a diverse outlook on what is being planned and developed.

M. Yochanna (✉)
Kibbutzim College of Education, Technology and Arts, Tel-Aviv, Israel
e-mail: miri.yochanna@smkb.ac.il

Y. Yondler et al. (eds.), *Cultivating Future-Oriented Learners*, Understanding Teaching-Learning Practice, https://doi.org/10.1007/978-3-031-63253-2_3

Collaborative activities and processes in teacher training offer the opportunity to expand future teachers' multicultural and diverse knowledge base and to give them the freedom to teach a variety of topics, regardless of the discipline they are training to teach. 'Collaborative learning encourages understanding, fosters relationships, builds self-esteem, reduces anxiety, and stimulates critical thinking' (Panitz, 1999 in Gonzalez-Lloret, 2020, p. 261). The preservice teachers' experience in collaborative work is vital as 'school is a communal working organization, and for the teachers, collaborative competency is one of the key components of their expertise' (Havu-Nuutinen et al., 2019, p. 583).

Teaching English as a foreign, second or international language (EIL) requires a vast array of techniques, activities and ideas. It offers the teacher an opportunity to think outside the box and to teach almost any subject they wish using English, thus exposing their learners to as much natural language as possible. Collaborative activities can 'promote what Swain (2000) termed "collaborative dialogue"' (in Gonzalez-Lloret, 2020, p. 261), by having the participants engage in problem solving and knowledge building activities and processes. This is further progressed through the polyphonic classroom or dialogue, based on what Bakhtin (1984 in Naot-Ofarim & Solomonic, 2016) refers to as the 'dialogical communicative model [which] entails the normative assumption that "good" communication transpires when subjects address and are responsive to each other' (p. 392).

'Furthermore, specifically among educators of additional languages, there is a consensus that a primary goal of teaching EIL should be to facilitate intercultural communicative competence (ICC) because of the reciprocal relationship between language and culture' (Topaz & Waldman, 2022, p. 203). According to Cobb (2016, in Mostafa, 2021), students who worked collaboratively developed good relationships with their peers, performed better and had better self-confidence than those who didn't. Collaboration among the students in the college classroom, as well as intercultural and international collaboration with other undergraduate students studying education, provides an opportunity for the students to work on and produce multicultural and diverse teaching activities as an ongoing process. These activities then offer the students a perfect platform for focusing on a multicultural and multidimensional learning platform for their future classes.

This chapter describes one of the collaborative processes the preservice teachers in the EIL program experienced in one of the courses. This changed over the years and two versions of this process are presented in this chapter.

Model and Theory Connection

Collaborative Learning Among Preservice Teachers

Growth of a teacher, especially a pre-service teacher, requires interaction with others, collaboration with others. Collaborative learning promotes collaboration with others and teamwork. In fact, 'research suggests that students learn more deeply and perform better on complex tasks if they have the opportunity to engage in more "authentic" learning' (Barron & Darling-Hammond, 2008, p. 3). The participants in a collaborative process learn how to communicate with their team members, how to negotiate, persuade others and to develop critical thinking. This aids in the development of innovative teachers, teacher empowerment, building the teacher's self-belief in their competence (Koiv et al., 2019) as well as their ability to impact their learners' education and progress.

An additional benefit of collaborative learning, especially for pre-service teachers, is learning about oneself, and brings oneself, their 'culture, values, beliefs, misconceptions, attitudes, behaviors, etc.' (Economides, 2008, p. 249). Collaboration with others, those from a similar background and others from different cultures or beliefs, both local and foreign, enables the participants to pay attention to their own abilities, their identities as language teachers, and their own culture and educational point of view. By working collaboratively, the pre-service teacher participants are able to learn about how they work in a group, how they work with others, where they are willing to be flexible, where more adamant. In addition, the participants learn how they can assist others and how others can assist them and that it's perfectly okay to accept help (Cohen et al., 1982; Cook et al., 1985; Hartley, 1977; Ginsburg-Block et al., 2006; Johnson & Johnson, 1989 in Barron & Darling-Hammond, 2008).

Moreover, collaborative learning enables the acquisition and development of leadership skills, teamwork skills, flexibility to change plans or ideas as well as an ability to develop a plan from start to finish. The opportunity to collaborate, negotiate and persuade, enables the participants to voice their ideas and their opinions, agreeing or disagreeing and understanding how others view the issues at hand (Barron & Darling-Hammond, 2008). These are all skills that are an integral part of a teacher training program.

Multicultural Collaboration

Collaboration in a multicultural and diverse setting offers significant learning opportunities and an opportunity to actualize their potential and raise their self-perception of themselves as teachers. The polyphonic classroom enables the distinct voices to enhance the classroom or group discourse, enabling more learning opportunities and awareness among the student teachers. The development of intercultural communicative competence (ICC) should be an integral element of a teacher training program (Topaz & Waldman, 2022). The exposure to cultural differences through collaboration, may lead to a more in depth understanding of one's own self; culture, language and teaching ability and develop ICC. 'Cultural values of individual learners in a heterogeneous group would impact upon the learning process and outcome of the entire group of learners (Change & Lim, 2002 in Economides, 2008, p. 250). In addition, they learn about their ability to collaborate and to discover what motivates them. Computer-supported learning also enables the participants to become proficient users of technology and technological pedagogical tools and to apply those in their own teaching (Chuang, 2016).

On the other hand, multicultural collaboration may affect participation and communication as different cultures regard these differently. This may affect collaboration, trust, sharing, knowledge transfer and may hinder the progress of the group. By engaging in more multicultural collaborations, and developing the teams with in depth thought and understanding of the cultures, the benefits outweigh the negative aspects (Economides, 2008).

However, intercultural communicative competence can be seen or defined as simply being able to communicate effectively in different cultural contexts but it's so much more. 'It also implies that language learners and language users be sensitive to their interlocutors' cultural norms, and be openly curious and non-judgmental during interaction (Byram et al., 2002 in Topaz & Waldman, 2022, p. 204). All preservice teachers, and especially EIL teachers, should develop ICC skills to become well-rounded educators.

Computer-Supported Collaborative Learning

Computer-supported collaborative learning enables a multicultural and diverse setting through collaboration with others from all over the world. It enhances 'peer interactions and teamwork in groups, and facilitates sharing and distributing knowledge and expertise among' (Chuang, 2016) the participants in the team. Real time online interaction, in which all participants are equally able to contribute, and which 'would try to foster participants' participation, interaction and engagement with collaborative tasks' (Economides, 2008, p. 245) is essential. The use of different digital tools enables the participants to learn about each other and the integration of these tools in the EIL classroom setting.

An additional aspect that has to be taken into consideration when using computer-supported collaborative learning is the ease of use and level of familiarity the students have with the digital tools being used (Lee et al., 2016). The tools used have to support self-regulated learning, social interaction, collaboration, diversity, and ease of management (Lee et al., 2016; Chuang, 2016). Thus, it's very important to ensure student familiarity with the digital tools being used or required in any task. Chuang (2016) found that addressing the gap through additional guidance and scaffolding could 'adequately ensure learning outcomes' (p. 872).

The Collaborative Model

The model described below was designed as a class task but over time developed into a multicultural polyphonic task that not only worked on material preparation for EIL classroom but as a tool for multicultural exchange among the participants.

This model made use of video clips available online that convey a message that could be considered universal, yet relies on cultural understanding.

Version 1: In Class Collaborative Version (F2F) (2019)

The participants in this group were all from the same college, studying together in their third year of a four-year program. In spite of that, the class make up was diverse, different cultures and students from different parts of the country. They met once a week, on campus, and worked collaboratively in the *future classroom space* (a collaborative, interactive physical space designed for face-to-face and digital learning, sharing and cooperation) at the college. Digital collaboration was done through a shared Google Drive, which enabled both ease and fluid collaboration.

Aims

The aims were for the students to work collaboratively, learning from each other and expressing their own ideas, to create a lesson that deals with a dilemma or social issue that is presented in a YouTube clip provided by the lecturer. Each clip dealt with a different social dilemma or issue, thus providing the students a shared starting point. Yet each student was able to gain their own understanding of the issue presented based on their own world view. This understanding enabled different ideas to be presented and discussed, and cultural points of view and understanding to be fore-fronted and highlighted. Digital tools were used to ease collaboration and sharing.

The process:

1. **Stage 1: Division into groups to enable collaboration**: The class was divided into small groups, randomly. Each group was given a clip. They were to collaborate on the planning of what to teach through the clip and how this could be done. Each group was to teach their clip and topic to the class and to prepare a post-viewing task. Of the participants, each group was assigned a different group which would be the ones to 'execute' the task that the group presents.

   - For example, Group 1 would teach the class, but only Group 5 would have to actually do the post viewing task. This group would then be evaluated by Group 1 according to the rubric.
     Each group was asked to:
   - prepare the teaching materials needed for the peer teaching lesson and to teach the class for about 10 min. This was to include the viewing of the clip.
   - explain the post viewing task. This included step by step instructions for the task and a rubric for evaluation.
     The division into collaborative groups enabled every group member to express their point of view, ideas and how they perceive the pedagogical aspects needed. Furthermore, it offered them an opportunity to negotiate their

ideas and to persuade others of their ideas, developing leadership skills and flexibility. Likewise, the opportunity to communicate in what Barron and Darling-Hammond (2008) call 'authentic learning' based on real life situations that may arise, presents itself. Furthermore, the use of the clip and the Google drive for collaboration included the use of digital tools to enhance their understanding of how these tools can be used in the classroom.

2. **Stage 2: Peer teaching for meaningful learning using digital tools**: Each group taught the whole class. They were to run the peer-teaching element thoroughly, including discussion and questions where needed. They presented their topic, their clip and their task. All of this was done using a variety of digital tools, as well as face-to-face teaching.

For example: The students had to fill in the dialogue based on the clip.

*Image 1: Write a dialogue based on the clip

Or fill in this questionnaire based on a different clip.

Each group was assigned another group in the class. This was the group that was to execute the post viewing task that their group presented and explained. As explained above, while the entire class studied together during the peer teaching section, only one group was asked to do the task. This, of course, was established beforehand. So, while Group 1 taught the whole class, only Group 2 was asked to do the post viewing task, and so forth.

This point was vital as the assessment of the effectiveness of the task was dependent on the whole group being able to take part in the production of the task they were given. Through peer teaching, the students co-taught and collaborated on their own plan experiencing the clarity of their task and its instructions, and if needed, to tweak it. The teaching was done via the collaborative digital platform in the future classroom space, which enabled all the students to see what was being done real time and to contribute their own ideas.

3. **Stage 3: Group production and collaboration on the task**: The groups who were taught were then given time in class to collaborate on the task, each group working on their corresponding task, and then be able to present their results to the class.

This enabled collaboration, discussion and interpretation of their understanding including different points of view and different cultural elements that may come into play.

4. **Stage 4: Presentation, assessment and feedback**: While each group presented their post-viewing task results, the group that developed that task, the ones who taught the clip, evaluated the group presenting, using the rubric they developed, and gave feedback both in writing and orally. This enabled the students in the teaching group, to consider all aspects of their planning, to evaluate both the product and their own work.

Being able to assess the results of their own task enables the students to reflect on their own planning, leading to the ability to rethink, make changes if needed and to gain deeper understanding of their own work. Giving feedback in a safe environment enables the development of leadership skills, which is vital for pre-service teachers.

- Instruction Page (See Appendix)
- Example

Version 2: Multicultural and Multilevel Collaborative Online Version (2021)

This version of the Model was a collaborative task across borders. The task was conducted jointly with four colleges in Israel and one university in Germany. Prior to starting the actual work with the students, the lecturers from each institution met to coordinate, collaborate and plan appropriately. The group make up was diverse and multicultural, including students from each institution in each group. They met once a week, on Zoom, and worked collaboratively in the shared Google Drive, which enabled sharing at a high level.

Aims

The aims were for the students to work collaboratively, learning from each other and about each other, to enable the participants to express their own ideas, to create a series of lessons, a mini teaching unit for the grade level of their choice, that deals with a cultural dilemma or social issue that is presented in the clip. Due to the nature of the collaboration, the use of digital tools enabled virtual exchange and collaboration that wouldn't be possible in a face-to-face situation. The use of diverse digital tools, using tools such as Zoom, Google drive, Flipgrid, WhatsApp and other tools, learning about them and making use of them not only to collaborate but as part of their units, broadened their digital pedagogical knowledge and enhanced their ability to collaborate.

The process:

1. **Stage 1: Division into groups to enable collaboration**: The students were divided into multicultural groups, including at least one student from each institution. The groups were to collaborate on the planning and creation of a mini unit by following step by step weekly instructions for a five-week-long collaboration. The unit was based on a theme determined by the group, connected in some way to the clip they received. These were YouTube clips, chosen by the lecturers in advance, for each group. The clips all dealt with some social dilemma or issue. This enabled different ideas to be presented and discussed, different cultural points of view to be shared, learned and understood as well as to expand knowledge regarding other cultures and people.
2. **Stage 2: Peer teaching for meaningful learning using digital tools**: The groups were to include microteaching of the clip within the group, along with the task that they created. The groups were to experience the activity that was planned. The aim of teaching their own group was twofold: 1. To experience teaching the clip and leading the discussion using digital tools, such as Zoom and sharing platforms; 2. To check that their plan is executable, especially in an online environment. This enabled them to experience virtual teaching and learning, which has become part of daily life.

    - For example:

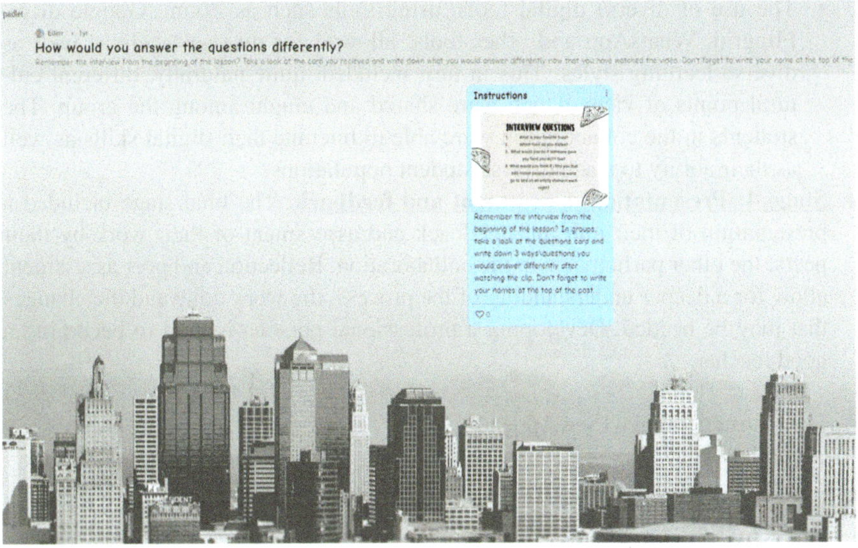

***Image 2: Padlet—How would you answer?**

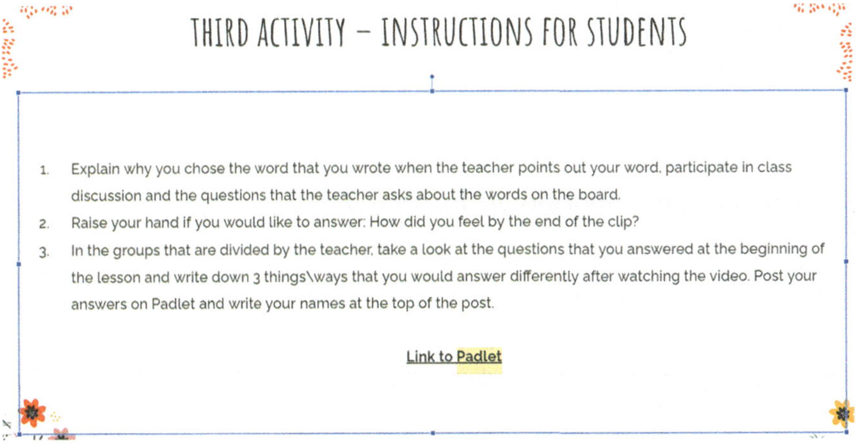

***Image 3: Instructions for students—Third Activity**

3. **<u>Stage 3: Inclusion and diversity, making sure to enable all equal access</u>**: This entire unit was to be designed heterogeneously, i.e. adapting the level to cater to the mixed abilities in their target class and the multicultural makeup of their target class. Through such a design, the students creating the unit were able to consider the need of all their students in class. As each group was asked to choose the grade level their unit would be best suited for, they had to have thought of this in advance, including the various student body makeup.

   - The use of diverse digital tools, using tools such as Zoom, Google drive, Flipgrid, WhatsApp and other tools, allowed for diverse levels as well as diverse learning styles. This in turn included, quite naturally, different cultural points of view, which were shared and taught among the group. The students in the collaboration were able to finetune their digital skills as well as their ability to teach diverse student populations.

4. **Stage 4: Presentation, assessment and feedback**: The final stage included a presentation of their unit and feedback and assessment of their work by their peers, the other participants in the collaboration. Reflection and peer assessment allow for a deeper understanding of the process, the work done and the changes that may be needed. Developing a professional persona is vital to becoming a good teacher.

- The Instruction Page (See Appendix)
- Example

Pedagogical Contribution of the Model

Awareness

Pre-service EIL teachers who engage in multicultural collaboration as part of their studies develop an awareness of other cultures and their differences in learning, communication and participation. Likewise, they enhance their multicultural social skills and expand their awareness of the study teaching needs of their own students.

Collaboration as Foundation for Future Teaching

The model presented works on collaboration of a team of pre-service teachers to create a teaching unit for a grade level of their choice. As future teachers, this is a vital skill. Most material preparation is done in teams, whether it's planning the course syllabus, designing evaluations or simply creating materials for class use. The ability to contribute to the development of teaching materials in the team one belongs to, to understand that other people have different points of view and they aren't necessarily wrong but just different, and the ability to explain oneself in a clear, non-judgmental manner is the essence of being a team player and eventually a leader.

The model fosters the notion of preparing similar teaching activities for their own classes, creating a multicultural, student-centered approach to their teaching, which is a major element in humanistic education.

Digital Tools

The integration of the digital tools enabled smoother collaboration. The use of Google Drive in both versions allowed easy collaboration and sharing, synchronously or asynchronously, as needed.

In the face-to-face sessions, the students were able to share their products in the future learning spaces, where each group had the opportunity to present their ideas to the others and received immediate feedback.

In the online version, the use of the Google Drive, Zoom and other digital tools such as WhatsApp and Padlet, among others, stressed the ease with which sharing has been enabled. The students communicated via WhatsApp with their group partners, they shared their ideas on the Google Drive and they had synchronous meetings on Zoom.

The use of these tools and the simplicity of their use within the group offered the students an opportunity to thing about how to use these same tools with their future students. Through the use of these simple tools, the groups were able to ensure everyone had equal opportunity to express themselves and an equal platform, creating a truly diverse collaborative opportunity.

In Short

Overall, this model challenged the pre-service student teachers on a few aspects: to collaborate with others that they may not necessarily know well, to take others' needs and points of view into equal consideration to their own, to plan a culturally diverse teaching unit, to negotiate with others and to teach them of their own knowledge, and lastly to understand where their own abilities lie (Fig. 1).

The amalgamation of Pedagogy, Content, Space and Technology create a multicultural polyphonic classroom through with the learners acquire new insights and develop abilities and understandings not available through the use of each element individually. The Pedagogy is based on collaborative learning and humanistic education, stressing the agency of each learner and their contribution to the group. The Space utilized is a multicultural online setting, integrating the use of diverse Technological Tools. These enable synchronous learning, expansion of both

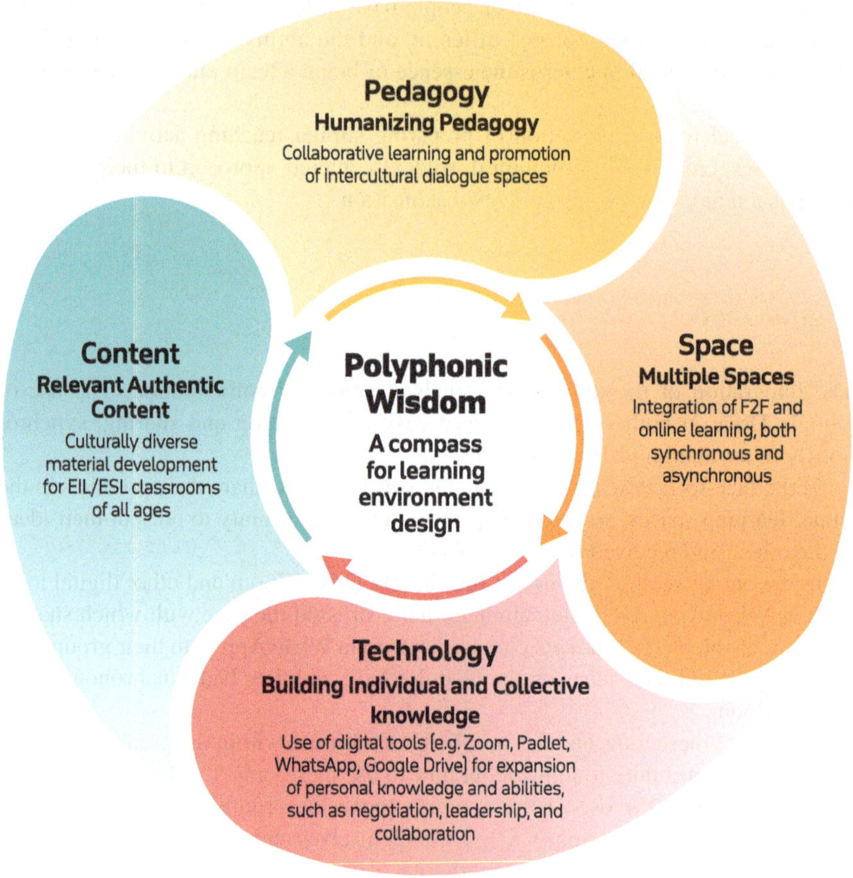

Fig. 1 Polyphonic model

personal and group knowledge and abilities. Furthermore, the Content, which focuses on the development of culturally diverse materials for classroom use, ensures each learner's voice is accounted for in the materials developed. The integration of each of the elements, Pedagogy, Space, Technology and Content, enables the development of truly culturally diverse yet harmonious teaching materials, all achieved through a Multicultural Polyphonic Classroom setting.

Challenges

The execution of this model presented a few challenges, but nothing that wasn't easily surmounted.

Planning

The first challenge was the specific planning, week by week, with an understanding of what might go wrong and how to deal with it should something happen. The main problem, especially in the face-to-face version, was attendance. At times, half of one group would be absent and then the group couldn't continue working properly. In an attempt to enable the work to continue, the representatives of the groups that were present in class continued and at times teamed up with others to get assistance when needed.

This challenge, absences, was remedied in the online version where the students were required to set up their own schedule for group collaboration time. Giving the students more responsibility enabled smoother work among the group members. It's a good idea to delegate and assign responsibilities to each student, so they feel more committed to the work.

Clear Instructions

The second challenge was writing up the detailed instructions needed to ensure all participants understood what was needed, including outside of class time. This meant creating a very detailed teaching guide for the students to follow, with step-by-step instructions, ensuring nothing is missing and nothing is vague.

To overcome this, when writing the instructions, it's a good idea to have a colleague read it and give you feedback as to whether the instructions are clear enough. Or alternatively, have a student read the instructions and give you feedback. After all, they are the target audience, so it's important that the instructions are clear to them.

Lack of Cooperation

The third challenge was the lack of cooperation among some of the groups. Many of the students felt, at times, that some team members weren't working as hard as others, or not contributing as much as others.

This required a discussion with the group to discover what was happening and why. Much of this was miscommunication among the group or cultural differences, where one student was waiting to be told what to do and others expected everyone to take initiative. Cultural differences had to be discussed and noticed. This enabled a learning opportunity by all.

It's very important to discuss the issues that arise, as they arise. Make sure the participants in a virtual exchange are aware that they have open channels of communication with you at all times.

Final Products

The final challenge was the level of material that was created. Naturally some groups created much richer and more extensive units than others.

A clear rubric was designed for use (See Appendix) and it was easy to assess as a result. The use of rubrics for assessment ensures objective, fair and reliable assessment of the students' work.

Conclusion

Multicultural and Multi-level Collaborative Tasks

Multicultural and multi-level collaborative tasks are an integral part of life in today's world. Most people work in teams and those teams are multicultural, even if everyone is from the same country. Different backgrounds, different points of view, different religions, ethnic backgrounds and cultures, make up the population of just about every country in the world.

Computer-Supported Environment

Planning and preparing a collaborative task that is both multicultural and focuses on planning of a unit should be an integral part of teacher education. Creating the task in a computer-supported environment further expands the abilities and the requirements of both future teachers and of their future students. Teaching twenty-first century skills to students, at all levels, as well as helping them become culturally aware of the diversity around them should be the objective of a good teaching program.

Diversity

The model described in this chapter focused on unit planning for an English as an International language class. This included planning the objectives, the activities, the reasoning, the materials and the assessment method required for evaluation in class. The groups were all given the same instructions but the diversity of the groups, the different topics that each clip offered, all led to extremely different and diverse units. The units all focused on an element of self-awareness and diversity in some manner, and all taught language, English in this case, in accordance with the requirements in the instructions.

Knowledge

The units showed the different abilities and knowledge of the participants on a number of aspects: the multicultural knowledge, the pedagogical knowledge, and the language ability in English.

On a Personal Note

Being able to guide preservice teachers to understand how to ‘see’ teaching opportunities in materials that aren’t designed specifically for that purpose, such as the clips presented to each group, gives me great satisfaction. When graduates continue to use the skills, they developed while working in a multicultural setting in my courses, expand their understanding of the diversity that exists in any classroom setting and as a result are better teachers for it, I feel I’ve done my job well.

Appendix

Instruction Page

Version 1: In Class Collaborative Version (F2F) (2019)

Task 3: Clips as a Teaching Tool
Each group gets a clip. Your group has to decide how to teach it in one lesson to our class and which materials to use to do so. You are to plan a creative post viewing task for the students and they are to share it with the rest of the class in some format, taking advantage of the space we are in.

This activity is divided into three parts:

1. *Your group will prepare the teaching plan for this clip.*
2. *One group in the class will be chosen to actually do your task.*
3. *That group will present and your group will evaluate their results.*

1. *Part 1: Day 1*
   (a) *Decide what you would like to teach using this clip.*
   (b) *State clear objectives / goals / aims. Why are you doing this and what do the students get out of it?*
   (c) *Prepare the teaching plan and the materials for teaching this clip.*
   (d) *Teach the clip to the class. You have 10 min max.*

   (e) *Write up step by step instructions for the creative post viewing activity.*
   (f) *Prepare a rubric for evaluation.*
   (g) *Explain the task to the group chosen to do the task.*

2. *Part 2: Day 2, first half*

   (a) *Each group will watch the clip they've been designated.*
   (b) *The group has to read the instructions and do the task given.*
   (c) *All members in the group have to participate.*

3. *Part 3: Day 2, second half*

   (a) *After half an hour each group will present their product / results.*
   (b) *The time limit is 10 min per group.*
   (c) *The group that prepared the activity has to evaluate the students' product using the rubric they've designed.*
   (d) *Give feedback on the presentation.*

You will be evaluated by me according to the criteria on the next page. Use them as a checklist.

Day 1:

Criteria	*Value*	*Done*
Logical teaching plan	*10%*	
Clear aim / goal / objective for plan	*15%*	
Clear step by step written instructions for the students	*30%*	
Teaching of clip clear and easy to follow within the 10 min time limit	*15%*	
Evaluation rubric valid for the task	*20%*	
Explanation of task to group clear and easy to follow	*10%*	

Day 2:

Criteria	*Value*	*Done*
The group was able to follow the given instructions	*20%*	
The group worked within the time limit allotted	*10%*	
The group presented and showed clear understanding of what was expected	*30%*	
The evaluators gave clear and constructive feedback	*30%*	
All the members in the group participated	*10%*	

Instruction Page

Version 2: Multicultural and Multilevel Collaborative Online Version (2021)

Clips as a Teaching Tool

In your group you are to prepare a short teaching unit on a theme you choose based on the clip your group received.

Your group has to work together following the instructions below and to create the materials needed to teach.

You are to decide the grade level / age group you are aiming for. Likewise, you are to decide how many lessons you'd like this unit to be. It should be at least 4 lessons but you are welcome to do more if your plan requires it.

The entire plan, with all the details as listed below, are to be placed in the google slides for your group.

Week 1 [Week of April 25th-April 30th]:

1. *Step 1:*
   (a) *In your groups, discuss the issue of teaching culture and integrating it into the English classroom.*
      (i) *How did you learn about other cultures when you were in school?*
      (ii) *How are you studying about other cultures in your current studies?*
      (iii) *Write up the points that you all have in common.*
      (iv) *How would you integrate the topic of other cultures into your teaching now and in the future?*
      (v) *Upload your group decisions / ideas to your group's google slide.*
2. *Step 2:*
   (a) *Watch the clip and decide what theme you would like to teach using this clip.*
   (b) *How would you integrate the notion of different cultures into the theme you have chosen?*
      (i) *Would the theme be related to differently in different cultures?*
      (ii) *Is the theme common or familiar in the different cultures in the group?*
   (c) *What does this theme show about your different cultures in the group?*
   (d) *How does the clip lend itself to the teaching of this theme?*
   (e) *Why are you teaching this theme and what do the students get out of it? State clear objectives / goals / aims.*

(f) *Write up the ideas and the upload to your group's google slide.*

3. *Step 3:*
   (a) *On the Group Forum on Moodle [link]:*
      (i) *Discuss how your group felt during this process by reflecting on what went well and what was more challenging.*
      (ii) *Add any other reflection you desire.*

4. <u>*Due date*</u>*: These steps need to be completed by Sunday, May second, 2021.*

Week 2 [Week of May 2nd—May 7th]

5. *Step 1:*
   (a) *Prepare a general outline of the unit about the theme you've chosen, using the clip as the opening session.*
      (i) *Your unit should include the following:*
         1. *The opening task using the clip*
         2. *The integration of at least three more digital tools for the unit [link to list of options]*
         3. *Vocabulary relevant to the theme*
         4. *A reading or listening text*
         5. *Work on the reading or listening*
         6. *Work on the vocabulary*
         7. *A creative post reading / listening task*
         8. *Assessment*
      (ii) *Your outline should be on the group's google slides.*
   (b) *Prepare the opening session, the one in which you use the clip.*
      (i) *Write step by step instructions on what has to be done.*
      (ii) *This section MUST have a short task for the students to do as a group.*
         1. **This might be a good place to add a cultural element to the task, if it fits.*
6. *Stmep 2:*
   (a) *Together, as a group, decide how you are going to teach this section of the unit.*
      (i) *You are going to teach each other.*
      (ii) *Divide into two small groups within your group.*
         1. *One group will teach the activity.*
         2. *The other group will be the students.*
      (iii) *Decide how your group is going to teach, you are free to choose how this is done.*

1. *E.g. You can each teach a part, you can do it in pairs, you can have one person teach and the other aid in some other way, etc.*

(iv) *Record yourselves teaching this activity on zoom (no more than 10 min) and upload the recording to your google slides via a link.*

7. *Step 3:*

(a) *On the Group Forum on Moodle [link]:*

(i) *Discuss how your group felt during this process by reflecting on what went well and what was more challenging.*

(ii) *Add any other reflection you desire.*

8. <u>*Due date:*</u> *These steps need to be completed by Sunday May ninth, 2021.*

Week 3 [Week of May 9th—May 14th]

9. *Step 1:*

(a) *Prepare the detailed teaching plan.*

(i) *You can use the following chart to help you organize your plan.*

Grade ______ class ______.

Topic: ____.

Lesson 1	***Lesson 2***	***Lesson 3***	***Lesson 4***
Subject: ***Objective:*** ***Activities:***	***Subject:*** ***Objective:*** ***Activities:***	***Subject:*** ***Objective:*** ***Activities:***	***Subject:*** ***Objective:*** ***Activities:***

(b) *Prepare a general overview with overall objectives for the unit*

(i) *What do you want your students to be able to do.*

10. *Step 2:*

(a) *Prepare the lessons that make up the unit*

(i) *Ensure each lesson complements the previous one*

(ii) *Ensure there is a clear build up of the material being taught and worked on*

(iii) *Incorporate easier and more challenging tasks, or versions / instructions at different levels for each task, to enable all the students to work at their own level*

(iv) *Include scaffolding where appropriate, to aid those who need it*

(b) *Each lesson should include a step-by-step plan - Link to CEFR Descriptors*

(i) *The plan has to be clear and detailed enough to enable the reader to understand*

(ii) *Write clearly what has to be done in each activity*

(iii) *Clearly write what language issues are being worked on*

1. *What vocabulary*
2. *Which text / listening text are you using*
3. *Which digital tool you are using and why*

11. *Step 3:*

(a) *On the Group Forum on Moodle [link]:*
(i) *Discuss how your group felt during this process by reflecting on what went well and what was more challenging.*
(ii) *Add any other reflection you desire.*

12. *Due date: all lesson plans for your unit need to be completed by Sunday, May 16th, 2021*

Week 4 [Week of May 16th—May 25th]

13. *Step 1:*

(a) *For each lesson plan, there must be at least one operative objective and one pedagogical objective for each of the lessons*
(i) *Explain what you want the students to be able to do with the language by the end of each lesson*
(ii) *What is your pedagogical reasoning behind your choices?*

(b) *For each lesson, create the materials for the lesson in detail*
(i) *The teaching materials*
(ii) *The text*
(iii) *The questions and instructions*

14. *Step 2:*

(a) *Prepare an assessment for the unit which includes:*

(i) *Clear details for their task that is evaluated*
(ii) *A rubric for evaluation*

15. *Step 3:*

(a) *On the Group Forum on Moodle [link]:*

(i) *Discuss how your group felt during this process by reflecting on what went well and what was more challenging.*
(ii) *Add any other reflection you desire.*

16. *Due date: all detailed lesson plans for your unit (including materials/texts/questions) need to be completed by Sunday, May 23rd.*

Week 5: Prior to final session on May 31st.
Presentation by May 28th

17. *Film a video presentation of your unit, explaining the main theme, objectives and activities that lead up to the final task.*

(a) *You have 1.5–2 min to present your unit in the video.*
(b) *You have creative freedom to present in any way you desire.*
(c) *Upload your videos to the google drive. [link]*

May 30th

18. *Watch the videos*

19. *Fill in the evaluation form for each*

Final Session: Synchronous Meeting Monday, May 31st

By June 6th—complete final reflection form

Examples of Ideas for clips:

The present: https://youtu.be/3XA0bB79oGc - group 1
The bridge: https://youtu.be/YNOnFsnjYhY - group 12

Task Checklist

Due Date	*Task*	*Done*
April 21st	*Padlet post - picture and 2 fun facts*	
April 30th	*Meet and coordinate*	
May 2nd	*First week assignment 9*	
May 9th	*Second week assignment*	
May 16th	*Third week assignment*	
May 27th	*Fourth week assignment*	
May 31st	*Group clip*	
June 6th	*Evaluation of peer group unit - google form*	

Due Date	*Task*	*Done*
April 20th	*Post personal introduction on Padlet*	
April 21st	*First synchronous session on zoom* *Meet your group and get to know each other.*	
April 28th	*Have met and coordinated the joint work within the group* *Division of labor*	
May 2nd	*First week assignment is due on Google slides* *First reflection to be posted on forum*	
May 9th	*Second week assignment is due on Google slides* *Second reflection to be posted on forum*	
May 16th	*Third week assignment is due on Google slides* *Third reflection to be posted on forum*	
May 25th	*Entire plan to be completed and shared on Google slides* *Final reflection to be posted on forum*	
May 28th	*Prepare group clip and upload to Google drive*	
May 30th	*Watch and complete evaluation for each group (google form)*	
May 31st	*Synchronous session on zoom* *Summing up, reflection and feedback*	
June 6th	*Evaluation of peer group unit - google form*	

Assessment Rubric

Criteria		*Comments*	*Value*
Week 1	*Teaching plan*		*/15*
	Reflection		*/5*
Week 2	*Teaching plan*		*/15*
	Reflection		*/5*
Week 3	*Teaching plan*		*/15*
	Reflection		*/5*
Week 4	*Teaching plan*		*/15*
	Reflection		*/5*
Final presentation			*/15*
Final reflection			*/5*

References

Barron, B., & Darling-Hammond, L. (2008). Teaching for meaningful learning: A review of research on inquiry-based and cooperative learning. In *Powerful learning: What we know about teaching for understanding*. Jossey-Bass.

Chuang, H. (2016). Leveraging CRT awareness in creating web-based projects through use of online collaborative learning for pre-service teachers. *Education Technology Research and Development, 64*, 857–876. https://doi.org/10.1007/s11423-016-9438-5

Depalma, R. (2010). Toward a practice of polyphonic dialogue in multicultural teacher education. *Curriculum Inquiry, 40*, 3. https://doi.org/10.1111/j.1467-873X.2010.00492.x

Economides, A. A. (2008). Culture-aware collaborative learning. *Multicultural Education & Technology Journal, 2*(4), 243–267. https://doi.org/10.1108/17504970810911052

Gonzalez-Lloret, M. (2020). Collaborative tasks for online language teaching. *Foreign Language Annals, 53*(1). https://doi.org/10.1111/flan.12466

Havu-Nuutinen, S., Kervinen, A., Uitto, A., Laine, A., Koliseva, A., Pyykko, L., Impoi, P., & Aittola, T. (2019). Pre-service and in-service teachers' experiences of inquiry-based primary science teaching: A collaborative team teaching model. *Journal of Baltic Science Education, 18*, 4. https://doi.org/10.33225/jbse/19.18.583

Koiv, K., Liik, K., & Heidmets, M. (2019). School leadership, teacher's psychological empowerment and work-related outcomes. *International Journal of Educational Management, 33*(7). https://doi.org/10.1108/IJEM-08-2018-0232

Lee, B. N., Abdullah, S., & Kiu, S. N. (2016). Supportive learning: Linear learning and collaborative learning. *TOJET: The Turkish Online Journal of Educational Technology, 15*, 2.

Mostafa, S. (2021). ESL cooperative learning activities using technology in the UAE. *Journal of Asia TEFL, 18*, 2. https://doi.org/10.18823/asiatefl.2021.18.2.27.719

Naot-Ofarim, Y., & Solomonic, S. (2016). Educational polyphony. *Studies in Philosophy & Education, 35*, 385–397. https://doi.org/10.1007/s11217-015-9491-2

Senyshyn, R., & Martinelli, A. (2021). Learning to support and sustain cultural (and linguistics) diversity: Perspectives of preservice teachers. *Journal for Multicultural Education, 15*, 1. https://doi.org/10.1108/JME-02-2020-0015

Topaz, B., & Waldman, T. (2022). Internationalization for nurturing intercultural communicative competencies in pre-service teachers. In D. Yitzhaki, T. Gallagher, N. Aloni, & Z. Gross (Eds.), *Activist pedagogy and shared education in divided societies: International perspectives and next practices*. Brill-Sense.

Trausan-Matu, S., Stahl, G., & Sarmiento, J. (2007). Supporting polyphonic collaborative learning. *e-Service Journal, 6*(1), 59–75.

Social Media, Embodiment, and Movement to Create a Holistic Teacher Training Experience

Tami Seifert

Introduction

Intensive and broad use of social media sites has recently increased significantly. We use social media for learning, acquiring, and sharing information, creating and preserving social ties, and connecting with local and international users, all without any time and distance limits (Greenhow & Askari, 2017; Halverson, 2011; Manca & Ranieri, 2013). Along with their notable advantages, the unique characteristics of social media may expose children and teenagers using them to risks they are often not equipped to cope with (Derrick, 2008). Consequently, social media and other digital environments confront teachers and teacher training institutes with a pedagogical challenge that requires intimate acquaintance with different virtual environments. They must be conversant with their operation and theoretical principles, integrating them into teaching-learning-assessment processes and mediating them (Anderson, 2019; Seifert, 2016). Familiarity of this kind would help teachers apply the virtual space in teaching and educate students to use social media and their potential in a controlled and sensible way, reducing their potential risks.

The present chapter introduces a teaching model reflecting the polyphonic wisdom model (Fig. 1) implemented in a post-graduate course titled "Social Networks in Educational Contexts" offered at a teacher-training institute. In the spirit of polyphonic training, the primary purpose of the course is to acquaint teachers with various pedagogical social media and network implementations in teaching. This would help them reflect on their conduct with the students, develop critical thinking, shape stands concerning the use of such environments, apply sensible online behavior, observe privacy, and protect information. Social networks are rhizomatic rather than linear, allowing for great flexibility and dynamism in connecting varied content. In

T. Seifert (✉)
Kibbutzim College of Education, Technology and Arts, Tel-Aviv, Israel
e-mail: tami.seifert@smkb.ac.il

Y. Yondler et al. (eds.), *Cultivating Future-Oriented Learners*, Understanding Teaching-Learning Practice, https://doi.org/10.1007/978-3-031-63253-2_4

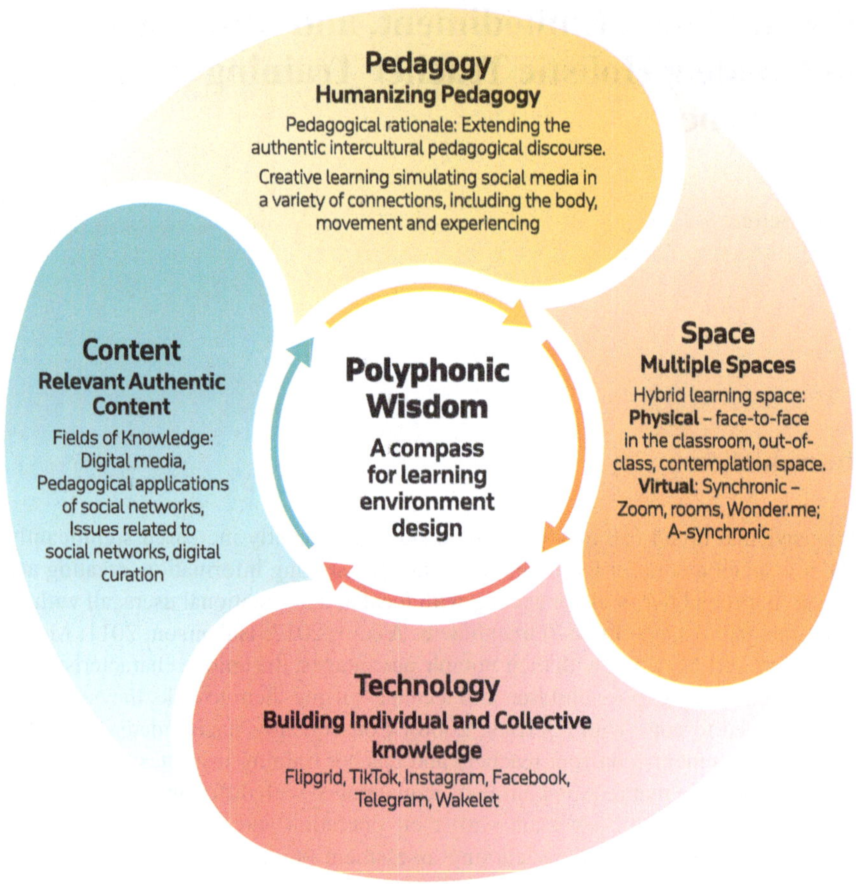

Fig. 1 The framework of the model used to achieve various learning purposes

expressing this dynamism, we used physical and virtual movement to impart some course contents and incorporate social experiences into the learning. Before the COVID-19 pandemic, the course was given face-to-face. It comprised one synchronic session and four a-synchronic international activities. One learning unit that was shared with a student group from the United States aimed to illustrate the network's complexity from a broader perspective and extend the intercultural discourse related to the social networks. The COVID-19 restrictions necessitated flexible thinking and changing the course teaching and learning modes and international collaborations. Consequently, hybrid teaching included adjustments to ensure optimal adaptation of the synchronic and a-synchronic face-to-face sessions to the teaching mode. Complex as social networks are, educators must recognize their advantages, risks, and potential unfavorable effects and foster a participation culture aware of media use implications.

As mentioned, the course model in Fig. 1 illustrates polyphonic wisdom by presenting the complex experience of social network activity and the ambivalent reactions it elicits. It sheds light on points that exposure to experiential, social, physical, and intercultural aspects could strengthen. The model proposes ways to utilize social networks that yield an inclusive, engaging, and creative teaching paradigm for implementation in the physical or virtual space in a broad intercultural context.

The model serves as a conceptual framework for a course that teaches social media and networks authentically through communication with students from various countries. Over the course, students creatively experience various theory-based pedagogical applications on social media and networks. They also experience first-hand some network aspects: eye contact, interaction, interpersonal contact, communication, understanding social network messages, pre-and post-course stands about social network use, convenience and inconvenience zones, and potentially threatening and dangerous spaces. The course's concluding activity divides the class into three zones: convenience zone, non-convenient zone, and danger zone. The students move between these zones according to a scenario or behavior presented to them. Intercultural contacts and experiences gained over the course enrich the personal, interpersonal, and intercultural perspectives about social media and networks and their incorporation into school learning. The course develops the students' critical self-awareness and stands about social media and network use. Over the learning, students adapt and personalize the contents, learning environments and tools, teaching modes, implementation, and assessment to their needs as teachers and those of their students. In the process, they expand their cognitive, social, experiential, physical, and intercultural practices. All of the above indicates combining two central polyphonic paradigm foci: Enhancing the learners' agency in broadening their knowledge independently and allowing them to follow their preferences and skills in connecting to the learned material while structuring their acquired knowledge via social interaction. This combination promises to offer a much-needed response to the constantly changing learner needs, and enable acquiring skills and capacities that ensure optimal functioning in a global, technological, and multicultural environment.

Theoretical Background

Using Social Media and Networks in Teaching Toward Collaborative, Stimulating, and Engaging Learning

The polyphonic paradigm and social networks share the principles of communication, collaboration, and connectivity. They both emphasize interaction and a dynamic and flowing give-and-take between people. Social network structure relies on interconnections and discursive exchange between users. Similarly, the polyphonic paradigm regards learning as an interactive collaborative process. They both advocate open communication, flexibility and dynamism of voices, and multiple perspectives. They share the values of collaboration, creativity and dialogue. Social networks are the most widespread online activities. We link on, get news, and share content, making the social networks the most up-to-date news sources. They offer informal communications, and professional learning communities utilize them as well. Einstein said, "We cannot solve our problems with the same thinking we used when we created them." Indeed, social networks enable us to base our actions on new contacts, maintain and bolster existing ones, identify connections and patterns other than our own, and synthesize this varied information. Applying social networks in teaching promotes a model characterized by independent learning and offering varied communication and collaboration opportunities (Rogers et al., 2007; Seifert, 2016; Sheely, 2006). Students take part in structuring their knowledge meaningfully, which helps them internalize the learned material (Mayer, 1984). Incorporating social networks in teaching promotes constructivist learning based on collective wisdom and a connective learning approach (O'Reilly, 2005; Siemens, 2005). Additionally, social networks are essential to combining social processes with teaching to match the students' speech and thought and offer them lifelong learning relevant to their needs in a changing reality. Their application promotes involvement and enhances control and ownership of discourse and knowledge (Bozarth, 2010; Veletsianos & Navarrete, 2012). They boost collaborative values (Bouton et al., 2021), higher thinking levels (Anderson & Krathwohl, 2001), and self-efficacy. The technological environment enables realizing purposes that are impossible to achieve without it. Studies of the influence of teacher self-efficacy on classroom processes indicate that teachers with high self-efficacy tend to incorporate more often innovative pedagogies, including social networks (Kelleci et al., 2018), into their teaching (Zee & Koomen, 2016). Additionally, the high self-efficacy of teachers in applying techno-pedagogy and social-media learning has contributed to their professional evolution. They developed enhanced lifelong learning skills (Anders, 2018), as did the student-teachers they guided (Kan & Murat, 2020). The literature indicates that self-efficacy may be a decisive factor in the success of those learning to integrate technology and collaborative learning in their classes (Ronen et al., 2006).

A study that summarized several years of social network use in teaching (Seifert, 2016) found that teachers who experience optimal social network applications during their training and continue to develop guided activities on social networks may also lead innovative pedagogy and redesign the learning in spaces they and their students are familiar with. Such teachers can reassure the policymakers and promote a challenging albeit controlled use of social networks while observing privacy and information protection rules. Teachers must be familiar with social network features such as availability, accessibility, effectiveness, collaboration, sense of community, student empowerment, creativity, and pleasure to promote dynamic, relevant, and experience-based teaching. At the same time, they should be aware of concerns about using them and exposure to different teaching modes.

First-Hand Experience of Social Network Complexity: Contribution of the Physical Body Aspect of Learning

Movement is an inseparable part of our everyday life at any time or place. A person moves spontaneously, aware or unaware of moving. Moving enables us to live, function, defend ourselves, adapt to the environment and harness it to our needs, acquire knowledge, act effectively, create ties, stay healthy, and be comfortable. Studies indicate that learning through body movement is meaningful (Seifert & Yaron, 2019). Body movement supports and contributes to verbal learning. The moving body affects perception and representation. During information processing, personal perception and action assist in structuring that information's representation (Merleau-Ponty, 1962). Movement allows for engaging with the sensory, motor, kinesthetic, and transformative space. By exploring movement, one can express curiosity, perseverance, and commitment (Deans, 2016). Gros (2014) describes how thinkers like Rousseau, Kirkegaard, and Kant walked to enhance their personal and professional health. Henry David Thoreau, an eighteenth century American writer, poet, and philosopher, walked for about 4 h every day throughout his adult life. He wrote in his diary, "Methinks that the moment my legs begin to move, my thoughts begin to flow..." (Thoreau & Blaisdell, 2011). Nietzsche, a walking enthusiast, declared that "Only thoughts reached by walking have value" (Nietzsche, 2007, p. 9).

The human body's movement in the physical space differs from movement in the virtual space, which enables expressing the dynamism of the learners' virtualcharacter. In students, such experiences stimulate rhizomatic thinking (Deleuze & Guattari, 1987) that resembles polyphony in representing complex, critical, and multidimensional thinking. Such thinking is compatible with learning on networks, encouraging learner agency by creating new, unexpected links. This thinking mode offers multiple entry and exit points. It connects different contents, allowing every content junction to connect with another casually and irregularly, thus generating dynamism and ramified movement in space. Studies indicate that we remember information better if we memorize it while moving (Paul, 2021).

Intercultural Aspects of Social Media and Network Applications

Wise and competent technology use can bring about a paradigmatic change in teaching and learning. Educated use of social media and networks can potentially improve teachers' personal and professional skills and bridge between cultures, knowledge resources, and different viewpoints. Incorporating interactive technological tools that express voices, speech tones, and body language in the virtual space strengthens the learners' sense of connection and increases their interaction. Two social media that facilitate such communication are the Flipgrid and Facebook environments. There are many advantages to using Flipgrid. It offers visuality, accessibility, flexibility, involvement, motivation, and a convenient option for participation tracking. Facebook has potential pedagogical value and may professionally advance teachers and teachers-to-be. Intercultural activity can deepen acquaintances and enhance the learning experience and authentic pedagogical discourse of teachers-to-be. During the activity, students familiarized themselves with some ISTE2017 standards (Trust, 2018). These standards use an innovative approach to exploring the pedagogical aspects of teleprocessing incorporation into teaching. It offers students the twenty-first-century skills they need to succeed in the digital era: creativity and innovation, information literacy, communication and collaboration abilities, critical thinking, problem-solving, and decision-making. The intercultural learning included discussion-based peer learning through short video clips in a Flipgrid environment that enables uploading synchronically and a-synchronically recordings, texts, audio, and video files, and commenting on the uploaded clips. The Facebook environment served to share and discuss them on the social network educational enterprises involving Israeli teachers who also developed part of them. Intercultural activity has enhanced confidence and authenticity by using video clips that overcame the language barrier of the Israeli group. The collaboration has also improved digital media literacy, meaningful learning, and command of social media both individually and through application with the students. Exposure to another culture emerged as powerful since it intensified the authentic use of social media and offered students of both countries another perspective on teaching and learning.

Teaching Mode: Connected, Unconnected, and Those Between

In the spirit of polyphonic wisdom, the presented model enables teachers to exhibit their capacity to synergize between space, technology, content, and pedagogy. Through this synergy, learners interact while embracing the humanistic values of containment, multiculturalism, and dialogue. Learners' agency in social media and network applications interrelates the learning space and reality, providing learners a response to social network issues and challenges they contend with. The learners' physical, experiential, social, and intercultural cognitive involvement yields insights into their online conduct, enabling them to adapt the emerging interaction, communication, and connection types to their future students. Figure 2 summarizes the theoretical foundation of the model.

Purpose of the Model

The model displays the theoretical aspects and complex experience of using social media and networks in teaching-learning-assessment, including intercultural contexts. While some warn against their inherent dangers, others note their immeasurable educational potential. The model design aims to confront the students with

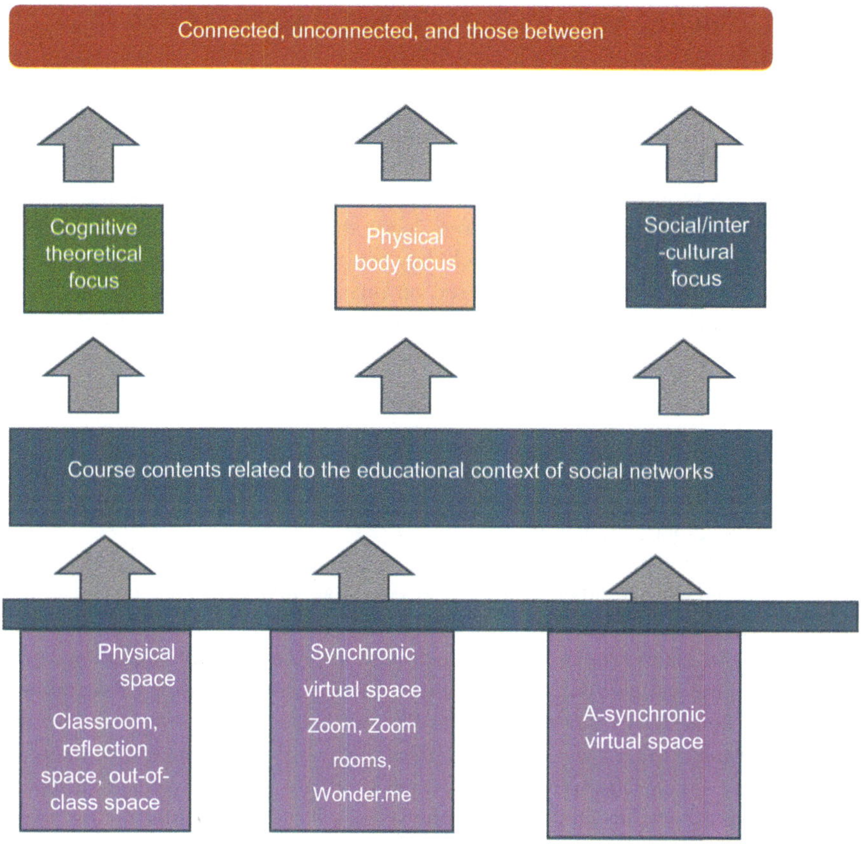

Fig. 2 Theoretical foundation of the model

issues emerging over using social networks and encourage them to shape their stands about applying them in teaching-learning-assessment.

Model Stages

Online teaching, learning, and assessment require extra attention in planning the learning process. While certain aspects lend themselves naturally to face-to-face sessions, synchronic and a-synchronic online sessions must preserve interpersonal contacts and interaction. In response to this challenge, the proposed model incorporates cognitive, social, and physical components to deepen the learners' involvement, interest, and motivation and boost their learning self-efficacy.

Below is a description of the model stages.

Stage 1: Building Knowledge About Social Media Theories and Issues

The students are introduced to the theoretical basis of the course and experience various social media and network applications and activities in the classroom, out of class, and in a reflection space. They share their personal experiences and knowledge and probe personal stands. Students learn about the connectivism theory and engage in classroom activities in which they position themselves in a netlike form under the lecturer's guidance and based on questions posed to them. This stage requires cognitive, emotional, physical, and social involvement and gains them the following:

1. A physical body experience that combines movement in the classroom space simulating a social network with its communication, contacts, and dynamism. The students position themselves according to their residence location, teaching experience, the age-group they teach, types of networks they are active on, intensity of social network activity, etc.
2. Theoretical cognitive knowledge about social network characteristics, users' online behavior, and other issues and aspects that come up.
3. Initial exploration of social-network-based activities, characteristics of the activity and the environment, and discussion of ways to adjust them to students through physical and social involvement. Critical contemplation of social networks. The activity takes place in class, out-of-class, and in the synchronic and a-synchronic virtual space. Students experience the Wonder.me environment as part of the synchronic activity. Wonder.me simulates phygital video-chat spaces that serve as synchronic group meeting spaces. Participants entering this space connect to its video cameras and microphones, and can choose to join or not participate in a conversation with an individual or a group of participants. When two or more participants are near each other, they are able to hear and see each other and interact. The moderator can communicate with all the groups. In this environment, the backgrounds may change according to need. The activity is adjusted to social network features. Students move around the virtual space according to the changing background and activities. This exposes them to the various issues and opinions of their peers and the challenges of working with students, and requires them to think critically, examine and shape their stands.
4. First-hand experience of the social network. This workshop activity occurs in the reflection space. Students perform a guided activity that regards eye contact and communication in the screen era. The workshop includes several experiential activities with physical, cognitive, and social involvement of the students. The students perform several guided exercises involving eye contact while they move, after which they form groups. Each group receives an expression related to communication in the screen era, such as text messages, selfies, or phone alerts. They dramatize them individually, in small groups, and finally all together.

5. Creative representation of the social network space. Experiential activity to evaluate the contents learned in the course. This collective activity occurs outside of the classroom. Students review the concepts, environments, theories, and contexts they have encountered over the course. A term or expression related to the course content is stuck to the forehead of each student who does not know what it is. The students move about, ask questions, and answer the questions of their co-learners until they find out what their expression is. This mode of evaluating the learned material enables pooling the collective knowledge, practicing question phrasing, noting peer answers, and reaching conclusions based on the varied applications, implementations, and contexts encountered.

This individual and collective stage occurs in the classroom, out of class, synchronically and a-synchronically, and in the reflection space. It covers collective humanizing aspects like network and activity selection, discourse, dialogue, brainstorming, and creative critical thinking in devising an activity. The environments used include Wakelet, Pinterest, Instagram, Flipgrid, Facebook, Wonder.me, and Zoom, and different means are applied, such as balls, paper, colors, plasticine, hoops, and music. Knowledge assessment at this stage leans on a conversation through which students find the terms attached to their foreheads. Students must be attentive to their peers' voices while structuring the activity through a dialogue that empowers the participants. These activities and applications teach students how to use social media more wisely in learning.

Stage 2: The Intercultural Context of Social Networks

At this stage, the students communicate with foreign counterparts, in a synchronic or a-synchronic collaborative activity that allows for personal and group intercultural acquaintances over the learning and implementation process. In a joint activity carried out with American students, the Israeli students developed cognitive, social, and intercultural skills in several steps:

A. The Israeli and American students formed two-person teams and interacted in pairs. The Americans introduced themselves in a short Flipgrid clip to which the Israelis reacted. They remained in contact until the end of the activity.
B. The Israeli students proposed enterprises on Facebook and described tthem. The American students reacted to each proposal, enriching the group exchange. On both sides, the teachers also posted their reactions.
C. The American students posted a TikTok-applicable pedagogical activity, and the Israeli students commented on it and suggested how to expand and improve it.
D. The two groups held a synchronic Zoom meeting. Initially, they briefly described their whereabouts and pinpointed them on a shared map. They later met in a Wonder.me environment and held small-group discussions using the changing backgrounds, thus navigating several environments with experiential, cognitive, social, and intercultural involvement.

The assessment included Israeli feedbacks on the American TikTok activities. By receiving three or four feedbacks, the students could upgrade their activity and gain new insights.

Stage 3: Student-Led Pedagogical Application and Assessment of Social Networks

At this stage, students develop the ability to design pedagogical social-network applications, displaying their creativeness using various social network environments and activities. Through collaboration, interpersonal communication, and using pedagogical models best fitting specific social networks, they implement the connectivism theory and the constructivist approach. Over the activity, the students apply most of the physical, cognitive, and social aspects they have previously experienced. They work in different environments and use creative teaching modes that engage the learners, encourage dialogue and critical thinking, and allow for work in various group types.

After testing each of these applications, the learners discuss ways to implement them in different fields with their students, thus personalizing the learning experience. Collaborative work with their peers is an opportunity to explore favorable implementation methods for later use with their students. This stage also emphasizes the significant interdependence between the pedagogical activity's nature and selecting a suitable environment. The collaborative exploration may occur in different learning spaces applied in the course, i.e., synchronically, a-synchronically, in the classroom, and out of class. Physical venues include the classroom, the reflection space, and out-of-class spaces. Online synchronic spaces include Zoom, Zoom rooms, and Wonder.me.

Using an a-synchronic online space enables students and teachers to perform the activities at the most suitable times and places. The various available techno-pedagogical tools enable the learners to use these activities as models that inspire their future work with their students. Relevant environments include Flipgrid, TikTok, WhatsApp, Instagram, Facebook, Telegram, Wakelet, and Wonder.me. Students discover various aspects of the network while keeping aware of controlling security and anonymity issues. Assessment at this stage combines self-assessment, lecturer assessment, and three anonymous peer assessments.

The described training stages represent the central concepts of the polyphonic wisdom approach. They assist educators in understanding the complexity of incorporating technology in teaching while showing them how to use multiple environments that reflect our complex reality. Exploring the mentioned learning environments encourages learners to apply their digital literacies independently and in teamwork while acquainting them with varied content worlds and democratic values for their personal and collective good.

Challenges and Practical Tips for the Model's Implementation

The described model covers the course contents, techno-pedagogical aspects, learning-teaching-evaluation spaces, and implementation of teaching modes adjusted to the teaching purposes or ad hoc learning spaces encountered at various stages. Below are the challenges that emerged at the different stages of the model's implementation, and practical tips to content with them.

Stage 1: Theory and Related Issues

1. One challenge at this stage is deciding how to present the theoretical background. An optional way used was mapping theoretical articles by their interconnections, similar to a social network. This required delving into the articles' contents to find interconnections to enable presenting them as a network. Highly flexible thinking and attentiveness to creative student thoughts was imperative. Another challenge was finding theoretical articles that established how to apply each environment. We recommend allowing space for different ways of thinking and associative connections between sources.
2. Experiencing varied social media and networks: Teachers must bring examples of optimally applying social networks in teaching. The example applications must relate to knowledge, learning space, and activity nature and be user-friendly. Teachers may be surprised to discover that some students are not acquainted with networks considered to be widely used and known. The teachers should uncover little-known layers and creatively associate the network with various pedagogical and educational uses. Once students have formed stands regarding the application of social networks in teaching, they must test their mastery of the contents introduced in the course. The challenge here is reviewing the terms, environments, and activities encountered over the course to make sure that students utilize them. As they try to discover the content of the expressions written on the stickers, they rehearse the entire course content world.
3. First-hand experience of social networks: At this stage, students must challenge themselves and articulate various aspects of the screen era that have become part of our daily routine. In the workshop, students temporarily distance themselves from daily life, put aside all technological and other means, and use the body to express situations related to the overuse of social networks and screens. They also form a physical space that simulates the social networks' virtual space to assess network convenience, inconvenience, and risk zones while moving, followed by making a justifiable choice of space. Such exercises require being attentive to learner differences. Some learners with certain blocks may surprise themselves by discovering new aspects during the activity despite the challenge

and the effort this takes. Others discover the benefits of physical activity, allowing them to express themselves optimally. We recommend moderate warming-up activity to dissipate tensions and create a pleasant atmosphere for the benefit of the whole group.

Stage 2: The Intercultural Aspect of Social Network Use

Before launching an international collaboration, the teacher must check the extent of the selected network's use by the foreign counterparts. The issue of time differences must be considered. Language gaps may delay the usual pace of reaction on social networks. The participating parties from institutes abroad must agree on a common language and be ready for face-to-face, written, and video communications to stay in contact. Such contacts make the Israeli students realize the importance of improving their ability to express themselves in English. It would be advisable to team up the students who master the English language with those who do not to strengthen the group as a whole.

Stage 3: Pedagogical Uses of Social Networks

The challenge here is planning and utilizing optimally different digital media and social network environments to best fit the relevant content and selected environment. Session configuration is of the utmost importance and must be meticulously chosen, whether face-to-face, in or outside the classroom, in the reflection space, and if it is online—whether synchronic or a-synchronic.

The Model's Contribution

Utilizing social networks in teaching has high potential. Teacher trainers can benefit from social networks for informal learning and professional development that could serve as the basis for international enterprises and instill these methods in student teachers. The rapid growth of social networks, whose effect has been called "tectonic" (Shirky, 2008), meets the social needs of people, as described in Maslow's need hierarchy (Maslow, 1970). They include the need for self-expression, belonging to a group or a community, gaining peer appreciation and social status, achieving personal purposes, creativity, and self-actualization.

The model contributes by offering an opportunity to practice via social networks using various forms of independent, collaborative, and group work, whose added value and utility derive from the nature of the activity. These uses support collaboration in learning, strengthen socio-emotional aspects, and boost peer learning. This is an opportunity for teachers to address issues they encounter while using social networks for work. They can discuss them in depth while sharing personal dilemmas and establishing personal stands.

The model assists students to grow as learners, collaborators, and designers of learning environments. If optimally applied in teaching, social networks can promote flexibility, interaction, motivation, and involvement (Seifert, 2016). They bolster personal and professional capacities and bring together different knowledge resources, cultures, and perspectives. Incorporating informal learning environments can authentically boost communication, collaboration, knowledge sharing, common interest fields, privacy, self-expression, access to different perspectives, active participation, and reflective thinking, developing lifelong learning skills.

Summary and Conclusions

The challenges of applying content, pedagogy, and learning spaces are significant, requiring thorough acquaintance with each. In addition to knowledge acquisition, the model develops vital skills that equip the students with digital literacy, pedagogical thinking, and self-efficacy. Learners may enjoy adding physical expression to their tool box. The model also advances cognitive, social, and intercultural skills, offering students a dynamic, progressive learning experience. Incorporating cognitive, social/intercultural, and physical aspects in learning has fascinating and valuable creative educational implications for self-experience. They are the model for eventual work with their students in a non-stressful, enjoyable learning atmosphere that triggers thinking. The model challenges the traditional educational models to reexamine their underlying pedagogy and rethink methods that could prove beneficial to students in an educational system.

A Personal Note

I have chosen to dedicate this chapter to introducing a model capable of advancing students' cognitive, social, physical, and intercultural practices. I strongly believe that teachers who enjoy teaching can instill the joy of teaching in their students. The learning space comprises different variables and components that interweave and support each other. Designing the learning process as a content mixture that promotes the acquisition, internalization, and organization of the learned material to facilitate memorization was challenging. Activity combining body experience, sociability, and interculturality with cognitive characteristics assists these processes and the interpersonal relations developed in learning frameworks, deepening the learners' interactions among themselves and with me. I permit myself to define the learning space as a rhizome (Deleuze & Guattari, 1987) whose form is a simultaneous occurrence of meaningful processes and moves that interact in facilitating and empowering dynamic, varied, and unexpected learning processes. In that, it resembles the non-hierarchic social network communications that also attend to information production and dissemination.

References

Anders, A. D. (2018). Networked learning with professionals boosts students' self-efficacy for social networking and professional development. *Computers & Education, 127*, 13–29.

Anderson, T. (2019). Challenges and opportunities for use of social media in higher education. *Journal of Learning for Development, 6*(1), 6–19.

Anderson, L. W., & Krathwohl, D. (Eds.). (2001). *A taxonomy for learning, teaching and assessing: A revision of bloom's taxonomy of educational objectives*. Longman.

Bouton, E., Tal, S. B., & Asterhan, C. S. (2021). Students, social network technology and learning in higher education: Visions of collaborative knowledge construction vs. the reality of knowledge sharing. *The Internet and Higher Education, 49*, 100787.

Bozarth, J. (2010). *Social media for trainers: Techniques for enhancing and extending learning*. Wiley.

Deans, J. (2016). Thinking, feeling and relating: Young children learning through dance. *Australasian Journal of Early Childhood, 41*(3), 46–57.

Deleuze, G., & Guattari, F. (1987). *A thousand plateaus*. Translated by B. Massumi. University of Minnesota Press.

Derrick, W. (2008). Online social networks: Educational benefits and dangers. *Distance Learning, 5*(1), 43.

Greenhow, C., & Askari, E. (2017). Learning and teaching with social network sites: A decade of research in K-12 related education. *Education and Information Technologies, 22*(2), 623–645.

Gros, F. (2014). *A philosophy of walking*. Verso Trade.

Halverson, E. R. (2011). Do social networking technologies have a place in formal learning environments? *On the Horizon*.

Kan, A. Ü., & Murat, A. (2020). Examining the self-efficacy of teacher candidates' lifelong learning key competences and educational technology standards. *Education and Information Technologies, 25*(2), 707–724. https://doi.org/10.1007/s10639-019-10072-8

Kelleci, O., Kulaksiz, T., & Pala, F. K. (2018). The effect of social network-supported microlearning on teachers self-efficacy and teaching skills. *World Journal on Educational Technology: Current Issues., 10*(2), 115–129. https://doi.org/10.18844/wjet.v10i2.3456

Manca, S., & Ranieri, M. (2013). Is it a tool suitable for learning? A critical review of the literature on Facebook as a technology-enhanced learning environment. *Journal of Computer Assisted Learning, 29*(6), 487–504.

Maslow, A. H. (1970). *Motivation and personality*. Harper and Row.

Mayer, R. E. (1984). Aids to text comprehension. *Educational Psychologist, 19*(1), 30–42.

Merleau-Ponty, M. (1962). *Phenomenology of perception* (p. 182). Routledge & Kegan Paul.

Nietzsche, F. W. (2007). *Twilight of the idols with antichrist and Ecce Homo*. Wordsworth Editions.

O'Reilly, T. (2005). *What is Web 2.0: Design patterns and business models for the next generation of software*. Viewed March 2006, verified 7 Jan 2010. http://oreilly.com/web2/archive/what-is-web-20.html

Paul, A. M. (2021). *The extended mind: The power of thinking outside the brain*. Eamon Dolan Books.

Rogers, P. C., Liddle, S. W., Peter, C. H. A. N., Doxey, A., & Brady, I. S. O. M. (2007). A web 2.0 learning platform: Harnessing collective intelligence. *Turkish Online Journal of Distance Education, 8*(3), 16–33.

Ronen, M., Kohen-Vacs, D., & Raz-Fogel, N. (2006, June). *Adopt & adapt: Structuring, sharing and reusing asynchronous collaborative pedagogy.* In Proceedings of the 7th international conference on learning sciences (pp. 599–605). International Society of the Learning Sciences.

Seifert, T. (2016). Involvement, collaboration and engagement: Social networks through a pedagogical lens. *Journal of Learning Design, 9*(2), 31–45.

Seifert, T., & Yaron, S. (2019). Movement literacy as a first language. In *Handbook of research on media literacy research and applications across disciplines* (pp. 220–233). IGI Global.

Sheely, S. (2006). Persistent technologies: Why can't we stop lecturing online? In L. Markauskaite, P. Goodyear, & P. Reimann (Eds.), *Who's learning? Whose technology? Proceedings of the 23rd ASCILITE conference* (pp. 769–774). CoCo, University of Sydney.

Shirky, C. (2008). *Here comes everybody: The power of organizing without organizations.* Penguin.

Siemens, G. (2005). Connectivism: A learning theory for the digital age. *International Journal of Instructional Technology and Distance Learning, 2*(1), 3–10.

Thoreau, H. D., & Blaisdell, B. (2011). *Thoreau: A book of quotations.* Dover.

Trust, T. (2018). 2017 ISTE standards for educators: From teaching with technology to using technology to empower learners. *Journal of Digital Learning in Teacher Education, 34*(1), 1–3. https://doi.org/10.1080/21532974.2017.1398980

Veletsianos, G., & Navarrete, C. (2012). Online social networks as formal learning environments: Learner experiences and activities. *The International Review of Research in Open and Distance Learning, 13*(1), 144–166.

Zee, M., & Koomen, H. M. (2016). Teacher self-efficacy and its effects on classroom processes, student academic adjustment, and teacher well-being: A synthesis of 40 years of research. *Review of Educational Research, 86*(4), 981–1015. https://doi.org/10.3102/0034654315626801

Part II
Ecohumanistic Awareness: Caring for the Glocal Environment

Exploring Natural Resources Through Transformative Sustainability Education

Dafna Gan and Adiv Gal

Background

The teacher training system must undergo profound change processes (Bartolic et al., 2021) to respond to ongoing worldwide social and environmental occurrences (Ruiz-Mallén & Heras, 2020), such as ones related to global warming, reduced biological diversity, and air, water, and soil pollution (Mehri et al., 2018; Ogar et al., 2020). Environmental changes engender socio-cultural ones as, for example, in the southern hemisphere, where inhabitants have turned into climate refugees due to the desertification of large areas (Atapattu, 2020). In turn, social changes affect the environment. Thus, globalization processes result in cultural and political homogenization and give rise to trends that inspire a consumption culture, regard technology as the ultimate solution for every environmental issue, put individual personal convenience at the center, and prefer increasing personal capital over investing in collective resources (Angelova et al., 2021; Garfolo & L'Huillier, 2017; Jahanger et al., 2021; Wani, 2011). These trends undermine collaboration and solidarity and cause damage to the natural and human environment. Environmental and social changes, which cause ecological, economic, cultural, and current health crises (Marouli, 2021), also affect education systems, confronting educators with the need to rethink their paths to contend with the new challenges (Marouli, 2021; Wals & Benavot, 2017) in a fast-changing world (Göçen et al., 2020).

The need to find a response to these challenges while taking into account student differences and applying fast-developing technologies requires educators to be flexible in their teaching. They could achieve such flexibility by adopting varied teaching modes and pedagogies (Hannah & Rhubart, 2020; Omare et al., 2020; Öztürk et al., 2020) and a polyphonic approach attentive to several simultaneous voices in

D. Gan · A. Gal (✉)
Kibbutzim College of Education, Technology and the Arts, Tel-Aviv, Israel
e-mail: adiv.gal@smkb.ac.il

Y. Yondler et al. (eds.), *Cultivating Future-Oriented Learners*, Understanding Teaching-Learning Practice, https://doi.org/10.1007/978-3-031-63253-2_5

different contexts (Schwarz-Franco, 2019; Khosronejad et al., 2023; Naot-Ofarim & Solomonic, 2016). The contexts addressed in this article regard students (the learners), teaching processes (pedagogy), and natural resources (the environment). A polyphonic approach assists in contending with various challenges and ultimately allows the schools designed for the industrial epoch to function (Göçen et al., 2020).

School teachers' changing needs have implications for teacher training systems, obliging them to change the traditional theory and implementation of training methods (Olimov, 2021; Vitranen et al., 2021) and adjusting them to the twenty-first century reality (Marouli, 2021). The required conceptual transformation must include redesigning the teaching system of teacher training institutes while particularly emphasizing the aspiration for a society that lives in harmony and respects the environment and human (Marouli, 2021).

Kibbutzim College of Education has designed a post-graduate environmental education program to equip its graduates with the theoretical knowledge and applicative tools to address the social and environmental challenges. To this end, we developed a model based on the theoretical transformative sustainability education approach. It combines outdoor learning with digital pedagogy in collaborative strategies that follows the polyphonic approach.

Using digital pedagogy allows the students to familiarize themselves with the environment while spending time in it. They practice self-learning and learning in collaborative small groups, listening to different voices. The lecturer organizes the activity and creates a learning platform that avoids frontal teaching as much as possible and focuses on natural resources. Staying alone in the various learning spaces, the students are personally responsible for learning under the lecturer's remote guidance. Thus, the primary advantages of the model are that students develop a polyphonic-oriented learning capacity, acquire comprehensive knowledge, and develop critical thinking and understanding. Experiencing this learning process allows for an educational transformation in the students' various fields of interest. It deepens their theoretical-pedagogical understanding and enables them to instill similar pedagogies in their own educational field.

The Theoretical Model of the Course "Natural Resources in an Era of Environmental Crisis"

In conceptualizing the course discussed in this article, we followed the theoretical model of Expósito and Sánchez (2020) (Fig. 1). It is a tree scheme with two meanings. First, the tree's three branches represent content, theoretical approach, and teaching modes and spaces. The tree is a fitting metaphor for the course, representing the natural environment, continuous growth, power of development, change, and dynamism of social and environmental processes. The second meaning of the tree, which is also close to the course's subject matter, is that it symbolizes the services the ecological system bestows on humanity free of charge.

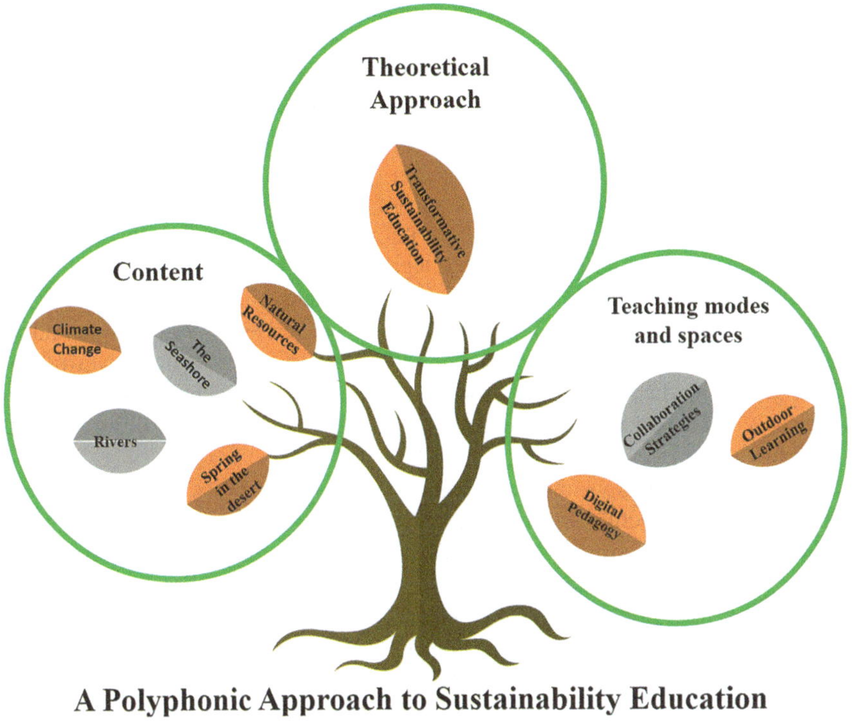

Fig. 1 The tree model—the conceptual framework of the course

The theoretical branch of the tree concerns transformative sustainability education and the environment. Transformative education is, by definition, a meaningful learning process that generates a behavioral change in the learner. It has several key characteristics: Focusing on learning processes (how people learn), examining the learning results (what was learned), and pinpointing conditions that promote learning (best ways to support the learning process) (Mezirow, 2003). Hence, transformative education underscores the learning experience that shapes the learner, brings about a conceptual change, and affects the learner's future work. Transformative teaching differs from the learning methods commonly used in higher education institutes, whose basis is knowledge transfer (Lammers & Murphy, 2002). Another difference between transformative and traditional higher education is the emotional component integrated into transformative learning. Emotional learning is simultaneous to cognitive learning and adds meaning to it. In fact, emotional learning complements the cognitive learning processes (Kroth & Cranton, 2014).

Combining the transformative education theory with sustainability ideas forged the relatively new scientific concept of transformative sustainability education (Burns, 2015). This concept allows for rethinking our life on the planet and reshaping our ontological and epistemological ideas amidst the environmental crisis (Williams, 2018). From an ontological perspective, transformative sustainability education encompasses the entire environmental system, the mutual relations between humanity and the environment, and broader views on cultural, social, economic, and political aspects (Lange, 2018). From an epistemological perspective, transformative sustainability education underscores the changes in people's perception of their place in the world and their relations with other people and the natural universe (Lange, 2018).

Transformative sustainability education has several characteristic features, which facilitates meaningful learning, transform knowledge that unites humanity with the environment for a sustainable future (Dagan-Buzaglo & Swirski, 2011; O'Neil, 2018). It also results in a favorable learning experience that uses the learner's life experiences as a starting point for transformative learning. Rational discourse, another feature of transformative sustainability education, advocates investigating the in-depth significance of the participants' different worldviews and expressing their ideas. Critical thinking is the tool for shaping the learner's worldview (Kroth & Cranton, 2014).

There are several ways to instill transformative sustainability education. Among them are using reflective writing, metaphors, and literature to encourage critical awareness, research, group projects, role-playing, case analysis, simulation, and yoga. These teaching modes, which may be implemented in the classroom or in other venues, have implications for cognitive processes, memory, the learning experience, behavior, and perception of educational phenomena (Kitchenham, 2008; Mezirow, 2003).

In transformative sustainability education, the teacher is a guide tasked with empowering the learners and encouraging them to embrace. It is an approach that emphasizes the learner's desire to make changes to the social order via groundbreaking thinking and joint creation of new knowledge (Expósito & Sánchez, 2020). It encourages visionary thinking about change and learning from experience via critical analysis and a deep understanding of past developments and the roots of change. The process shed light on past successes and failures in social, cultural, economic, and environmental contexts and tests potential alternatives for creating a sustainable world for people and nature. Over the process, students develop creative thinking and are urged to propose significant changes to reduce the environmental crisis.

Contents of the Course

The course engages with three natural resources: the seashore, rivers, and the desert. All natural resources are constantly under pressure due to human activity. Over the course, students examine the three mentioned resources on the local, national, and international levels, also addressing the burning issue of climate change.

Teaching Modes and Learning Spaces of the Course

Outdoor Learning Covers various modes of learning away from the classroom that complement or contribute to classroom learning (Malone, 2014). Such learning may involve various knowledge areas such as reading, writing, literature, mathematics, science, art, environmental education, health, drama, and social sciences (Dyment, 2005). Outdoor learning can encourage transformative learning.

Digital Pedagogy In addition to outdoor learning, the course applies various techno-pedagogical principles (Öztürk et al., 2020) via using digital tools, including shared work files, mobile phones, and digital games. Digital tools assist in navigating, locating information, checking answers, and collaborative learning. Most of the applied techno-pedagogical tools are games that require group member collaboration, such as "The Race to The Million".

Collaborative Learning The different levels of collaboration regard independent learning, learning in pairs, small groups, and as a whole student body. Collaborative learning also includes joint design of products, such as a concept map, and group discussions. Collaborative learning allows for listening to different voices, reflecting the polyphonic approach that encourages learners to be attentive to various opinions in parallel (Schwarz-Franco, 2019).

Stages of the Theoretical Model Implementation in the Course

The program of the post-graduate course "Natural Resources" reflects the three model branches: content (natural resources), pedagogy (outdoor learning, digital pedagogy, and collaborative learning) and theory (transformative learning). The course aims to instill a holistic perspective and integrative understanding of human natural resource exploitation on the local, national, and international levels. Students engage in an in-depth multidimensional scientific analysis of capitalism and its effects on natural resources exploitation, environmental degradation, and deepening social gaps. Among the complex issues addressed in the course are ones related to left and right political wings, capitalism and socialism as worldviews, local and global aspects of the social and geographic center and periphery, conservation vs. development of global natural resources, and religion and environmental features of population growth. These issues are examined in light of the Israeli governments' management of natural resources that belong to all the state citizens and are affected by globalization processes. The program also delves into the dilemmas around social and environmental justice, analyzing the effects of capitalism on Israel's government. Combined, all these topics illustrate the existing polyphony in matters of natural resources. The course program's three stages implement the theoretical model over field trips that introduce each a different environmental resource.

Stage 1: Collaboration as a Pedagogical Principle Lacking in Society: The Seashore Example Over the field trip, students learn about environmental dilemmas related to Israel's seashore. Numerous entities are in competition over this thin strip of land: The Israel Defense Forces (IDF), industrial bodies, settlements, nature reserves, marinas, and more. In many cases, they block access to the beach, obliging the citizens to pay for accessing and enjoying it. Yet, the seashore is a national natural resource owned by all the citizens. This illustrates to the students the dire social and environmental results of lack of collaboration, dialogue, and attentiveness to others and the struggles they entail.

To demonstrate the dilemmas concerning various uses of the seashore, the students participate in the digital game "Race to The Million". The game mirrors the principles of transformative education, where learning occurs through experience, with the teacher as a guide emphasizing the need for collaboration and dialogue and the advantages of brainstorming and joint work. The students thus realize how the management of the seashore resource lacks all these advantages. Small groups and the whole class both work in collaboration. Students receive beforehand questions related to the seashore. Each student must answer one question. The whole picture emerges when all the answers are put together. The students post their answers on a joint google file, and receive the meeting point for the session on the beach only after posting the correct answer. During the "race," the students divide into small groups and have to pass six spots along the Tel Aviv coast, each telling part of the seashore story as a natural resource. To advance to the next spot, they must solve a riddle they receive by scanning a QR code with their cellphones (Figs. 2 and 3). They cannot go to the next stop unless they solve the riddle. The answers given at

Fig. 2 Students scanning a QR code on a Tel Aviv beach as part of outdoor techno-pedagogical learning

Fig. 3 A QR code attached to the fence of a military base on the Tel Aviv shore —

each spot are added to a joint work file to which the teacher has access. The teacher is in touch with the students via a WhatsApp group, allowing giving directions if needed. In an alternative evaluation process, all the groups meet on the beach at the end of the "race" and jointly prepare a concept map based on the information gathered through the learning. Pedagogy-wise, this illustrates the significant weight and contribution of each individual (in a polyphony, every voice is meaningful) in creating a whole picture. This makes for a collective rather than individual evaluation process that conveys the educational message that collaboration is a central principle in teaching and resolving environmental and social issues.

The varied teaching environments and pedagogy help uncover the moral dilemmas in managing the seashore resource while addressing authentic human issues that require both collaboration and a respectful dialogue, such as dealing with climate change. These all represent transformative sustainability education.

Stage 2: Dialogue and Beyond-Human Right for Equality—The Example of Rivers This field trip takes the students to Alexander river which flows from Samaria in the Palestinian Authority to the Mediterranean via Israel. Its course exemplifies the need for a dialogue between the two political entities and contemplating the river's right for water. The students critically discuss the justification for the prize granted to the Alexander River Rehabilitation Project. They delve into the dialogue between the two involved political entities (the Palestinian Authority and Israel) and local bodies, such as local councils and the Drainage Authority. They learn that human needs are equal to the needs of nature and encounter the polyphonic approach through an in-group dialogue and listening to other voices in meetings with key figures involved in the works carried out in the river. The visit carried out in groups, begins by investigating the biotic and abiotic elements (Fig. 4) to understand the river's needs and entitlement to water (beyond human rights of

Fig. 4 Exploring Alexander River

equality). To better understand human needs, they examine the mutual relations between Man and the river, i.e., the human effects on the river and vice versa. Among the pedagogical means for learning these topics are encounters with key figures that call for attentive empathy and sensitivity to different voices, exploring the river, sketching its surroundings and the forces affecting it, and a dialogue between the course participants. Drawing and its subsequent discussion enable the emotional expression of individual voices, critical thinking, and learner dialogue, all representing different modes of understanding the topic. Drawing is an alternative evaluation tool that helps understand mutual individual relations and the interrelations in the class as a whole. Using smartphones and digital tools to analyze the river's flora and fauna embodies digital pedagogy. At this stage, students must demonstrate humanistic sensitivity towards humanity and nature. These means reflect the combination of transformative sustainability education with a polyphonic approach.

This field trip also refers to handling climate changes, this time from the perspective of the river and its water. The students encounter a teaching mode that enhances their reflective skills and develops empathy for others and for nature as part of social emotional learning.

Fig. 5 Field trip of the old aqueduct in the Natural Reserve in the desert

Stage 3: The Desert as a Critical Thinking Setting and Behavioral Change Motivator Critical thinking is essential for transformative sustainability education and motivation of behavioral change. To exemplify it, students go on a desert field trip to the Dead Sea area, where they learn about springs in the desert and the uniqueness of an oasis that is a source of life for nature and human. The spring in the nature reserve benefits the area's vegetation and animals. Some of the water passes to the local industry making the water available to consumers throughout Israel. The learning is mostly outdoor (Fig. 5), and drawing serves as a pedagogical tool. The field trip focuses on ethical education for responsibility, considering nature and the other, human sensitivity, and modest relations with nature. Students develop critical thinking by understanding the various interests and realizing that they can become involved and bring about change. Students examine the water division between the needs of the reserve and the local industry, gaining insights by discussing the reserve's capacity to accommodate visitors without risking its delicate balance. Critical thinking is also applied in contemplating the dilemma of jeopardizing the Dead Sea, the lowest spot on the planet. The learning processes allow for switching from dual to complex scrutiny of environmental components. Students undergo an interdisciplinary intellectual education toward understanding the complexity and mutual relations between natural and human systems. Summary evaluation at the end of the course involves group work to put together a digital concept map that incorporates the complex power relations with Israel's natural resources. The map product embodies critical thinking, collaborative work, dialogue and discourse, and the principles of a polyphonic transformative sustainability education.

In conclusion, the three described model stages lean mainly on outdoor learning spaces that combine digital pedagogy and collaborative strategies. The course's theoretical approach, based on polyphonic transformative sustainability education, aims to enable openness, experience, and critical thinking that would urge post-graduate environment education students to act toward reducing the environmental crisis and climate changes occurring around us.

Advantages of the Course Model

One student summarized the advantage of combining different learning spaces, various levels of collaboration, and varied pedagogical tools, saying: "I liked the division into actual encounters in the field, learning from home on Zoom, traveling together … Several teaching and learning modes and varied experiences … contributed significantly to creating an optimal high-quality learning experience … It was fun." These words reveal that the course's emotional and cognitive response allowed optimal learning. Another student summarized the course similarly: "The course was wonderful in its richness, content, teaching methodologies, learning fields, and teamwork … I would be delighted if it has a sequel in the next school year." She thus noted that the learning modes facilitated content learning and made her wish for a continuing course. These quotes prove that the students derived a positive experience from the course. It would appear that lecturers who wish their students to have a positive learning experience should expand outdoor learning and collaboration levels and utilize different pedagogical tools.

Observing the course model from the polyphonic wisdom perspective (Refer to the polyphonic wisdom model provided in the theoretical chapter of the book) reveals that separately and together, its stages reflect this wisdom in their humanistic educational approach and constructive social approach. These are the two pillars educators lean on to create synergy between the four components of the polyphonic concept: Multidimensionality, technology that facilitates collaborative and personal knowledge building, authentic content, and humanistic pedagogy. In other words, the flower model corresponds to the tree model (Fig. 1), whose alternative spaces (outdoor and digital ones) and technological choices boost learning topics related to transformative sustainability education. This approach fosters personal and social responsibility for natural and human systems, understanding and accepting the perspectives of others, openness, holistic critical thinking, and methodically guided self-education that helps learners achieve their goals.

Theoretical and Practical Contribution: Implementation Tips and Summary

The described theoretical model combines theoretical elements of polyphonic transformative sustainability education and a pedagogical approach that advocates outdoor learning, digital pedagogy, and collaborative strategies. These are all implemented in a higher education teacher-training institute. The model illustrates how varied pedagogical ideas combine with humanistic ideas of dialogue, attentiveness, containment, and empathy among people and between humanity and nature. It has a twofold contribution to education and teacher training. First, it develops critical thinking and encourages teachers and their students to become active in struggling with the environmental crisis. Second, it enables course participants to implement the various parts of the model in their respective education fields and in different contexts. Moreover, the model is adaptable to other knowledge fields and outdoor spaces. One student testified, "I am already implementing the pedagogical tools I acquired in the course in the classes I teach."

Challenges and Implementation Advice

Various learning spaces, different collaboration levels, and a number of pedagogical tools may prove complex to apply, explaining why there are numerous challenges in implementing the described model. To begin with, the teacher must cope throughout the course with ongoing uncertainty. Outdoor learning takes both the teacher and the students out of their comfort zone, i.e., the classroom with its seats and writing board. Outdoor learning is affected by inconsistent weather conditions such as high or low temperatures, blazing sun, no shade, wind, rain, and uncomfortable sitting. Another major challenge is that the lecturer has difficulty controlling the teaching processes. The greater the uncertainty, the greater the risk of reduced lecturer control. Together and separately, uncertainty and reduced control make outdoor teaching more difficult, impairing the ability to predict what voices the polyphonic learning will include.

In such circumstances, the teacher must be sufficiently flexible to respond to the different challenges. For example, in a field trip that explored sand as a natural resource, the lecturer was asked about a sand crab that popped up suddenly. Although the creature's connection to the field trip topic was remote, the teacher thought discussing it was important for a broader understanding of the learned subject.

Another challenge of outdoor learning is that the teacher must always be ready to make concessions. These may concern content (unlike classroom learning, completing the missed material later is no option), teaching location (if an exploration spot is unavailable for unpredicted reasons, returning to it would not be possible), or disrupted timetables (such as ones due to traffic jams).

Teaching in various spaces with varied pedagogical tools and different levels of collaboration requires investing considerable time in preparing the course and each of its sessions and carrying them out. The teacher must perform a preparatory field trip and scout the planned itinerary, see to receiving security authorizations, make transportation arrangements and deal with the drivers, appoint a second escort, make sure that spots for bathroom stops are available on the way, and choose digital or other pedagogical tools to suit the learned content rather than have the tools dictate the content.

In summary, teaching in various learning environments, at different collaboration levels, and with varied pedagogical tools enhances learning. However, a teacher who wishes to enrich his teaching, as was done in the "Natural Resources" course, must be flexible in his behavior and give up the convenience of the classroom. While contributing to the students, this eventually also benefits the teachers, as we learned from the participants of a similar course and as the research literature indicates. It takes courage to cope with uncertainty and reduced control and muster the flexibility required for outdoor teaching. A lecturer who wishes to benefit from the advantages of this model must not recoil from diving in. Notably, experience reduces the sense of environmental alienation in teachers and students and increases the confidence required to face the complexity of outdoor learning. Inviting educators experienced in this kind of teaching to join the activity can also be helpful.

Given the advantages of the model presented in this article, it is of the highest importance to incorporate a pedagogy based on transformative sustainability education in all the teacher-training programs and not only in programs pertaining to environmental education or the sciences. Open spaces are vital for learning, particularly if technological means help develop twenty-first-century skills and manage the environmental crisis. We therefore recommend looking for ways to impart the principles of this type of education to already working teachers in the system. Among the ways to achieve this are continuing teacher education courses, guiding teachers in their routine work, and urging policymakers to adopt such pedagogical principles.

A Personal Note

In preparation for writing this chapter, we contemplated the design of this course and defined its unique theoretical and practical model. Through this contemplation, we managed to improve its implementation and presentation to the students while at the same time deepening the students' understanding of its contents and enabling them to apply the learned material in other situations, according to the local, national, and international influence circles. Using outside spaces and digital technology for collaborative learning illustrated the power of these tools and highlighted the need to design additional courses based on this model. We strongly believe that the model and the chapter describing it can assist other educators in taking advantage of our experience and help instill complex issues related to the environmental crisis into the education system's pedagogical practice.

References

Angelova, M., Dimitrova, T., & Pastarmadzhieva, D. (2021). The effects of globalization: Hyper consumption and environmental consumer behavior during the Covid-19 Pandemic. *International Journal of Economics and Business Administration, 9*(4), 41–54. https://doi.org/10.35808/ijeba/733

Atapattu, S. (2020). Climate change and displacement: Protecting 'climate refugees' within a framework of justice and human rights. *Journal of Human Rights and the Environment, 11*(1), 86–113.

Bartolic, S. K., Boud, D., Agapito, J., Verpoorten, D., Williams, S., Lutze-Mann, L., Matzat, U., Moreno, M. M., Polly, P., Tai, J., Marsh, H. L., Lin, L., Burgess, J. L., Habtu, S., Rodrigo, M. M. M., Roth, M., Heap, T., & Guppy, N. (2021). A multi-institutional assessment of changes in higher education teaching and learning in the face of COVID-19. *Educational Review*, 1–17. https://doi.org/10.1080/00131911.2021.1955830

Burns, H. L. (2015). Transformative sustainability pedagogy: Learning from ecological systems and indigenous wisdom. *Journal of Transformative Education, 13*(3), 259–276. https://doi.org/10.1177/1541344615584683

Dagan-buzaglo, N., & Swirski, S. (2011). *Education reform: Making education work for all children*. Adva Center—Information on Equality and Social Justice in Israel.

Dyment, J. E. (2005). Green school grounds as sites for outdoor learning: Barriers and opportunities. *International Research in Geographical and Environmental Education, 14*(1), 28–45. https://doi.org/10.1080/09500790508668328

Expósito, L., & Sánchez, J. (2020). Implementation of SDGs in university teaching: Course for professional development of teachers in education for sustainability for a transformative action. *Sustainability, 12*(8267), su12198267.

Garfolo, B. T., & L'Huillier, B. (2017). Ethics, globalization, and the role educators play. *Athens Journal of Education, 4*(3), 211–222. https://doi.org/10.30958/aje.4-3-2

Göçen, A., Hatice, S., Mustafa, E., Eral, S. H., & Perceptions, M. H. T. (2020). Teacher perceptions of a 21st century classroom. *International Journal of Contemporary Educational Research, 7*(1), 85–98.

Hannah, L., & Rhubart, C. (2020). Teacher perceptions of state standards and climate change pedagogy: Opportunities and barriers for implementing consensus-informed instruction on climate change. *Climatic Change, 158*, 377–392.

Jahanger, A., Usman, M., & Balsalobre-lorente, D. (2021). Autocracy, democracy, globalization, and environmental pollution in developing world: Fresh evidence from STIRPAT model. *Journal of Public Affairs*, e2753. https://doi.org/10.1002/pa.2753

Khosronejad, M., Weber, L., & Ryan, M. (2023). Teacher learning as a polyphonic endeavor: A context sensitive model of teacher professional development. *Teachers and Teaching*, 1–16.

Kitchenham, A. (2008). The evolution of John Mezirow's transformative learning theory. *Journal of Transformative Education, 6*(2), 104–123. https://doi.org/10.1177/1541344608322678

Kroth, M., & Cranton, P. (2014). Stories of transformative learning. In *Stories of transformative learning*. https://doi.org/10.1007/978-94-6209-791-9

Lammers, W., & Murphy, J. (2002). A profile of teaching techniques used in the university. *Active Learning in Higher Education, 3*(1), 54–67.

Lange, E. A. (2018, February). *1. RiverSpeaking: The spiraling of transformative and restorative learning toward kinship ethics*. https://doi.org/10.3920/978-90-8686-846-9.

Malone, K. (2014). *An evidence based research report on the role of learning outside the classroom for children's whole development from birth to eighteen years*.

Marouli, C. (2021). Sustainability education for the future? Challenges and implications for education and pedagogy in the 21st century. *Sustainability, 13*(2901), su13052901.

Mehri, A., Salmanmahiny, A., Reza, A., Tabrizi, M., Mirkarimi, S. H., & Sadoddin, A. (2018). Integration of anthropogenic threats and biodiversity value to identify critical sites for biodiversity conservation. *Geocarto International, May*, 1–16. https://doi.org/10.1080/10106049.2018.1475510

Mezirow, J. (2003). Transformative learning as discourse. *Journal of Transformative Education, 1*(1), 58–63. https://doi.org/10.1177/1541344603252172

Naot-Ofarim, Y., & Solomonic, S. (2016). Educational polyphony. *Studies in Philosophy and Education, 35*(4), 385–397.

O'Neil, J. (2018). Transformative sustainability learning within a material—Discursive ontology. *Journal of Transformative Education, 16*(4), 365–387. https://doi.org/10.1177/1541344618792823

Ogar, E., Pecl, G., & Mustonen, T. (2020). Science must embrace traditional and indigenous knowledge to solve our biodiversity crisis. *One Earth, 3*(2), 162–165. https://doi.org/10.1016/j.oneear.2020.07.006

Olimov, S. (2021). The innovation process is a priority in the development of pedagogical sciences. *European Journal of Research Development and Sustainability (EJRDS), 2*(3), 86–88.

Omare, E., Imonje, R. K., & Nyagah, G. (2020). Teacher qualification, experience, capability beliefs and professional development: Do they predict teacher adoption of 21. *International Journal of Curriculum and Instruction, 12*(2), 639–670.

Öztürk, G., Karamete, A., & Çetin, G. (2020). The relationship between pre-service teachers' cognitive flexibility levels and techno-pedagogical education competencies. *International Journal of Contemporary Educational Research, 7*(1), 40–53.

Ruiz-Mallén, I., & Heras, M. (2020). What sustainability? Higher education institutions' pathways to reach the Agenda 2030 goals. *Sustainability (Switzerland), 12*(4), 1–18. https://doi.org/10.3390/su12041290

Schwarz-Franco, O. (2019). Polyphonic teaching: The ability to facilitate multiple voices as a crucial teaching skill. In *Sonic studies in educational foundations* (pp. 87–108). Routledge.

Virtanen, A., Valtonen, T., Hoang, N., Sointu, E., Piia, N., Sanna, J., Kati, M., & Johanna, P. (2021). How pre-service teachers perceive their 21st-century skills and dispositions: A longitudinal perspective. *Computers in Human Behavior, 116*, 106643. Contents. https://doi.org/10.1016/j.chb.2020.106643

Wals, A. E. J., & Benavot, A. (2017). Can we meet the sustainability challenges? The role of education and lifelong learning. *European Journal of Education, 52*(4), 404–413. https://doi.org/10.1111/ejed.12250

Wani, H. (2011). Impact of globalization on world culture. *Journal of Humanities and Social Sciences Studies, 2*(2), 33–39.

Williams, L. (2018). Transformative sustainability education and empowerment practice on indigenous lands: Part one. *Journal of Transformative Education, 16*(4), 344–364. https://doi.org/10.1177/1541344618789363

Sustainability, Literature and Art in Various Spaces: "Between the Trees and the Non-trees"

Netta Baryosef-Paz and Dafna Gan

Introduction

Based on polyphonic teaching, eco-humanist approach, and the holistic perception of education, this chapter presents a pedagogical model that integrates various fields and partnerships within different spaces of teaching and learning. The framework of the model revolves around sustainability education and encompasses literature, visual arts, music, environment, and society. We present this model, which is based on a course entitled "Sustainability and Art," in a holistic manner, navigating between the concrete and the imaginative, and bridging technology with creativity.

"Between the Trees and the Non-Trees"/Agi Mishol

I am not travelling anywhere.
I am too instable to be uprooted
From my contexts
And the laziness within me aspires to perpetuate
Its state
To continue and dwell in its familiar space
In twilight time
On the staircase
When the imagination is satiated
And the hunters' eyes are already resting
In the niches of my head.
[…]
I am only present here
Between the trees and the non-trees

My door is wide open
And the soft night is invited into the house— (Mishol, 2003).

N. Baryosef-Paz (✉) · D. Gan
Kibbutzim College of Education, Technology and Arts, Tel-Aviv, Israel
e-mail: Netta.bar-yosef-paz@smkb.ac.il

Y. Yondler et al. (eds.), *Cultivating Future-Oriented Learners*, Understanding Teaching-Learning Practice, https://doi.org/10.1007/978-3-031-63253-2_6

The speaker in Agi Mishol's poem positions herself in a space that is an outcome of her linguistic (non-grammatical) invention: "Between the trees and the non-trees." She seeks to express her detached presence from an actual place, meaning her boundary-defying and hybrid location—not here and not there. It could also suggest—not quite in nature and not in a human-made place, not inside the house and not outside of it (but, rather, on the staircase). Similarly, in the model we propose: for us "Between the trees and the non-trees" represents the unmarked spaces we offer, spaces that merge into each other and are not arranged hierarchically or chronologically. They are spaces of urban nature alongside urbanized wilderness, which blend human-made and natural elements. The urban nature experienced by the students in the course is not an authentic nature of the land of Israel but a hybrid combination of human-made elements. Just as the speaker "is present here," observing, listening, breathing, and sensing—the course also offers a contemplative and introspective presence into the inner spaces of all participants and outward into the environment, blurring boundaries in a fluid manner. Indeed, the boundary-less perception of discipline, field, or profession is the most crucial response, in our view, to today's educational needs. In our surrounding world, education (as well as medicine, employment, and politics) is often divided into narrow, mechanistic, and technical disciplines. Instead of all these, the educational model detailed in this chapter promotes a holistic view that blurs boundaries, the same way as we should contemplate the natural environment. Indeed, the environment is presented in the course as part of the sustainability perception, which is a central axis in the course.

The term sustainability includes the environmental crisis deriving from the human pursuit of comfort, which is the epitome of ease and personal pleasure—from the use of disposables to private vehicle usage; from ceaseless consumerism to the preference for capital holders over a deteriorating nature. Like the poem's speaker "Between the Trees and the Non-trees," our inherent laziness aspires to perpetuate its state, and so does our imagination, which like our stomach is satisfied and idle.

In order to address the environmental crisis, sustainability education is the solution proposed by the model presented in this chapter. Sustainability education, hybrid pedagogical spaces, as well as literature and art—all these are described in this chapter discussing the unique teaching model implemented in the course, designed for Visual Arts Master's program at Kibbutzim College of education. We, the authors of this chapter, created and developed this course collaboratively, and we wrote this article together, word by word, paragraph by paragraph—as a genuine joint creation.

Theoretical Background

The course, as well as the chapter, relies on two complementary theoretical pillars: holistic pedagogy and ecohumanism. The first is pedagogical, practical, and applied, while the latter is conceptual. The course's context is the environmental crisis, which is the most pressing global issue today. Threats loom over the globe; coastal cities face submersion, populations are affected by disasters, inundations, or infrastructure collapse, and are forced to migrate. Species and natural ecosystems are disappearing and becoming extinct. The crisis is complex, and the related issues are so intricate and laden with conflicting interests that sustainability education, which was previously practicable, cannot continue as before and requires change.

Today, there is a tendency in sustainability education courses in higher education to focus on acquiring scientific knowledge related to topics such as climate change, biodiversity loss, pollution, and technological methods for addressing it (Albareda-Tiana et al., 2018). Even though efforts have been made in the field of sustainability education for over 40 years, the situation on Earth is not improving and, in fact, is worsening significantly.

What is required here is a holistic perspective—of ecological issues and of the learning individuals and their place in the socio-cultural world as well as in the natural environment. Holistic education is a profound form of education that addresses the whole person on all dimensions—physical, intellectual, aesthetic, emotional, and spiritual—offering hope for the prosperity and growth of our wondrous planet as a whole, including all its inhabitants—human and non-human alike. An essential component of this educational approach is the connection to the environment. Holistic education aims to be in harmony with nature, enabling teaching and learning focused on interdependence and connection to nature (Hare, 2006; Miller et al., 2019).

Therefore, we claim that the holistic approach to sustainability education—an approach that is evolving and developing recently—is preferable for many reasons. This approach provides a way to cope with the complexity of the current environmental situation, directing the shift in the educational paradigm from reductionist to holistic. Consequently, it involves treating knowledge and its acquisition as holistic. Teachers should be aware of the natural connections between science, ecology, society, and spirituality (Echegoyen-Sanz et al., 2021; Sterling, 2010).

Holistic education is built on four learning foundations: learning to learn, learning to do, learning to live together, and learning to be. The totality expresses itself at different levels—individual, societal, and natural (Mahmoudi et al., 2012; Sterling, 2010). Some important principles in this educational approach include freedom of choice, respect and autonomy for the learning individual, centrality of experimentation and experience, cooperative learning, participatory democracy, and global citizenship. If we want future educators to be capable of applying a holistic approach in their work, they must develop creativity and constructive thinking.

Research indicates that the holistic approach has brought about changes in educators' environmental attitudes (Echegoyen-Sanz & Martin-Ezpeleta, 2021), by developing practical skills in the field of sustainability and educational skills for integrating the subject into the education system. Moreover, such an approach aligns with the goals of the United Nations for Sustainable Development (Albareda-Tiana et al., 2018). The holistic approach offers a way to cope both with the subject's complexity and with the emotions arising when teaching such a multidimensional subject. Placing the learner at the center of the learning process, as done in our course, is one tool for achieving this. Thanks to the fact that our students are educators themselves, they have the opportunity for the subject's application in their schools.

Side by side to the principle of holism, the second theoretical pillar is ecohumanism. The term ecohumanism consists of two components representing two different worldviews. According to the humanist approach, individuals form social and political relationships based on a moral commitment to human dignity, equality, and fair opportunities for everyone to live a life of development, self-fulfillment, and meaningful participation in society. Based on the sustainability approach, which includes the ecological perspective, humans use natural resources and engage in economic development with the appreciation of natural systems and the protection of the environment. This worldview focuses on the interconnected relationship between humans and the environment, with a sense of care and responsibility for harmonious relations between the human species and the natural environment (Brody et al., 2013). This approach also embodies a commitment to the long-term and optimal existence of social and natural systems, contributing significantly to the prosperity of nature and humanity. It provides insights into solutions, both to prevent catastrophes and to avoid recurring and escalating crises in infrastructures that had not initially been built sustainably (Aloni et al., 2023).

Ecohumanism is a holistic ethical perspective on sustainability, combining responsibility for the fate of nature and humanity. It is an ethics and pedagogy that, based on the respect for human dignity and social justice, natural systems, and biodiversity, works to promote the prosperity of the natural world and the quality of life for all humans. As educators seeking to nurture young generations and equip them with insights, sensitivities, and abilities for a life of quality, we need to be connected with humanistic values, social justice, peace pursuit, democratic citizenship, healthy lifestyles, and environmental sustainability (Aloni et al., 2023).

Ecohumanism is implemented in various ways, including active listening and a dialogical culture, that were particularly present in our course. Active listening is respectful, curious, perceptive, sensitive, empathetic, and interpretative. Like the making of art, this form of listening observes before changing, contemplates before inventing, and listens before adding its voice. It is an open-minded approach to things as they manifest themselves, according to their nature and uniqueness, avoiding imposing a scrutinizing gaze and manipulative utility. A dialogical culture replaces the approach of success at the expense of others with an approach of agreement and coexistence with others. This is true also for the relationship between ecology and humanism, and for interpersonal and intercultural relationships. Dialogues are built on foundations of mutual respect, goodwill, reciprocity, trust, empathy, and attentiveness. They reject authoritarian, coercive, and controlling methods, including the consumerist obsession, all of which common to human behavior in general and towards the natural environment specifically. Instead, they construct agreements through reasoning, humanity, fairness, and harmony. The model we propose aims to translate the philosophical ideas of ecohumanism and holistic education into educational action in the teacher training field, with the intention that educators will instill the pedagogy they experienced in the course into their educational work (Aloni et al., 2023; Shor & Freire, 1987).

A Polyphonic Teaching Based Approach to the Course: Holism and Ecohumanism

The course "Sustainability Education and Art", embodies the polyphonic teaching: it generates synergy among various voices (individual and collective, in different spaces and with different tools) that integrate into a coherent educational rationale. This allows the development of the polyphonic perspective of both learners and educators. The holistic course revolves around axes from the concrete to the abstract, from the internal to the external, from the existing to the imaginary, and vice versa. It engages in reflective and introspective components, yet it is also dependent on interaction among the diverse voices. The course explores imagination, art, and literature, however it is also grounded in ecological, environmental, and cultural knowledge. It takes place in physical pedagogical spaces as well as virtual spaces.

The course is non-hierarchical, non-chronological, and its spaces intertwine in layers, at various times and seasons, in different modes of interaction and throughout time, resembling the polyphonic perspective. Holism is manifested in several encounters in the course, each containing different aspects of pedagogical spaces. The course aspires for a product that allows the learner to reflect on oneself as a student as well as an educator who integrates sustainability and holism into his/her teaching. The educational spaces in the course are interwoven, blending into one another, and emerging from each other, as we demonstrate below.

The course includes the following spaces: cultural and artistic spaces (music, singing, storytelling, visual arts, and cinema); virtual space (Padlet, Zoom, moodle forum, Google Docs, and virtual exhibition); spaces of place and time (museum, classroom, and outdoors); spaces of observation and imagination (mindfulness meditation, contemplative writing, and silent walking); and, finally, holistic pedagogy spaces (learning to learn, learning to do, learning to live together, and learning to be). The course takes place both synchronously—on Zoom, in the classroom, and outdoors—enabling collaborative learning, and asynchronously—through students' individual visits to the actual exhibition in the gallery or museum—facilitating individualized learning, translating the acquired concepts into personal insight and individual interpretation for both art and sustainability.

Co-teaching is a central feature of the course, creating a common space between the two lecturers, as well as separate spaces that each lecturer shares with the students. The mutual space is primarily an expression of interdisciplinarity: lecturers come from different fields of knowledge, and possess diverse worldviews. The collaborative space created includes several dimensions. Firstly, the lecturers collaborate in course planning, thinking, and teaching—each allowing a genuine space for mutual influence: it involves continuous and conscious listening throughout all stages, flexibility, and flow. Secondly, the students collaborate during the lessons (in teams and in the plenary). Thirdly, the space between students and lecturers (in the classroom, outdoors, on Zoom, and in other virtual spaces) is also collaborative: for example, students collaboratively create the final task. The final product is the learning process's peak. It is a presentation, which can be an art creation (e.g., fashion design and fashion products made from packaging of snacks, a video including environmental and situational references to a desert sculpture garden, or an art video about consumer culture). It can also be an analysis of such works. In both cases, the students link their product to the sustainability principles of the course. These examples illustrate how the course and the proposed model enable learners to practically apply humanistic values, encouraging environmental and social responsibility. Concurrently, working on the products inspires communication and collaboration among learners, creating communal products while cultivating collective knowledge for the common good. Thus, we may claim that creating synergy among the four components—collaborative lecturers, students, spaces, and final product—is the ability to operate with a polyphonic teaching.

Thus far, we have presented our course's structure. In what follows, we outline its thematic features. Representing the lecturers' fields of knowledge, the course integrates sciences, education, leadership, and music on the one hand, and the relationships between literature, reflective pedagogy, and ecocriticism on the other. Overarching this variety of themes is sustainability education, defined by UNESCO, as focusing on developing and strengthening the abilities of individuals, organizations, and countries to make the right choices that will lead to sustainable development. As such, it deals with changing the learners' perception of the world and their ethical awareness, enabling them to make the world safer, healthier, and more flourishing. In light of this, the course addresses concepts such as ecocriticism (environmental humanities), anthropocene, ecocentrism-biocentrism-anthropocentrism, environmental crisis as a social opportunity, climate change, and consumer culture. It introduces students to several contemporary literary and visual art works that represent these environmental themes. Students explore the subject through reading theoretical texts and literary works, observing artworks, and engaging in independent creation.

The Teaching Model: The Course's Structure

A way to look at this course is to see it as a two-stage process. The first stage (Experience-Observation-Experience) emphasizes the experience arising from listening to music, reading poetry, outdoor learning, and contemplation. This stage generates the perception of polyphonic voices, enabling the expression of each and every voice. The second stage (Analysis and Application through Personal Interpretation) offers an opportunity for a nuanced expression of personal and group insights. This is a stage of harmonious connection amongst all voices, creating synergy interrelating all voices as they are expressed in the aforementioned spaces, knowledge, pedagogies, and technologies.

Stage I: Experience-Observation-Experience

The course opens with the sounds of the harpsichord: before the greeting, introduction, or presentation of the participants and lecturers, Dafna played a prelude from the work "L'Art de toucher le clavecin" by Francois Couperin.[1] Afterwards, Netta read the poem "Apocalypse I" by Yonit Naaman,[2] and the students were asked to introduce themselves using a line from the poem (Naaman, 2018). These pieces of art—poems on the environment and musical pieces describing natural phenomena—inspired a lesson which combine both thematic and pedagogical features significant to the course: music and literature generated observation, listening, free contemplative as well as structured writing, drawing, and, finally, an attentive discussion. In other words, the students practiced various types of attentiveness and response.

Subsequently, we ventured outside to a tour of an office building near the campus, for a dialogue-rich encounter between humans and mostly neglected urban space. The products of this tour inside and outside the tower—written segments, still photographs, video clips, and performances—were presented on a collaborative digital board. The digital tool creates a new collective creation that is more extensive and powerful than the sum of its parts. It allows all students (even those who could not attend the tour) to be part of it, upload photos from their personal surroundings, and create an additional rich discussion. One insight derived from this lesson is the power of literature and art to direct our gaze to those phenomena we choose not to see—environmental, social, and cultural.

Such a phenomenon is illustrated in a series of poems, portraying cleaning workers (specifically women). In this lesson we opened with an activity rooted in contemplative pedagogy. Students were guided into a meditation that evolved into guided imagination: "Think about a cleaning lady. Imagine the situation—her workplace, what a day in her life looks like, her personal appearance, her likes and dislikes. Perhaps it's a cleaning lady you know, one you always see, or maybe it's one you've only seen from a distance. Maybe the cleaning lady is you. We all play the role of a cleaning lady at some point." At the end of the meditation, we asked the

[1] The music by Francois Couperin reflects harmony without polyphony. It is music grounded in the common sonority without distinct differentiation of internal voices. In contrast, Johann Sebastian Bach (whose works were also part of the course) incorporates polyphony in almost all of his compositions.

[2] Naaman's poem is a clear expression of orchestrated polyphony that expresses excess both in content and form—long lines, almost cramming the edges of the page, semantic, phonetic and syntactical repetitions, and an attractive (and repulsive) description of all types of pastries, creating the effect of hyper-consumerism and simultaneously criticizing it.

students to share the emotions and bodily sensations without revealing the entire situation. The exercise was influenced by mindfulness meditation practice, utilizing this separation between emotions, bodily sensation, and thought to achieve a clearer awareness of the experience.

Following that, we asked the students to create a poem based on the vocabulary (taken out of the existing poem) we supplied them. The students shared their poems on a collaborative digital board. Afterward, we read the original poems and conducted a thorough and profound discussion. Reading comprehension was enhanced by the technique we adopted: the students had essentially wrote the poem (in multiple versions) before reading it. This lesson achieved an internal and interconnected perspective on social injustices, addressing environmental justice and social justice, which are essential components of the concept of sustainability. For this reason, we chose meditation, reflective writing, and personal sharing: an inner exploration of how these issues relate to each person individually.

To summarize stage I, presenting the holistic idea of environment-arts-sustainability, we met with an environmental artist. She presented the scientific basis for her work—the sixth extinction and the Anthropocene and shared her own art as well as myriad artwork from around the world. Human presence in nature, the detrimental impact of human beings, and the beauty of nature were all present in the artworks. Her presentation illustrated the principles of ecohumanism, such as observing the interconnections between science and art, relating gender equality in human affairs to equality among all species, and admiring nature and its representation in art.

Underlying the experience-observation-experience is creating a sequence that begins with sensory exposure to an artwork (for example, visual), its integration with artworks from another field (literary, for example), and—following this exposure—allowing participants to express themselves. Thus, we implement the principles of ecohumanism, including attunement, slowing down and presence, as well as the attentive dialogue.

Stage II: Conceptualization and Application Through Personal Interpretation

This stage dealt with understanding through personal interpretation of environmental phenomena and literary and artistic works. In this stage's first lesson, we asked students to go out to city streets and define what sustainability education is through observation and drawing. In the asynchronous lesson that followed, they had to independently view a virtual exhibition, connect it to a chapter from Zygmunt Bauman's seminal *Wasted Lives* (2003), and discuss the issues arising from it with their peers in an online forum. A similar online discussion took place in another asynchronous lesson where they had to visit an exhibition in a gallery or a museum. After the visit, they had to choose one exhibit, relate it to sustainability education, and participate in the forum. In the discussion with their peers, they compared the exhibits and the selected concepts. The forum allows the students to learn about themselves, about others, and gain new and refreshing perspectives on the subject. As mentioned before, the course's final assignment is an original personal creation or analysis of an existing work (from literature or art) linked to sustainability education and the concepts taught, demonstrating knowledge and integrating sustainability with art. Additionally, its mode of presentation expresses the principles taught in the course.

In general, in this stage we return to the environment in order to observe and comprehend through visual imagery a central concept. After discussing the concept and clarifying it, we can discuss it in other virtual spaces, integrating observation of artworks and the application of social-economic and environmental theories. The stages in the discussion are crucial: (1) observing artworks and formulating a personal response; (2) publishing the response; (3) viewing others' responses and engaging in a comprehensive and in-depth discussion. The final product is an integration of everything learned: observation, creation, and relation to abstract concepts.

The Theories and Their Application

The model's applied and theoretical contributions are intertwined. Firstly, the collaborativeness—characterizing both theoretical approaches in the model (ecohumanism and holism)—is practically implemented. Collaborative teaching allows students to learn better and we lecturers also function as role models. Secondly, according to the holism and ecohumanism each student is a complete and full world, and when placed in different learning spaces, there is an added value and further possibility of applying theoretical ideas.

We conduct each lesson, and explain every concept according to the holistic perspective. However, the topics as well as their representation in literary and visual arts are abstract and complex. Therefore, our role as instructors is to present all these dimensions both in their abstract form and in a nuanced and concrete manner, so that learners experience, feel, and understand the theme's entirety. For example, when discussing consumer culture and its environmental, social, and economic dangers we read a poem portraying excess as a major trope. Reading a poem involves an emotional, auditory, sensory, and intellectual experiences. A profound discussion emerges on the production, marketing, sale, and consumption of different products and the price that individuals and society as a whole pay as a result. All these are integral parts of sustainability.

Outdoor learning—a vital component in the course—is a holistic tool enabling profound and multifaceted exploration of sustainability. Sharing their experiences from a tour on a digital board, the learners managed to integrate the technological space with the physical and creative space. Their observation of the site-specific environment and elements of sustainability indoor and outdoor, sublimated into artistic representations. Going through this process, the students internalized the dimensions of urban sustainability of the campus's neighborhood.

Holistic observation, if applied, allows transitions between spaces—from the tangible to the creative, from the digital to the mental—and facilitates the understanding and conceptualization of the insights emerging from these transitions. Moreover, as educators in the twenty-first century, we cannot ignore the environmental crisis. Therefore, holism does not end with the personal learning of each student. Our goal is to motivate students to take action as educators, so they can learn by themselves but also be capable of translating their knowledge into action in the field where they work (kindergartens, schools, and informal education). An educator needs to find their personal way, through their perception, experience, approach, perspectives, skills, and training, in order to bring sustainability into practice.

For example, such a finding of personal expression is through the final assignment of the course, which requires the processing of concepts, ideas, pedagogical tools, and artworks learned in the course, along with the creation of a new element. This processing will allow them to concretely apply in the educational field the abstract principles they experimented with in the course. To summarize, the course implements polyphonic teaching as expressed in pedagogy, content, space, and technology (see Fig. 1: Polyphonic Wisdom Model), employing the principles of eco-humanistic perception and holistic pedagogy, such as dialogue, interdisciplinary approaches, and slowing down (Aloni et al., 2023).

Conclusion

My door is wide open
And the soft night is invited into the house –

These lines conclude Agi Mishol's poem "Between the Trees and the Non-trees", which we cited earlier. We interpret the title, as recalled, as referring to the holistic, interdisciplinary presence—both in the intermediate realm (between) and in the coexistence of nature and ecology (the trees) and the realm of poetry and literature (the non-trees); between the urban and non-urban, between the classroom and non-classroom, between the frontal and virtual teaching, synchronous and asynchronous learning. The poem's conclusion is primarily a declaration of openness and surrender that the speaker feels. Similarly, we felt the students' receptiveness and sincerity throughout the course. Indeed, the invitation (as appearing in the poem's last line) is for the continuation of the students' work, a continuation that arises from the openness of thought and heart. The invitation is primarily a hope and a wish that the students continue the process they have started in the course, engage in sustainability education through art, and pass on the holistic idea that sustainability is in everything. We also hope that the process is based on commitment and responsibility to individuals, nature, society and the entire environment. In addition, we, as instructors, look at the process we went through in the course sincerely and

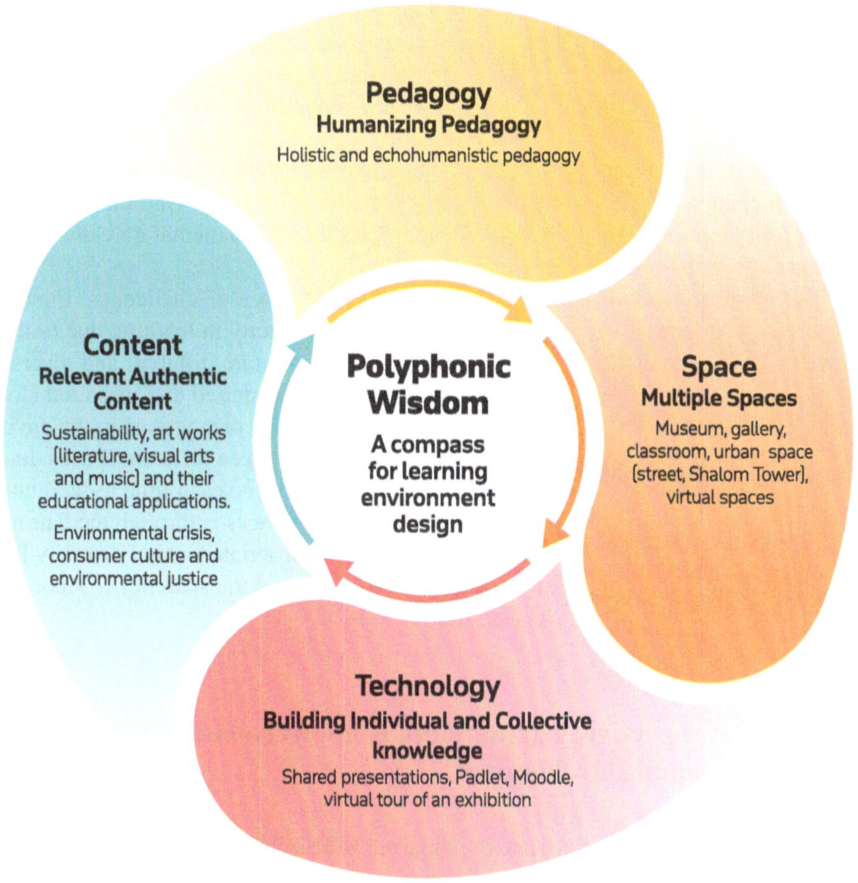

Fig. 1 Polyphonic wisdom model

gaze towards the future—how to improve, make accessible, and cope in the next course with the challenges detailed below.

Challenges and Coping Strategies

Since the dominant and accepted structure in teacher training is built on disciplines and specializations, holistic and interdisciplinary thinking poses a challenge for all of us. Consequently, holistic and interdisciplinary learning is difficult and challenging for students as well as lecturers. We are not accustomed to thinking in this way: we need a vision, a definition of clear principles, and predefined spaces. Therefore, once the principles are defined, the process continues with the students, and we continuously clarify these principles through the syllabus and subsequently throughout the educational process, in the various defined spaces, the interplay between them, and their ongoing dynamic existence.

Indeed, the flow and dynamism also create uncertainties, challenging both instructors and students. Dependence on weather conditions, urban spaces, and the functionality of the virtual space, increased the factor of uncertainty and demanded flexibility. Here too, collaborative work sometimes intensifies the difficulty of coping with changes, challenges, and making decisions on the go. One must be prepared for compromises and it is advisable to establish fundamental agreements in advance, fostering mutual trust and appreciation.

The hybridity and diversity in spaces create two types of challenges. Firstly, there can be a sense of fragmentation or a lack of continuity in learning due to the transition between spaces. Secondly, different spaces require different and diverse learning and teaching skills that sometimes need to be acquired and mastered (for example, digital skills, concentration skills when there are distractions in the environment, or mental flexibility for physical movement between different spaces during the lesson). The different spaces need to be reintroduced each time to facilitate learning and teaching. The way to deal with these challenges is through mediation. It is necessary to carefully select the spaces and the appropriate level of diversity for teaching partners and to mediate clearly with pedagogical transparency to students about the required skills before and after the lesson.

Personal Perspective: Partnership, Empowerment, and Professional Development

We choose to share our experience of preparing and teaching the course in the same manner that we taught contemplative lessons: sharing emotions, bodily sensations, and thoughts. The emotions that arise during the teaching process include excitement, joy, and empowerment—both from interacting with the students and the dialogue with the teaching partner. The sensations present in our bodies are those of openness, inner energy, and relaxed breathing. These feelings and sensations stem from a successful journey, collaboration through creation, and from new and surprising insights. All of these lead to feelings (both physical and mental) of personal and professional growth for each of us.

Empowerment also arises from the partnership between us. On one hand, this is a commitment that creates mutual dedication in all aspects of the project. It is a personal commitment based on a shared interest and a mutual promise not to abandon the partner and the project. On the other hand, at the same time, we also benefit from the shared responsibility between us for the initiative—planning, teaching, student care, and the overall responsibility for the course and its success.

We view the course as a work of art that both of us create together. The creation, collaborative work on it, the outcome, discussions about the outcome, and its reflections all lead us to much deeper contemplation than if we were each teaching separately. Involved in this are reflections that are not confined to individual considerations but extend to the collective brainstorming between the two of us, fostering broad learning for both of us. The interest naturally arises from the essence of each one's learning, knowledge, skills, and qualifications.

Mutual learning leads to a central theme in our model—we experience professional development both in "how" and in "what", both in content and in form. Consequently, collaborative teaching serves as a model for students who undergo holistic teaching that implements the principles of personal well-being, empathy, and dialogical engagement. Indeed, our collaborative creation serves as inspiration for the works presented by students at the end of the course.

References

Albareda-Tiana, S., Vidal-Raméntol, S., Pujol-Valls, M., & Fernández-Morilla, M. (2018). Holistic approaches to develop sustainability and research competencies in pre-service teacher training. *Sustainability, 10*(10), 3698.

Aloni, N., Alkaher, I., Assaf, A. B.-y., Paz, N., Gal, A., Gan, D., Lev, N., Margaliot, A., & Segal, A. (2023). Nature, humans and education: Ecohumanism as integrative guiding paradigm for values education and teacher training. In R. Rozzi et al. (Eds.), *Field environmental philosophy: Education for biocultural conservation*. Springer.

Brody, M. S., Dillon, J., & Wals, A. E. (2013). *International handbook of research on environmental education*. R. B. Stevenson (Ed.). Routledge.

Echegoyen-Sanz, Y., & Martín-Ezpeleta, A. (2021). A holistic approach to education for sustainability: Ecofeminism as a tool to enhance sustainability attitudes in pre-service teachers. *Journal of Teacher Education for Sustainability, 23*(1), 5–21.

Hare, J. (2006). Towards an understanding of holistic education in the middle years of education. *Journal of Research in International Education, 5*(3), 301–322.

Mahmoudi, S., Jafari, E., Nasrabadi, H. A., & Liaghatdar, M. J. (2012). Holistic education: An approach for 21 century. *International Education Studies, 5*(2), 178–186.

Miller, J. P., Nigh, K., Binder, M. J., Novak, B., & Crowell, S. (Eds.). (2019). *International handbook of holistic education*. Routledge.

Mishol, A. (2003). Bein-Ha-Etzim ve Ha-lo Etzim. In *Selection and new poems* (p. 171). HaKibbutz Hameuchad Publishing House and Bialik Institute.

Naaman, Y. (2018). Apocalypse I. In *If a hear falls* (pp. 26–27). Locus.

Shor, I., & Freire, P. (1987). What is the "dialogical method" of teaching? *Journal of Education, 169*(3), 11–31.

Sterling, S. (2010). Learning for resilience, or the resilient learner? Towards a necessary reconciliation in a paradigm of sustainable education. *Environmental Education Research, 16*(5–6), 511–528.

Part III
Dialogues in Action: Accepting Others' Perspectives

Four Mothers in the Face of Four Screens: A Multicultural Debate in the Digital Space

Efrat Harel

Introduction

In the past two decades, human migration has led to a noticeable increase in the number of children growing up in multicultural and multilingual communities, where they are exposed to more than one culture and language. In Israel, where Hebrew is the dominant language, many families speak other first languages, and according to the Central Bureau of Statistics (2013), there are more than 30 languages spoken as mother tongues in Israel. As a result, 14% of kindergarten children in Israel are immigrants, and in some cities, this number reaches 40% of kindergarten children (as of 2015). Tennbaum et al. (2020) surveyed many of the languages spoken in Israel, including English, Arabic, Russian, French, Yiddish, Spanish, Amharic, Romanian, Hungarian, German, in a study addressing the Ministry of Education's request to examine the language policy of multilingualism in the country.

Therefore, it is important that the education system and teacher training programs provide theoretical and practical information regarding multicultural understanding and implementing effective responses in the field, adapting study programs to the twenty-first century (Zohar & Bushrian, 2020). Consequently, the need to train early childhood educators is emphasized, as education for multicultural understanding in the children's preschool years has the potential to develop a tolerant, humanistic, and collaborative society (Zadunaisky-Ehrlich et al., 2016). The model presented in this chapter is based on a multicultural perspective aiming to address the global phenomenon of migration, which challenges education systems worldwide. This chapter focuses on early childhood in the context of bilingualism in Israel, translating theoretical perspectives into pedagogical-practical application. In

E. Harel (✉)
Kibbutzim College of Education, Technology and Arts, Tel-Aviv, Israel
e-mail: efrat.harel@smkb.ac.il

Y. Yondler et al. (eds.), *Cultivating Future-Oriented Learners*, Understanding Teaching-Learning Practice, https://doi.org/10.1007/978-3-031-63253-2_7

theoretical terms, the model presents four parental approaches regarding exposure to English as an additional language. In practical terms, students are required to arbitrarily support one of the approaches, think about relevant arguments, and ultimately decide in favor of the winning approach from their perspective. Therefore, the learning process in the model incorporates two key elements: mutual interaction among participants and maintaining individual identity, reflecting the essence of the polyphonic wisdom that integrates both aspects.

The added values of the model also express the polyphonic wisdom experienced by the students, that is synergy between space, technology, content, and pedagogy, within the humanistic context in the hybrid space. In this model, students undergo a lesson in which they study collaboratively, create, and react, engaging in learning both in physical and digital spaces, and acquiring technological tools. In such a lesson, the instructor serves as a facilitator rather than a conduit for knowledge transfer. Furthermore, students are required to exercise critical thinking, actively participate in group learning, and also express their unique voices. Throughout the process, each student as an individual is exposed to diverse perspectives and learns to give space to different viewpoints.

A Multicultural Perspective in Early Childhood

In the global era of the twenty-first century, we witness the accelerating phenomenon of migration worldwide. In Israel, the coexistence of many languages and cultures has been prevalent since its establishment, and, as a result, a diverse society with varied identities, opinions, and traditions has emerged. Education plays a central and crucial role in shaping and building a society globally, making the integration of immigrant children into the education system relevant.

Within the framework of preschools, children acquire beliefs, ideas, and learn to navigate in society. This learning forms the basis for their future paths. Given the diverse and multicultural nature of Israeli society, it is essential for educators to create an educational framework that is safe and open, allowing exposure to various cultural symbols. Such a framework will expose children to both their similarities and the uniqueness of each individual (Zadonisky-Ehrlich et al., 2016).

Multicultural perspective is one option for managing society, though certainly not the only one. Sever (2016) outlines five ways in which societies with cultural diversity can operate. Three represent patterns where cultures in society are not equal and, therefore, operate according to the assimilation model. In contrast, the other two ways refer to a multicultural society where cultural diversity is seen as a potential for mutual learning and development, thus reflecting a model that promotes equality and mutual respect.

The two patterns that promote diversity in society are called the "mosaic" strategy (Federative Pluralism) and the "chulent" strategy (Interactive Multiculturalism). In the "mosaic" approach, there is an acknowledgment that in every society, there is a mosaic of equal cultural groups, and there is no hierarchy among them. Therefore, each cultural group coexists alongside others, preserving its uniqueness without blending with others. In the second approach, cultural diversity is seen as a potential for growth, and therefore, the path to shared living occurs through interweaving. Hence, Sever refers to it as the "chulent" strategy, where each group maintains its identity and uniqueness but also engages in interaction and mutual influence. The model presented in this chapter is inspired by the "chulent" model. As detailed later, students in the course participate in discussions where various opinions and perspectives are heard, allowing each one a place for expression and mutual consideration, as befitting a multicultural model and current educational programs in Israel (Zohar & Bushrian, 2020).

As mentioned, the preschool serves as the primary platform for young children to experience the world and the social reality around them. During the early years, language development takes place, and young children need to acquire insights about the general discourse in the society and culture they live in. "The kindergarten teacher plays a central role in the development of children's language abilities and in promoting literacy discourse" (Zur et al., 2012, p. 281). Therefore, it is crucial, even at an early age, to expose children to a language-rich environment, social and cognitive experiences, and mediate the world in the best possible way for the children.

Since children spend many hours in the preschool, a lot is placed on the shoulders of the kindergarten teacher. In addition to her role as the manager of the preschool, she also needs to exhibit high empathy and acceptance skills and address the children and their parents' needs (Frish, 2012). In the literacy and mental aspects, Ziv et al. (2013) demonstrate how dialogue and mediation through books, conducted by the preschool teacher, foster social understanding among children regarding desires and thoughts of others. These skills are coined in the literature as 'Theory of Mind,' and their development is crucial for children's adaptation in society, including conflict management, problem-solving, and consideration of others' wishes. These abilities develop during the early years, particularly around ages 3–5 (Carpendale & Lewis, 2004; Symons, 2004; Ziv et al., 2008, as mentioned by Ziv et al., 2013).

It is essential to acknowledge that the early years serve as the foundation for our future as a society, and the more we demonstrate sensitivity to children's needs and integrate multicultural activities into their routines, the greater the potential for them to become responsible and empathetic adults. Supporting a multicultural perspective that encourages social justice and equality is emphasized in Banks' article (2014). According to him, the education system can and should serve as an example for the entire population by incorporating principles of equality and democracy. When a society promotes multicultural values, the likelihood of a sense of belonging and social commitment between individuals increases. This also applies to educational institutions: providing an inclusive and fair space for minority groups, such as children from homes where Hebrew is not spoken, enables them to identify with the local culture, eventually acquiring the second language, Hebrew, and integrating socially.

Indeed, multicultural education in early childhood education has increased over the past two decades. Vagner (2003) discusses the integration of bilingual children into the educational system during their early years. Recognizing bilingualism as an asset rather than a burden, Wagner suggests various activities that can be incorporated into the kindergarten setting. For instance, in the literacy aspect, one can establish a library with books in different languages, create rhymes for words in various languages, or develop bulletin boards with notices written in all the languages present in the preschool. Zilberberg (2003) described a long-term process she implemented in her kindergarten. Based on the understanding that "trust is acquired over time through repeated action and continuous involvement" (p. 77), she conducted home visits in collaboration with parents to create exhibitions, joint activities, and parties. According to her, these ongoing actions fostered openness and collaboration from both children and their parents, built trust, and created authentic social integrations.

In 2016, the Ministry of Education published a booklet titled 'Common Language in Kindergarten: Education for Culturally and Linguistically Diverse Children' (Zadunaisky-Ehrlich et al., 2016) to provide tools for the inclusive integration of new immigrants or children from non-Hebrew-speaking homes. Based on research indicating numerous advantages of bilingualism, such as cognitive benefits, broadened thinking, preservation of the heritage language and culture, etc., the booklet offers educational activity ideas to utilize the multilingual situation and positively enrich the multicultural kindergarten. The recommendations in the booklet stem from the understanding that the kindergarten is an ideal place to promote multiculturalism, as children experience equitable and respectful education on a daily basis, holding the potential to transfer multicultural behavior to other channels in society. An example of demonstrating tolerance towards a child who does not speak Hebrew at home is giving them the opportunity to express themselves in their mother tongue without pressure to speak only Hebrew. Furthermore, educators can encourage the child to teach them a few words from her home language, teach her peers in the kindergarten, and even invite the child's parent to demonstrate aspects of their culture. "Exposure to different languages increases the metalinguistic awareness of all the children in the kindergarten" (p. 29). In other words, such an approach generates curiosity among kindergarten children, fostering potential for closeness and friendships, not only among the children in the kindergarten but also among their parents.

The multicultural approach, both in general and specifically in the kindergarten setting, incorporates added values in a humanistic context. A kindergarten that fosters multicultural education not only acknowledges but actively promotes a humanistic perspective. This is because the kindergarten, which provides education for multiculturalism, allows space for diverse starting points, thereby accommodating a variety of perspectives from each child. It exposes children to different viewpoints and customs, engaging them collaboratively in a collective manner.

The value of humanism is crucial in educational institutions, where children are exposed to discourse practices, interact with peers and teachers, and engage in dialogue with their fellow learners (Ben-Yosef, 2009). According to Aloni (2015), the concept of 'humanistic education' encompasses a commitment to intellectual freedom, moral autonomy, and democracy. Educators who adhere to this type of education aim to liberate learners from societal stereotypes and social alienation, empowering them to realize their personal human potential for meaningful, autonomous, and fulfilling lives. As part of humanistic education, Aloni also elaborates on the concept of empathy, dividing it into two dimensions: emotional and cognitive. In the emotional dimension, empathy involves the ability to emotionally experience the feelings of others. In the cognitive dimension, it relates to our capacity as humans to understand the story, logic, and narrative of the other person. It not only concerns emotional experience but also encompasses a rational understanding of the existence of the other. Thus, the ability to take a broad perspective requires cognitive abilities, intellectual openness, and flexibility, in addition to emotional capabilities. In her book 'With whom did you play today in kindergarten', Becker (2009) explains the importance of developing empathy in early childhood. By the age of two, children already have the tools to influence and be influenced by others, to develop social understanding, and to form mutual relationships with their peer group. This ability has innate characteristics and is also influenced by the environment. Throughout childhood, children's relationships are also characterized by conflict management within the educational framework, as they express their positions and engage in understanding the perspectives of others. In fact, educators at all levels must be capable of empathy, as it is a moral foundation that nurtures effective communication (Winberger & Bakshi-Brosh, 2013; Jaber et al., 2018). These central elements, characterizing the development of young children, are found at the core of Sever's "chulent" model (2016) as an option for societal management: on the one hand, there is interaction among participants, empathy for the needs of others, and sensitivity to their desires. On the other hand, and in parallel, there is a preservation of individual identity and the cultivation of personal voice.

Acknowledging the significant impact of educators on children's development, the topic of multiculturalism has been directly integrated into the curriculum of early childhood education institutions over the past decade. At Seminar Hakibbutzim College, the course "Multiculturalism in Early Childhood" has been taught since 2012. With an aspiration to educate for optimal development and adaptation of children from diverse cultural backgrounds, the course emphasizes the social, cultural, and emotional aspects that educators need to address. Ultimately, a variety of activities and practical tools are developed to promote children's adaptation in educational settings.

As part of acquiring academic knowledge in the course, the benefits of bilingualism are discussed. These children gain linguistic and cultural richness, and demonstrate cognitive advantages even in infancy (Bialystok et al., 2009; Kovacs & Mehler, 2009). Therefore, the issue arises of exposing monolingual children to an additional language so that they too can 'taste' the experience of bilingualism. The model presented in this chapter is based on this issue and presents four options through which even a monolingual child can benefit from an additional language in their environment.

After several years of teaching the course, I sought ways to enhance the students' experience, aiming to create a different, collaborative, and stimulating learning experience that would effectively develop twenty-first-century skills and encourage students' thoughts both as a group and as individuals. Thus, the model described in this chapter was "born", based on the two fundamental principles of the "chulent" model (Sever, 2016): one emphasizing interaction among participants, active listening, mutual feedback, empathy for others, and identification with them. The second provides a framework for maintaining personal identity within diversity and nurturing the individual's unique voice. In order to implement the model effectively and address the quality of each learner, collaborative technology is used, both in the physical space of the Future Learning Space (FLS) and in the virtual space (Zoom). The three stages of the model and the emphasis at each stage are described in Fig. 1.

1

Building collaborative knowledge via division into "Four Mothers"

Building collaborative knowledge while fostering sensitivity and empathy towards others' opinions. Using a shared Google doc, students work in teams of 4 "homes", each "home" has a "mother" with an opinion on the linguistic matter. The opinion is predetermined by the facilitator (Efrat), and each group's task is to develop relevant arguments in favor of the opinion.

2

Mutual interaction through debate in the assembly

In the assembly, each of the groups presents their arguments to the other "parents." This stage is characterized by raising the level of engagement of the participants, who listen and mutually influence the shaping of their thoughts.

3

Preserving identity through self-reflection and connecting to one's inner truth

Conceptualization of the entire experience. Following the tumultuous discussions representing four opinions, each student is asked to vote for the opinion that convinced them, revealing their genuine view, and specify if their original opinion changed after the activity and why. The personal vote is conducted using a Google form, a tool that allows each student to participate individually.

Fig. 1 Description of the model: four mothers in the face of four screens: a multicultural debate in the digital space

Background

During the course "Multiculturalism in Early Childhood," students learn about the advantages of bilingualism in linguistic, cognitive, cultural, and social aspects. The pre-service teachers realize it is possible that parents of Hebrew-speaking children may aspire to expose their children to an additional language. The additional language under discussion is English, due to its status as a universal language worldwide and its prestige in Israel. Therefore, in the context and norms in Israel, it is logical for monolinguals' parents to seek how to expose their children to English as a second language from a young age.

Likewise, the concept of the "Four Mothers" has a historical connotation. While not all the population is Jewish, the term is mostly recognized by the students. In the biblical history of the Jewish people, there are three fathers: Abraham, Isaac, and Jacob, and four mothers: Sarah, Rebecca, Rachel, and Leah, each with their own unique story and personal nuances. Since the majority of the course participants are female students, and with the aim of incorporating a discussion of four different opinions, it was decided to use the four mothers, based on their original names, as representatives of four diverse opinions. Additionally, choosing names of familiar "mothers" adds a humorous aspect to the activity, especially when each "mother" is associated with an image of a recognizable figure (such as poets and singers).

The Framework Story of the Model

The activity includes about 20 female students, divided into four groups. Each group consists of 4–5 students, representing mothers of children who are a year and a half/2 years old. They are all Hebrew speakers, and it's important to them that their child won't have difficulty with English as they had experienced. They have four different options to expose the child to English, and they want to make an informed decision on the matter.

To this end, each group of mothers is asked to think about arguments in favor of the opinion they hold, based on both online sources and life experience.

The activity reflects an authentic issue relevant to many parents in Israel and around the world. Therefore, the issue at hand has the potential of leading to a genuine discussion connected to the complex reality.

The Stages of the Model and Its Implementation in Digital Spaces

The model presented consists of three stages, with a synergy between the domains: humanistic, collaborative, and the pedagogical-technological space, utilizing digital tools. In this, the model reflects a polyphonic spirit, as on the one hand, there is expression for the individual development of each learner, with attention to their voice and the application of humanistic values, and on the other hand, building knowledge occurs within social interactions, allowing space for a variety of voices. In the following lines, each stage will be presented with its various aspects, accompanied by images for illustration. Additionally, inspired by the "chulent" model, which emphasizes how each group maintains its uniqueness within the mutual interaction, we can see where the voice of the individual is heard.

Stage 1: Building Collaborative Knowledge Via Division into "Four Mothers"

The polyphonic wisdom is expressed right in the first stage, as there is interaction between the components of the polyphonic wisdom: practical content, multiple spaces (physical and digital), technology usage, and humanizing pedagogy. This stage deals with building collaborative knowledge while promoting sensitivity and empathy towards the opinions of others. For this stage, group work is conducted using a collaborative digital document, creating four different "houses" in the classroom. The areas of the "houses" are delineated with the help of mobile chairs that assist in constructing individual work circles for each group. Each group is tasked with formulating arguments in favor of their "opinion," providing supporting evidence, and articulating the arguments in the appropriate section of a pre-prepared collaborative document. This is done so that in the next stage, they can present their arguments to the rest of the class referring to the literature. At this stage, we can see the first element of the "Chulent" model (Sever, 2016), namely interaction, characterized by humanistic knowledge construction and empathy for the opinions of others (Aloni, 2015; Ben-Yosef, 2009; Ziv et al., 2013). The activity was carried out in the FLS, and an example of the physical space can be seen in Figs. 2 and 3:

The activity was designed for the FLS classroom at the college, equipped with screens, spacious mobile chairs, and digital tools such as tablets. In 2020, COVID-19 pandemic broke out, and teaching was shifted to remote learning, through digital means. Therefore, the model presented in this chapter was delivered via Zoom. It is important to note that both methods enabled collaborative knowledge construction and included multiple spaces, whether physically and digitally in the FLS, or online via Zoom. At this stage, the advantage tends to be in favor of the Zoom platform due to the division into breakout rooms, where group members work quietly and with absolute concentration in their private space.

Crucially, the digital space where arguments are consolidated, namely the shared Google document, is prepared in advance by the facilitating lecturer. The original document contains the four approaches to the issue, and the allocation of each approach by each group is random, according to the principle of 'first come, first served'. In other words, students may find themselves defending a view with which they do not necessarily identify.

Fig. 2 Building collaborative knowledge in the FLS

Fig. 3 Building collaborative knowledge in the FLS

In this context, the four options for exposing monolingual children to English as an additional language are:

(a) Enrolling the child in a kindergarten with English classes once or twice a week.
(b) Registering the child in a bilingual kindergarten that operates in two languages on a daily basis.
(c) Hiring an English-speaking babysitter in the afternoons, 3–4 times a week.
(d) Taking the task into the hands of the parents, who, despite not being native speakers of English, are willing to dedicate time to this task, such as purchasing English children's books and conducting conversations in English.

In fact, at this stage, the individual needs to wear a 'cloak' that is not necessarily 'tailored' to his exact measurements, as the parental choice she is defending may not necessarily be her real choice. For this reason, the facilitator of the activity might hear sentences such as:

but I don't even think that!

Alternatively:

Lucky me, I'm in a group that represents the opinion I agree with.

After a few minutes, a fascinating process unfolds where even those who didn't feel comfortable initially step into the role assigned to them and defend it. So far, the voice of the individual is heard, but not necessarily in a fair manner towards them, thus reflecting the peak value of humanism: a situation where a student is asked to defend an opinion they don't share and even oppose. This can foster the ability to put oneself in the other's shoes and empathize with them. It's important to note that the shared Google document is exposed to all, and even during the argument development stage, everyone can read each other's arguments and adjust accordingly.

Stage 2: Mutual Interaction through Debate in the Assembly

The polyphonic wisdom is also expressed in the second stage, where the use of pedagogy reinforces the experience of humanistic values. At this stage, the debate takes place in the plenary session, leading to increased engagement of the students. In the plenary, each of the groups presents their arguments to the rest of the "parents." Since the "houses" of the four mothers are located in different areas of the classroom, it's possible and desirable to approach their "homes" and screens to hear the arguments. One can also remain settled near each individual's group and observe the screens present in each area. Each "home" takes its turn to speak, but an open space is given to counter arguments and raise considerations against at every stage of the debate. In this way, the element of interaction comes into play, as this stage is characterized by an increased level of engagement of the participants, who listen and mutually influence each other's thoughts. In fact, the students listen to the arguments of the other three groups while presenting their arguments and respond to the arguments raised by the other teams during the debate. This way, the individual not only listens to their own true voice but also to other opinions and begins to exercise judgment and perhaps even flex their thinking, as arguments emerge that were not considered before the debate. Documentation from the debate stage, where arguments are presented, mutual listening takes place, and supportive or opposing responses are given, can be found in Appendix. This is relevant to both spaces: the physical FLS and Zoom.

At this stage, there appears to be an advantage to the physical space over Zoom, as in Zoom, one must choose whether to share the screen so that everyone can view the arguments presented by the representative or to remain in "gallery" mode so that the discussion will be as authentic as possible. In contrast, when everyone is in the same physical space, the document is projected onto two large screens, creating a more authentic dialogue.

In summary, the first two stages reflect learning processes of collaborative knowledge construction, increased empathy, and humanism, through mutual interaction and productive work within a dialogic discourse. In the next stage, individual judgment will be required, and therefore, listening to all arguments is essential.

Stage 3: Preserving Identity Through Self-Reflection and Connecting to One's Inner Truth

The third stage focuses on the conceptualization of the entire experience. After the tumultuous discussions representing four opinions, each student is asked to vote for the opinion that convinced them, regardless of the opinion presented by their group. Students were also asked if their original opinion had changed following the activity and why. The personal vote is conducted through the use of a Google form, a tool that allows each individual to participate independently. In the physical aspect, they return to individual seating, answer the questionnaire, and then collectively observe the results on the screen. By requesting each student to vote for the opinion that convinced them, personal judgment is exercised, not just collective. This has the potential to increase the awareness of each student and generate insights such as: *"I realize there are other opinions, probably different from mine, and I am asked to respect those as well"*. This stage effectively embodies the second element of the "chulent" model (Sever, 2016), which is maintaining identity within diversity. This principle resonates with the polyphonic wisdom by using technology and multiple spaces to enhance the experience of humanistic values through partnership, dialogue, and mutual respect for diverse voices. At this stage, one can see the deep thinking of each student with themselves, the need for conceptualization, and voting for an opinion that aligns with the individual's personal identity. By ensuring that the individual maintains their identity within the collective, they uphold another humanistic value, namely loyalty to the individual voice.

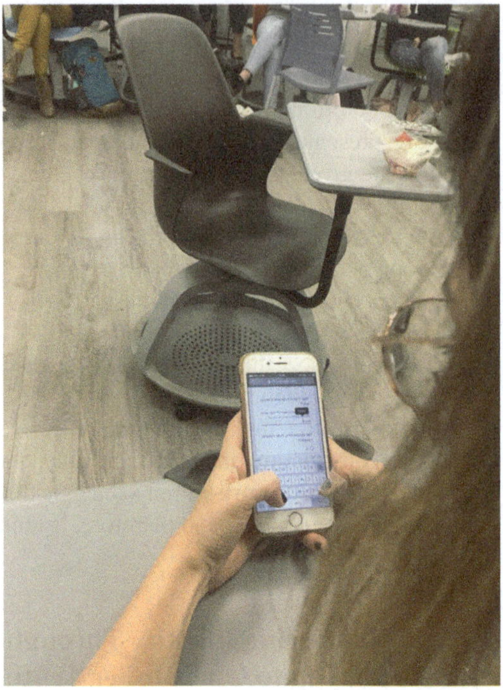

Fig. 4 Maintaining identity within diversity: a student responds to a personal questionnaire

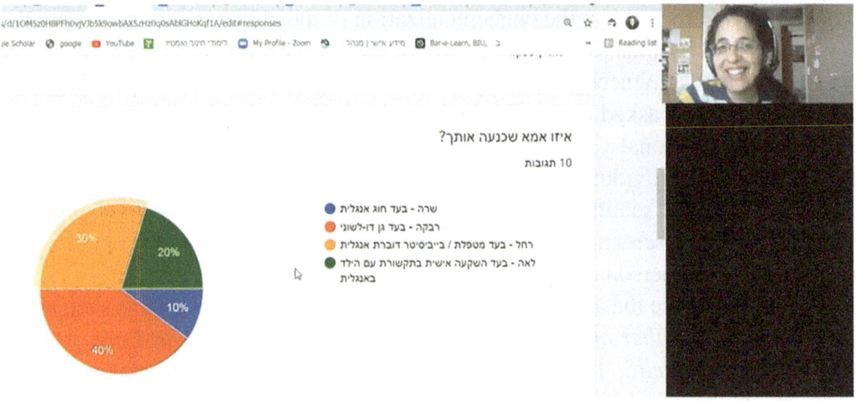

Fig. 5 Viewing the results following the participants' individual responses

At this stage, too, the technological tools served the objectives of the activity and intensified the humanistic-collaborative elements. In Fig. 4, you can see a student in the FLS, focused on responding to the questionnaire individually:

And finally, Fig. 5 illustrates a moment from the shared viewing of the results through screen sharing on Zoom (the question at hand was *'which 'mom' has convinced you'?*; blue (10%) signals an English class in the preschool; red (40%)—a bilingual preschool; yellow (30%)—an English-speaking babysitter; green (20%)—parents willing to dedicate time to this task):

At this stage, there is room for each participant's individual voice. There is excitement and curiosity regarding the prevailing, namely 'winning' approach, and an atmosphere of engagement among the participants, who applaud as the results are revealed. Examining the distribution of responses and accompanying verbal explanations—both in the physical space and on Zoom—fosters a dialogue that is vibrant, evolving, and nurturing, allowing different ideas to emerge and be legitimized.

As mentioned, in the third stage, the authentic voice of the individual is presented, following the first two stages where the individual is part of a group and may find themselves defending an opinion that is not their own. Here, they have the opportunity to maintain their uniqueness and consider their own personal judgment. This is the stage where participants are in the assembly, but each one individually responds to a Google-form questionnaire and answers four questions (2 close-ended, 2 open-ended), which are:

Which mother convinced you?
Explain why specifically this mother convinced you.
Has your original opinion changed as a result of the discussion?
If so, explain why.

Therefore, at this stage, the 'cloak' is removed, and the individual needs to be faithful to what persuaded them, regardless of the group they represented. Everyone sits in a circle/on Zoom, and after the voting is completed, they go over the results, with anyone who wants sharing where they stand in the process (for example, whether they agreed with the affiliated opinion).

Below are sample answers to the last two questions, whether the original opinion has changed and why:

No—*"I thought so from the beginning."*
No—*"Because I believe in her ideology. I think that a bilingual kindergarten is more effective than other options. At a very young age, even an English-speaking caregiver who is a native speaker is a good choice. Therefore, I am also in favor of Rachel."*
Yes—*"I heard the arguments of the bilingual kindergarten group, and I wasn't familiar with this idea. They presented an option that I think is better. Even the questions they asked me about my group aroused stronger negative thoughts in me than the positive ones I had."*

These examples illustrate the openness of mind and flexibility of thought that were significant throughout the entire process, reflecting the synergy between the humanistic-collaborative characteristics and identity preservation intertwined together in the model. The fact that the individual consistently wears a metaphorical 'cloak' and then learns to consider things with deliberation rather than just intuition, reflects the complexity and depth inherent in the model, demonstrating its connection to the theoretical framework and its contribution to the conceptual framework of the book and the field of education. Undoubtedly, educators will encounter diverse opinions and varied parental choices. I believe that an experience like this may lead to openness and acceptance of diverse viewpoints, as well as recognition of the beauty of human diversity and its ways of action. This highlights the contribution of the "chulent" model, both theoretically and practically, humanistic and collaborative, emphasizing the uniqueness of the individual in various stages of the experience.

In summary, each stage individually and all stages together in the model express a polyphonic wisdom that addresses two educational approaches: the humanistic educational approach and the socio-constructivist approach. These serve as two pillars shaping the educational path of the educator, who aims to create synergy between the four components of the polyphonic paradigm: multiple spaces, technology for collaborative and individual knowledge construction, authentic content, and humanizing pedagogy. In other words, the use of different spaces (physical and digital) and technological choices are intended to promote the learning of relevant content about parental choices based on a humanizing pedagogical approach. This approach encourages personal and social responsibility, understanding of others and acceptance of their viewpoints, openness, empathy towards people with different approaches, and self-directed learning guided consistently and systematically to achieve the goals set by the learners for themselves. This can be seen in Fig. 6.

Theoretical and Practical Contribution of the Model: Addressing Challenges and Added Values

As mentioned, the broader context of the activity presented in the model is parental decisions that educators are likely to be exposed to, and the need to accept and respect diverse parental viewpoints. Early childhood education for multiculturalism aims to develop a tolerant, humanistic, and collaborative society from its foundation, as kindergarten serves as a primary and significant framework for children (Zadunaisky-Ehrlich et al., 2016). Since the kindergarten teacher is at the forefront of educational action, it is important that her training process includes experiences of dilemmas, acceptance, and collaboration. Therefore, in this subsection, I would like to connect the model presented, its theoretical framework, and its contribution to the conceptual framework of the book and the field of education and teacher training practically. To this end, I will provide several tips that demonstrate how to address various challenges while connecting the components of the polyphonic wisdom: content, space, pedagogy, and technology utilization for this purpose. Reflecting on the key elements of the model, I will offer recommendations that encourage interaction, preservation of identity, and ultimately shared principles for the entire model.

Two tips encouraging mutual interaction:

Tip number 1: Initiate authentic activity that contributes to learners' practice

Tip number 2: Divide participants into groups arbitrarily in order to raise their empathy threshold towards others

The humanistic education (Aloni, 2015) aims for individuals to adopt the perspective of others, both cognitively in terms of open-mindedness and cognitive

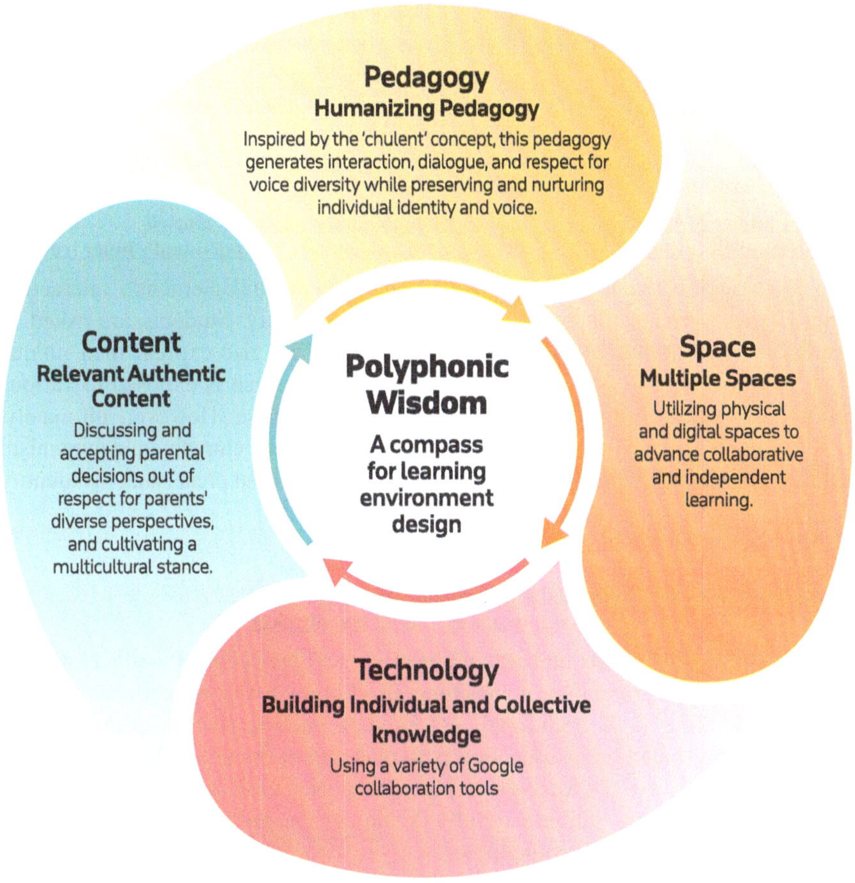

Fig. 6 The Polyphonic wisdom model

flexibility, and emotionally as well. In the spirit of humanistic education and inspired by the "chulent" model, the model "Four Mothers in the Face of Four Screens" combines collaborative learning and knowledge construction of pre-service teachers before they become educators. It addresses the pedagogical challenge of the need for experiential and authentic activities, with collaborative and humanistic values. In the presented activity, students learn through action and shared purpose, discuss a central issue inviting different perspectives in the context of the course content, namely bilingualism in early childhood. The bonding of each group is created around the "mother's" name, which carries a socially and culturally known meaning. In this way, it is reasonable to assume that students will remember the experience and content in the long term, which in turn may influence their choices as educators in the future.

The ability of the students to see the story, logic, and narrative of the four mothers leads to an emotional experience close to their practice, as well as to the existential rationality of something else. The ability to take perspective, not only in the emotional sense of empathy but also in a broader sense—cognitive, mental flexibility—expands the concept of empathy, as in its broader sense, empathy is a cognitive matter that requires mental flexibility and open-mindedness (Aloni, 2015; Jaber et al., 2018).

Two tips encouraging preservation of identity:

Tip number 3: Nurture the individual's empathy muscle towards himself
Tip number 4: Encourage connection and attentiveness to the individual's inner truth

The learning process in the model integrates two central elements: interaction among participants while maintaining individual identity. Students are asked to exercise critical thinking, engage in group learning, but also express their unique voice. Throughout the process, the student as an individual is exposed to various perspectives and learns to accommodate each perspective. However, ultimately, after mutual listening, the individual is required to cultivate empathy and humanism and to remain loyal to his truth by expressing his opinion and preserving his identity within the diversity.

Two tips arising from the entire model:

Tip number 5: Integrate collaborative digital tools in teaching
Tip number 6: Integrate multiple spaces: digital and physical

Educators in various fields set content objectives and pedagogical goals relevant to the context and age group they are teaching. In addition, today, educational tools are diverse, including both traditional and modern means, such as digital tools. Therefore, one challenge in education is to make appropriate and balanced use of digital tools that serve the lesson's purpose. We mustn't use digital tools as an end by itself, but rather, we should carefully define our teaching objectives and utilize those digital tools for the learning process.

The model presented in this chapter employs several digital and technological tools to achieve the activity's goals. These tools were relevant in both the FLS and the Zoom platform. The digital space included the use of Google Docs, where each group discussed and constructed their arguments collaboratively for shared knowledge building. To hear the individual's voice, a Google Form questionnaire was utilized. Technologies like computer screens, tablets, and personal mobile devices also facilitated the exploration of desired content by students. In the end, the participants found themselves involved in making parental decisions regarding exposing their children to English as a foreign language and were capable of accommodating diverse perspectives. This was achieved through a synergy of pedagogy starting with collaborative group work, continuing with discussions in the plenary, and ending with the expression of unique and personal opinions. Besides technology and pedagogy, both physical (mobile chairs, creating "homes," and returning to the plenary) and digital (using Google Docs and implementing the entire model on the Zoom platform) spaces served together to explore the desired content by students. Thus, authentic and meaningful learning was created, addressing pedagogical goals and the defined purpose in the content area being studied.

Tip number 7: Initiate a dialogue that combines interaction and preservation of identity in order to create the synergy between humanism and collaboration

The model presented in this chapter reflects the educator's perception as a facilitator who fosters a connection between two central elements: mutual interaction and identity preservation, as key aspects in bridging humanism and collaboration. By incorporating learners into diverse spaces, both digital and physical (multiple spaces), and using collaborative tools (technology), learners are invited to determine how they will work as a group and how they will express their personal voices (humanizing pedagogy). This dialogue, combining these elements, can take place in any topic relevant to learners' practice field (current content), making it authentic to learning and enhancing motivation. The educator's ability to create this synergy between the components of the polyphonic wisdom promotes both the humanistic educational approach and the socio-constructivist one.

Personal Perspective

The model addresses the challenge from which I initially started, namely the desire to create a different, collaborative, and stimulating learning experience that showcases twenty-first-century skills and provides a platform for both the collective and the individual. By combining various components, my experience as an instructor has been that we managed to create an innovative pedagogy with an impact on the professional and personal future of education students. This experience has significant added value for me. My role as an instructor is not only to impart knowledge but to function as a facilitator. Students learn through independent inquiry and collaborative thinking, and while I may "conduct the orchestra," they create the music themselves. This experience encouraged me to step out of my comfort zone and engage with digital tools that I was unfamiliar with, learn new things, and conduct lessons differently. Moreover, it involved applying the renewed thinking about teaching methods in other courses and contexts in teaching and research. I sensed that the students felt active as a group and as individuals, and engaged in critical thinking and creativity. This gave me a sense of empowerment as an instructor on both developmental and professional levels, accompanied by significant satisfaction. I hope that other educators will find inspiration in the model presented and seek to implement it in relevant contexts.

Appendix

In the physical space, each group of 'mothers' sits next to their 'home', and a representative from the group presents the arguments that have been formulated in favor of one of the approaches. For example, mom Rachel says: *"I want to hire a caregiver who speaks English as a mother tongue. I really think it's good because of the personal and tailored relationship the child receives. A caregiver is preferable to someone who doesn't speak the language and may create misunderstanding for the child.*" The rest of the 'mothers' listen to the arguments and can provide counterarguments at any given moment.

In the Zoom platform, all the groups meet in the plenary, and each group in turn chooses a representative to summarize the arguments raised in favor of the approach. In this space, too, the other 'mothers' listen and can raise counterarguments. For example, after mom Rachel presented her proposal to bring in an English-speaking caregiver in the afternoons, there were reactions from several mothers in the audience. Below is an example of a dialogue that arose between a 'mother' opposing the proposal and its supporters:

'Mom' A, who supports the idea of introducing the child to a bilingual nursery, says: *"At 8 pm., the kids are already asleep. At 4 pm., they finish their day in the preschool, so even during this short time, they will spend time with a caregiver? This way, they're with a caregiver all day long!"*

'Mom' B, representing Rachel, who proposes to hire an English-speaking caregiver, responds: *"But a babysitter is more personal, and it also depends on the age."*

'Mom' C, coming to her friend's aid, continues and says: "*The personal connection with the babysitter is not like in a preschool or club, where there are other children to teach the language. Here, it's a one-on-one relationship.*"

References

Aloni, N. (2015). Humanistic education. In M. A. Peters (Ed.), *Encyclopedia of educational philosophy and theory*. https://doi.org/10.1007/978-981-287-532-7_332-1

Banks, J. A. (2014). Diversity, group identity, and citizenship education in a global age. *Journal of Education, 194*(3), 1–12.

Becker, A. (2009). *With whom did you play in kindergarten? The social world of young children*. The MOFET Institute. (in Hebrew).

Ben-Yosef, O. (2009). *Circles of connection: Cultivating discourse culture in a humanistic educational institution*. The MOFET Institute. (in Hebrew).

Bialystok, E., Craik, F. I. M., Green, D. W., & Gollan, T. H. (2009). Bilingual minds. *Psychological Science in the Public Interest, 10*(3), 89–129. https://doi.org/10.1177/1529100610387084

Frish, Y. (2012). *The kindergarten teacher—As the kindergarten manager and educational leader—Management chapters*. The Religious Academic College for Education. (in Hebrew).

Jaber, L. Z., Southerland, S., & Dake, F. (2018). Cultivating epistemic empathy in preservice teacher education. *Teaching and Teacher Education, 72*, 13–23.

Kovacs, A. M., & Mehler, J. (2009). Cognitive gains in 7-month-old bilingual infants. *Proceedings of the National Academy of Sciences, 106*(16), 6556–6560.

Sever, R. (2016). Preparing for a future of diversity-A conceptual framework for planning and evaluating multicultural educational colleges. *Malta Review of Educational Research (MRER), 10*(1 Special Issue), 23–49.

Tannenbaum, M., Michalovich, A., & Shohamy, E. (2020). Toward a new multilingual educational policy in Israel: Attitudes and perceptions of teachers and students. *The Modern Language Journal, 104*(3), 581–600.

The Central Bureau of Statistics. (2013). *A collection of data from the 2011 social survey on Hebrew proficiency and language usage.*
Vagner, E. (2003). Bilingualism and multiculturalism—The implications of absorbing new immigrants in the preschool. In N. Kadman (Ed.), *Both in the kindergarten: A Guide for kindergarten teachers and staff* (pp. 29–37). Department of Publications, Ministry of Education, Culture, and Sports. (in Hebrew).
Weinberger, Y., & Bakshi-Brosh, I. (2013). The full empathic practice of teachers. *Giluy-Da'at, 4*, 97–123. (in Hebrew).
Zadunaisky-Ehrlich, S., Yifat, R., & Goverman, E. (2016). *A common language in kindergarten. Educating children from diverse cultural and linguistic backgrounds*. The Ministry of Education, Israel. (in Hebrew).
Zilberberg, H. (2003). *Multiculturalism in our kindergarten. Hed Hagan, 2*, 76–79. (in Hebrew).
Ziv, M., Smadga, M., & Aram, D. (2013). Reading a children's book in kindergarten by the kindergarten teachers and their reference to aspects of Theory of Mind. *Researchers @ Early Childhood—Levinsky College of Education, 1*, 48–72. (in Hebrew).
Zohar, A. & Bushrian, O. (2020). *Adapting curriculum and learning materials for the 21st century: Summary of the expert committee's work, current situation, and recommendations.* Yozma—Center for knowledge and research in education (in Hebrew).
Zur, B., Segal, M., & Rom, A. (2012). *So the child says: On the development of communication and language in childhood.* The MOFET Institute. (in Hebrew).

Experience with a Worthy Public Discussion, Based on the Ideas of Dewey

Guy Pinku

Introduction

We live in an era in which a great wealth of diverse information is accessible. However, this is a mixed blessing, since the amount of information is infinite and very complex. As a result, there is a danger that public discussions will become superficial and inflammatory. The danger increases due to the fact the information accessible to the public is not presented in a systematic manner. At times, the information is even biased, due to the author's agenda. To this, we can add the polarization between rival political camps. Oftentimes, this polarization is accompanied by tension and hatred between different groups in the population, due to aspects of demography (politics of identities).

Due to the polarization, each political camp is more attentive to the sources of information that support and entrench their position. The polarization, as a result, exacerbates the sharing of biased public information that, in turn, exacerbates the polarization, in a repetitive cycle. In this situation, the public finds it increasing difficulty to understand what will benefit them and to determine their real interest (Tucker et al., 2018). Moreover, this situation might even strengthen the danger that a populist leadership that does not serve the public good will emerge. In other words, it can lead to leadership that rests on superficiality of public discourse and political polarization in order to amass power instead of serving the public interest.

As a result, it seems as if John Dewey's proposal that was put forth over 100 years ago (due to a similar crisis) to educators to engage in a worthy public discussion remains relevant, perhaps even more so than before (Mason, 2017; Whipple, 2005). However, as I will present later on in the chapter, there is a pedagogical difficulty in implementing Dewey's proposal, due to the need to overcome prevalent habits of

G. Pinku (✉)
Kibbutzim College of Education, Technology and Arts, Tel-Aviv, Israel
e-mail: Guy.Pinku@smkb.ac.il

Y. Yondler et al. (eds.), *Cultivating Future-Oriented Learners*, Understanding Teaching-Learning Practice, https://doi.org/10.1007/978-3-031-63253-2_8

engaging in substandard public discourse. The proposed lesson plan uses digital tools and cooperative pedagogy in order to overcome this difficulty. It proposes designing conditions that encourage the creation of a worthy public discussion in the classroom—that is, a relevant, systematic, fact-based discussion of public issues that arouse division. Moreover, the proposed lesson plan meets educators' needs to find a suitable way to hold a discussion on divisive political issues in the classroom, as part of civic education in a democratic regime (Hess, 2009).

I will begin with an explanation of why Dewey argues that there is a need in education to hold worthy public discussions, and the essence of such education. I will then present the pedagogical difficulty in implementing his proposal. Finally, I will present a sample lesson plan designed to overcome this difficulty.

Why Is There a Need in Education for a Worthy Public Discussion?

In Plato's *Republic*, the philosopher presents the Achilles heel of the democratic regime (Plato, 1956, 375 B.C.): a demagogue might persuade the public to make decisions that contradict their interests. In his book, *Public Opinion*, the American publicist Walter Lippman (1922) echoes the fear that Plato voiced, arguing that **the character of the public discussion does not make it possible for the public to make decisions that are in their interests**. In John Dewey's book, *The Public and Its Problems* (1954), the philosopher and educational reformer dealt with this criticism, calling it the most serious criticism of democracy. Indeed, Dewey, who can be called democracy's 'poster boy', believed that democracy is not only a technical means of governance, but also a significant, ethical ideal of managing shared life. Dewey argued that there is a need to overcome the difficulty presented by Lippman by engaging in worthy public discussions.

What Is a Worthy Public Discussion?

Education for a worthy public discussion is based on Dewey's perception of the essence of a democratic society. Democratic society is like a puzzle that is comprised of different and unique pieces. The diversity of the pieces contributes to the wealth and beauty of the entire picture. Variance and diversity have a positive influence on public discussion. In dialogue between individuals who hold different positions, the participants hone, or even change, their positions. This complex interaction that includes exposure to different positions and responses to them, and that leads to the honing or a transformation of the initial position, contributes to the participants' development and corresponds to the wealth of ideas in society (Dewey, 1968). Dewey's perception and the polyphonic wisdom model correspond to one another.

According to both Dewey and the polyphonic insight, the unique voice of the individual develops, and is based in and constructed against the background of openness and empathic listening to different voices. Dewey argued that this is an ethical ideal of a democratic society and is actually the source of its strength.

Dewey proposed a number of characteristics found in a worthy public discussion. Similar to a scientific discussion, a public discussion needs to be relevant. The participants in the discussion need to research together a well-defined disagreement that is up for discussion. Like a Socratic ideal dialogue, this is not a discussion, in which the participants come with a solution or a crystallized idea. In the discussion, it is important that the group members influence one another as they engage in the joint process of research and crystallization of positions. In other words, a worthy public discussion is not a battlefield between people with different ideas, who are entrenched in their positions and attempt to subdue the opponent, but rather is a shared investigation that is based on cooperation and trust (DeCesare, 2012; Dewey, 1954).

There is affinity between the idea of a worthy public discussion, according to Dewey, and the *Veil of Ignorance*, proposed by John Rawls (2010). Rawls presented a hypothetical script in which a group of people comes together to decide if the social contract is fair. Rawls argued that in order to improve and reach a more exact process, it is important to put into place a veil of ignorance concerning the identities of the group members. Group members do not need to be aware of their identity or their social-economic status. That is, they engage in the discussion as if they had not yet been born, when talking about society's laws and the way society is administered. In other words, the participants do not know if they are women or men, rich or poor, White, Asian or African, etc.

In such a situation, Rawls asserts that there is motivation to create a fair balance between the interests and the needs of different population groups. For example, when a person does not know if they are rich or poor, they will want to balance economic inequality (that has the goal of encouraging economic growth), while maintaining certain characteristics of the welfare state. Alongside Rawls, Dewey suggested a notion of 'veil of ignorance in discussion', such a discussion is characterized by an intentional adoption of ignorance or bracketing of people's positions. As a result, a space for empathic listening to the other's viewpoint is created. Placing one's opening position in brackets and being willing to listen makes it possible for people 'to think together' about how to find balanced solutions.

The Difficulty in Education of Holding a Worthy Public Discussion

A number of years ago, in the course, *Progressive Educational Thought*, which dealt with the theory and praxis of progressive education, I tried to implement Dewey's model of education for worthy public discussion in a classroom of students of education in the Kibbutzim College (the class was comprised of Jewish and Arab students). In the beginning, I presented the topic of worthy democratic discussion, according to Dewey. Afterwards, the students were divided into work groups. Each group received a version of the Nation-State Law, one article that supported the law and one article that opposed it. My request from the students was to hold a public discussion, according to Dewey's proposal and to reach agreement in the group, in relation to the law.

The exercise didn't work. The lesson was a total failure. The students did not create thinking groups for the study of the dilemma and did not work together to consider different possible solutions. After a few minutes when the group members were 'polite', intense arguments began; each participant was certain that she was right. Because of this failure, I reached the conclusion that Dewey had a good idea. However, as often is the case of good ideas, it was not an idea that could be implemented.

In order to help students accept the idea and praxis of a worthy public discussion, there is a need to overcome the deep-rooted perception and habits of public discussion as a battleground in which there are opposing stances. The perception of a public discussion as a battlefield, as opposed to being a dialogical space, is a significant characteristic of the political polarization found in the present-day era (Tucker et al., 2018). Hence, it is illogical to expect that after a presentation of a worthy public discussion, based on Dewey's ideas, students will shed their deep-rooted customs connected to inferior public discussions and enter into a matter-of-fact discussion.

A Sample Lesson Plan: A Proposed Solution for Engaging in a Worthy Public Discussion

Due to my failed attempt to employ the direct approach, I understood that an indirect approach was needed. Instead of beginning with the theoretical rationale, the lesson should begin with experiencing a worthy public discussion. This makes it possible to then present the theoretical rationale. In other words, I decided to rely on Dewey's pedagogy: learning that is based on experience. Nonetheless, how is it possible to create an experience of engaging in a worthy public discussion without directly asking the students to engage in such a discussion? The solution is to create the conditions for such a discussion—conditions that include systematic thinking about the arguments for and against positions, which are unconnected to the initial position of the student. This helped me come up with the idea of creating groups of students who write arguments in favor of stances that are not theirs. I understood that this exercise needs to be undertaken in an indirect manner (as I had learned that it is difficult creating a discussion that is fitting for Dewey's ideas by explicitly asking students to act according to them). In essence, I hoped that, as a result of the group experience, each student would spontaneously think about the idea of a worthy public discussion.

The proposed lesson plan, which is detailed here, harnesses technological pedagogical tools and components of cooperative learning in order to create an experience of engaging in public discussion, based on Dewey's proposal and corresponding to the polyphonic wisdom model. It is only after this experience that the students are explicitly taught about the theoretical rationale that Dewey proposed for worthy public discussion. The assumption is that indirect acquaintance with the rationale, via the experience, will lead to the internalization of the idea (Table 1).

The Preliminary Stage: Clarifying the First Stance

Approximately 1 month before the course began, the students received a questionnaire about their position toward an educational model of the democratic school. The democratic school was chosen as a topic for activity for two reasons: the students had learned about the model in their course on progressive educational thought, and the topic had often aroused intense division. The pre-lesson questionnaire had one question: "What is your opinion of the democratic school?" The respondents were asked to choose one of four possible answers:

The first choice: It is an excellent idea. We need to aspire that all schools will adopt the democratic school model.

The second choice: It is a good idea. Each school should be able to decide if the democratic school model fits them.

The third choice: It is not a good idea. The democratic school model is not suitable for most schools.

The fourth choice: It is a problematic idea. Democratic schools need to return to the traditional model.

Table 1 A sample lesson plan: a proposed solution for engaging in a worthy public discussion

1.	**Thinking about different positions.** In the beginning of the lesson, the students are divided into groups that write arguments that support positions that are different or even contradict their own initial positions
2.	**A critical discussion about different positions**. After the groups finish writing down their arguments, they return to the plenum. In the plenum, the students hold a critical discussion of the positions and the arguments that support them
3.	**Self-assessment.** After the discussion ends, the students are asked to answer an online questionnaire. The questionnaire relates to change of initial position and the participant's opinion about the goal of the activity
4.	**Presentation of the theoretical rationale.** In this stage, the instructor presents the rationale and goal of the classroom activity, explicitly explaining how the activity is part of a worthy public discussion, based on Dewey's work

It can be assumed that the students did not connect this very short questionnaire that was sent via WhatsApp to the lesson they would be attending. As we will see, the goal of the pre-lesson questionnaire was to ensure a relevant division of the students into working groups in the classroom.

The First Stage: The Thinking About Different Positions

The course was held online, via Zoom, a format that made it easy for the students to move between the different pedagogical environments. In the beginning of the lesson, after the task was explained, the students were divided into four groups, and each group had its own Zoom 'room'. Each group received access to a shared document in Google Docs, in order to construct their knowledge. The groups received a description of a character, which included the character's name, a description of their role, their position and a picture of the character. The students in each group were asked to read aloud the character's position and to write three distinct, persuasive arguments that support the position. There were four characters in total.

The first character was *Sarah, a representative of the NGO for the democratic schools*. Sarah believes that all schools need to run according to the democratic model. That is, they need to slowly 'abandon' the traditional model. The second character was *Rachel, a representation of the NGO for Equality in Education*. Rachel believes that each school should have the right to freely choose the traditional model or the democratic model. In other words, if the school chooses the democratic model, this should not have a negative impact on the funding they receive from the government. The third character was *Rivka, a representative from the Ministry of Education*. Rivka believes that the current situation is the right one. She believes that there should be democratic schools, but that they should not receive full government funding. In other words, while there needs to remain acceptance of the democratic schools, the acceptance should remain informal. The fourth figure is *Leah, a representative of the NGO, Returning to Traditional Education*. Leah believes that all of the schools need to run according to the traditional model. In other words, they need to slowly 'abandon' the democratic model.

The students were divided into groups, according to their responses to the questionnaire. The students were intentionally separated in a way that ensured that they would have to construct arguments for positions that differed from their own positions, perhaps even ones with which they disagreed. The participants were also asked to try to see the world as the character did and to write down the most persuasive arguments they could think of, regardless of the students' own positions.

Working together in the small groups made it possible for all of the students to demonstrate their strength (when thinking about the position, when phrasing the arguments, and when they presented their work in the plenum). Moreover, they were able to express their thoughts, to try to persuade others and to become persuaded themselves. As a result, a synergy was created between the humanistic vision of the democratic community that was investigating the topic together (in accordance with Dewey's ideas) and the polyphonic wisdom model.

Writing arguments for a position that the students had to present was highly significant for them—especially for those who disagreed with a position they had to support. This task unraveled the Gordian knot between support and identification with a certain position and the unwillingness to think about other positions. The participants in the group 'adopted' the character's mindset concerning a position that differed from theirs. As a result, they undertook their task in a matter-of-fact way and considered different arguments. The task, in essence, was to think about why they should accept such a position, one with which they disagree.

This situation is different from the norm, in which a public discussion becomes a battle over opposing positions, as each individual is 'locked' into their stance. In other words, the mission of writing down the character's arguments released the students from focusing on the customary question: "What do I think about this position?" and they were, thus, able to focus on the question: "What are the arguments that support this position?" This question helps people abandon the common inferior habits of thinking about public issues, in which they first ask themselves what their position is, and then search for arguments that support their position. Discussions could improve if people were to consider the opposite option: "First, I will consider the arguments and then I will determine my position." 'Adopting the mindset' of the character whose position is different disconnects people's identification and tendencies from thinking about the topic.

The Second Stage: A Critical Discussion About Different Positions

After the groups finish writing down their arguments, they return to the plenum. In the plenum, each group is asked to read aloud the character's position and to present in their own words (that is, not to read from the page) two central arguments that support the position. After this presentation, a critical discussion about the arguments is held. Are the arguments persuasive (Should they be accepted? Is their truth to them?) Do they indeed solidify the position of the character? (This question relates to validity.) In this stage of the lesson, the conditions for a worthy public discussion are created, based on Dewey's terms. The participants think clearly about the issue on the agenda, as they rationally review the arguments concerning the different positions. This situation creates openness and, perhaps, even empathy toward the opposing stance. Moreover, working on the arguments and thinking about the strength of the argument from different aspects (the veracity and validity of the arguments) serves as an educational lesson and gives the participants the opportunity to exercise systematic and rational thinking.

The Third Stage: Self-Assessment

After the discussion ends, the students are asked to answer an online questionnaire, using Google Forms. The questionnaire opens with an open question, which asks the student to briefly describe their experience and feeling during the group preparation of the arguments. They are then asked: "Of the four positions that were discussed concerning the model of the democratic school, which one do you support?" This made it possible to compare the answers to the pre-questionnaire. Then the student was asked if she changed her position, due to the classroom activity. Students who responded that they had changed their position were asked to explain the reasons for this change. Finally, the students were asked for their opinion about the goal of the activity (this was an open question).

After this, the students return to the plenum. The instructor and the students review the questionnaire results together. Here, a special emphasis is put on the answers concerning the change in position, due to the class activity, as well as hypotheses concerning the goal of the activity. At times, the instructor asks the students, who are interested in doing so, to present and explain their answers. The personal reflection, which is followed by the group reflection, makes it possible for the participants to think independently about the process and to try to understand it. Here people are asked to think about something that is usually hidden from sight—to think about the shape of the discussion and not about its content.

The aim of this activity was to raise awareness and to focus attention on *the way* the systematic and relevant discussion developed and, as result, to bring the participants to think independently about Dewey's ideas concerning engagement in a worthy public discussion. Moreover, this corresponded to Dewey's pedagogy, according to which, understanding and internalization are created from experiences, and not from a theoretical description or preaching (Dewey, 1975).

The Fourth Stage: Presentation of the Theoretical Rationale

In this stage, after the experiential infrastructure was laid and the participants engaged in reflection, the instructor presents the rationale and goal of the classroom activity, explicitly explaining how the activity in which the students participated is part of a worthy public discussion, based on Dewey's ideas. In this stage, the problematics of engaging in a public discussion in democratic society, the dangers of this difficulty and the educational solution that Dewey proposed—education for a worthy public discussion—are presented. The lesson, itself, is, in essence, an example of how to implement such a solution. It is 'the opposite' in pedagogical terms, since the message is first transmitted through the experiential form, hinted at when students are requested to engage in reflective thinking and it is only at the end that the rationale is explicitly explained.

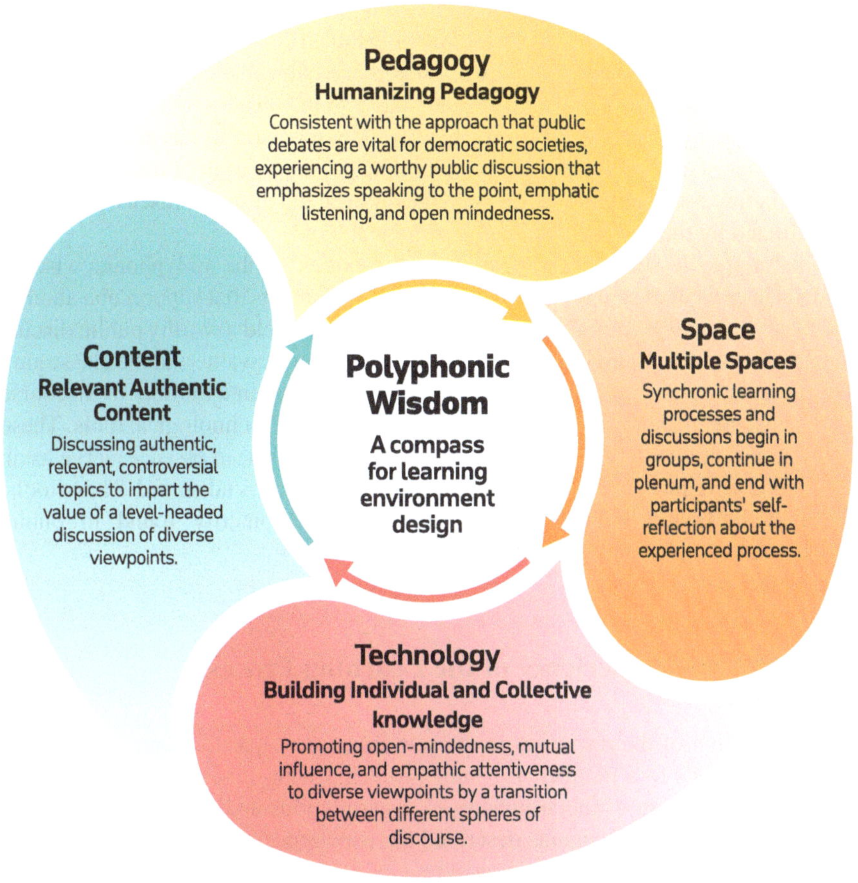

Fig. 1 Polyphonic wisdom model

The proposed lesson plan corresponds to the polyphonic wisdom model (see Fig. 1).

The proposed model is designed to advance education for a worthy public discussion, inspired by Dewey's ideas. It aims to advance education for relevant discussions about present-day important issues. The participant in a worthy public discussion does not come to the discussion with an 'unmovable' position; instead, the person crystallizes her position, based on the discussion as it unfolds. The idea of a worthy public discussion corresponds to the polyphonic wisdom model: it is important to educate the individual to solidify her position by listening to a discussion, which includes a multiplicity of voices.

Public discussions are often 'battles between positions'. Therefore, it is difficult to create a worthy public discussion in the classroom. This kind of discussion is very different from usual public discussion and serves as a kind of repair. In order to overcome this difficulty, the proposed lesson plan offers a number of discussion spaces that create the conditions for a worthy public discussion.

To begin with, the small groups work together to formulate arguments for positions they **do not** support. Afterwards, they move to the plenum to present and critically examine the different positions. Finally, they move on to the assessment and self-reflexive stage of the process. The preliminary examination of the participants' stances in the discussion and the movement between the different discussion spaces is facilitated by the employment of technological tools.

The sample lesson presented above corresponds to the polyphonic wisdom model. Here, we find synergy between the four components that support one another and make one another possible. In order to learn how to hold a worthy public discussion in a democratic society (which reflects the humanistic value), in the classroom, the students discuss content that usually arouses division, in a number of discourse spaces that are made possible through the employment of technological tools. These technologies are needed: they create discussion spaces that, in essence, serve as an artificial environment in which a worthy public discussion is advanced. These tools, furthermore, help overcome the inferior habits customarily found in public discussions.

The Students' Experience of the Learning Process

An examination of the responses to the self-assessment questionnaire, concerning the activity, leads to a number of results. To begin with, many of the participants described the writing of the arguments as a harmonious and positive process. For example, one of the participants described her experience in this way:

> Together, the group members performed the work in the group. I felt that each one had a place to express her personal opinion. Overall, our opinions were identical and it was enjoyable to discuss the topic and to hear the additional sides and other arguments.

Secondly, many of the participants described the difficulty in thinking positively and writing down arguments in support of a position, which they do not support. They noted that, from this aspect, the task was challenging. Thirdly, some of the students described how thinking about the arguments that their character might say created the understanding that 'there is something logical' about their position. In essence, 45% of the participants asserted that the class exercise led them to change their position on the topic. Changing one's position was also evident in the differences between the pre-course questionnaire and the post-plenary discussion questionnaire on attitudes. These findings indicate that formulating the arguments and discussing the stances that do not match one's position create openness for consideration of a different stance, and even an attitude change.

Moreover, it was found that most of the students hypothesized that the goal of the activity was to become exposed to other opinions concerning the topic. Two of the students even precisely described the rationale of the lesson (before it was explicitly explained). One of them wrote: "In my opinion, the goal of the activity was to expose us to different opinions about supporting or resisting the existence of democratic schools so that we could form our own opinion." A second participant wrote: "[the goal of the activity] was to show that it is possible to explain every opinion based on its reasons and that it is important to hear different opinions than mine and to understand them." These responses and the overall understanding that the goal of the activity was to expose the students to different opinions demonstrated that the students understood (with different degrees of explicitness) Dewey's idea about worthy public discussions, before the idea was explained. Therefore, it appears that the theoretical explanation at the end of the class was meaningful for the students: it explained an idea that was hazy in the beginning, to one degree or another, for the students. However, as the participants' responses showed, they eventually understood the idea by themselves, because of their classroom experience. In other words, the results demonstrate that the pedagogical approach of the model lesson (learning through experience) was indeed manifested in the proposed model.

The Educational Importance of the Proposed Model

In the proposed model, abstract philosophical ideas are transformed into concrete activity, by reliance on technological tools. The model makes two contributions. To begin with, it engages in democratic education, according to Dewey's perception. Secondly, the model offers complex ways to turn educational ideas into concrete action (by employing technology), and it demonstrates that it is possible to find a way to implement a significant educational idea. In other words, we should not give up on focusing on significant educational ideas, even if they are abstract or if it is challenging to find a way to implement them.

A third importance of the model is that it attempts to overcome the failure of holding worthy public discussions in the classroom. In such a discussion, the students express their opinions and there is a debate (which, in the best-case scenario, remains polite). This reflects the battlefield of different positions. In other words, discussions in the classroom about important present-day topics repeat the customary and problematic script, which reflects usual public discussions. That is, unconsciously, the education furthers inferior habits concerning public discussions. The proposed model describes how to create a revolutionary change: the instructor and students investigate together a burning public issue, not in order to persuade the other, but rather to understand together the different stances.

Based on Lippman (1922), Dewey (1954) raised a significant problem that is characteristic of our times (Mason, 2017). On the one hand, this is an era of complexity, characterized by access to a great deal of information. On the other hand, there are many clever biases of information. In such a situation, the public has difficulty understanding what is in its best interest, a difficulty, which continues to increase. It is not easy to acknowledge that public discussions fail. A person who yells out 'There is a problem' may be considered elitist, or even, a person who opposes democratic decisions. (Most politicians deny that a failure exists and argue that 'the people are smart', while hiring experts in public opinion that will succeed in confusing the people.) However, putting one's head in the sand will not solve the problem. If we do not admit that there is a problem, the problem will not disappear. Indeed, this problem threatens the existence of the democratic regime (as prophesized by Plato, in *The Republic*).

It appears that a change in the way we engage in public discussions will strengthen the democratic regime. Dewey (1954), who believed in democracy as an ethical ideal, presented the serious failure of public discussion and offered an educational solution. I propose adopting this solution and present a way to implement his idea (there may also be other ways to do so, of course). Perhaps it is naïve to believe that education can bring about change. However, as educators, we have no choice but to believe this is so.

Concrete Proposals

The lesson includes movement between different pedagogical environments (beginning in the plenary, working in small groups, engaging in personal reflection and afterwards returning to the plenary) and the use of work tools—Google Docs and Google Forms. Therefore, an online framework, such as Zoom, is the most suitable platform for carrying out the lesson. This platform makes it possible to move quickly and easily between the different pedagogical environments (for example, between the discussion in the whole group and in the smaller groups). Moreover, the participants have immediate access to the online format and the Google work tools. I believe that undertaking the lesson face-to-face would take more time—the online framework takes 90 min—and make the tasks more complicated.

I will now relate to each stage of the lesson, and add points that should be emphasized.

<u>In the preliminary stage</u> of administration of the questionnaire, in which each student notes their initial position, it is important to send out the questionnaire about 1 month before the class. Furthermore, it is important to do so in an unobtrusive way, without creating a connection between the questionnaire and the future lesson. It is important that the participants remain unaware of the manipulation—as much as possible—concerning their division into groups that is based on *their responses to the preliminary questionnaire*.

In the <u>first stage of the lesson</u>, there are a number of points to be emphasized concerning the instructions to the groups about the task of writing of the arguments. To begin with, as noted above, regardless of the participants' initial positions, they are asked to see the world through the character's eyes and to write down arguments that are the most persuasive. Secondly, it is important to stress that each argument must be different, with each one adding something unique. Thirdly, it is important to check that there is indeed a clear connection between the arguments and the position that the character presents, i.e., that the arguments indeed strengthen the position that the character presents.

When the students write down their arguments, the instructor moves between the rooms. In the beginning, the movement is quick, in order to encourage the groups to begin their work and to clarify the instructions, if there is a need to do so. Afterwards, the movement between the rooms is more relaxed and includes thinking together and a discussion of the arguments. Moreover, it is recommended that the instructor leave the rooms and read the shared Google Doc every now and then. In this way, the instructor can examine the rate of the progress of each group and help the groups working at a slower speed. I usually allocate 15 min for the work in the groups and add another 5–10 min, according to need.

In the second stage of the critical discussion of the different positions, it is important to see whether the discussion is dynamic and moving forward. The instructor should make sure that as many students as possible are participating in the presentation of the arguments concerning the position. It is further important to make sure that as many people as possible are participating in the following discussion of each position.

During the third stage of the self-assessment, when the students are answering the questionnaire, I turn off the video and audio functions on Zoom, in order to give the students privacy (the questionnaire is anonymous). While going over the responses, in the plenary, in which the Google Forms are shared (in essence, this is a summary of the Google Forms that presents the answers to each question), I read some of the answers and ask the participants to add things and comment. I spend more time on the last question that deals with thinking about the goal of the lesson. It is essential to encourage interest and thinking about this, since it is important for the students to reach insights, due to their experience.

The fourth stage is the presentation of the theoretical rationale. This is a stage that is intentionally short, since the participants are usually tired by this time. Therefore, I keep the presentation to 15 min. At times, if I feel that the students are tired, I end the class and begin the next lesson with this stage. From my experience, moving the explanation to the next lesson does not impede their understanding of the rationale of the approach.

On a Personal Note

I teach philosophy in a college for teacher training. I have learned that there is a tension (illusory, in my opinion) between the subject that I teach, in specific, and the humanities, in general, and the use of diverse pedagogy and technological tools. Philosophy is a classic and rationale area of study. There is a Socratic belief that all that anyone needs in order to learn philosophy is to present reasonable arguments in an explicit manner. As a result, employment of technological tools is perceived as similar to a rhetorical temptation that harm the essence of the discussion's rationale. I do not agree with this.

Abstract ideas and value often require concrete experience in order for people to understand and internalize them (Dewey, 1975). Giving a theoretical presentation and directly appealing to reason may fail (even though I do not believe that this failure will lead to the execution of the teachers, as Socrates was). In my opinion, it is relevant to use the proposed model in teaching, because diverse pedagogy and use of technological tools (that reflect the polyphonic wisdom model) can create a relevant experience for the students that advances internalization of the ideas. It is difficult to achieve internalization via a direct request. Therefore, I want to encourage my colleagues who teach humanities to use diverse pedagogy and technological tools, in order to advance a humanistic vision. Communication and turning to experience, which are advance by technological tools, do not stand in opposition to humanistic values of rationalism and autonomy. As I described above, it is important to create conditions in the classroom that will make a rational discussion possible. Technological tools open up new possibilities for the creation of these conditions. Therefore, I recommend that we, who teach the humanities, think about these tools not as constraints of the pedagogical era in which we live, but rather as an authentic way to overcome pedagogical difficulties in teaching the humanities. I wish to add that the technology can facilitate teaching the humanities, just as it aids teaching the natural sciences. The technology is not the enemy of the humanities: it is a friend.

References

DeCesare, T. (2012). The Lippmann-Dewey 'debate' revisited: The problem of knowledge and the role of experts in modern democratic theory. *Philosophical Studies in Education, 43*, 106–116.

Dewey, J. (1954). *The public and its problems*. The Swallow Press.

Dewey, J. (1968). *Democracy and education* (Y. T. Helman, Trans.). Bialik Institution.

Dewey, J. (1975). *Moral principles in education*. Southern Illinois University Press.

Hess, D. E. (2009). *Controversy in the classroom: The democratic power of discussion*. Routledge.

Lippmann, W. (1922). *Public opinion*. http://www.howardnema.com/wpcontent/uploads/2016/08/lippmann.pdf

Mason, E. L. (2017). The "Dewey-Lippmann" debate and the role of democratic communication in the trump age. *Dewey Studies, 1*(1), 79–110.

Plato. (1956). *Plato's writings* (Vol. 2, Book 7) (Y. G. Liebs, Trans.). Shoken.

Plato. (2000). *The Republic*. Translated by Tom Griffith. Edited by G. R. F. Ferrari. Cambridge, UK: Cambridge University Press.

Rawls, J, (1999). *A Theory of Justice: Revised Edition*. Cambridge, MA: Harvard University Press.

Rawls, J. (2010). *Justice as fairness* (D. Agam-Segel, Trans.). Yediot Ahronot (Hemed Books).

Tucker, J. A., Guess, A., Barbera, P., Vaccari, C., Siegel, A., Sanovich, S., Stukal, D., & Nyhan, B. (2018). *Social media, political polarization, and political disinformation: A review of the scientific literature*. SSRN: https://doi.org/10.2139/ssrn.3144139

Whipple, M. (2005). The Dewey-Lippmann debate today: Communication distortions, reflective agency, and participatory democracy. *Sociological Theory, 23*(2), 156–178.

Reading and Playing: Promoting Reading of Literature via a Digital Game

Lily Glasner

Introduction

Fiction literature introduces us to characters defined by their love of reading. Suffice it to recall two of them—Esther, a girl so possessed by a reading mania that she is unaware of the reality around her (Zarhi, 1976), and Nuri, the youth who loves life and adventure and is depicted as an avid reader (Michael, 1975)—to realize that readers are not one and the same. Their tastes and reading habits may differ significantly. Yet, what defines them both is their choice to read books. In the academic sphere, it seems natural to expect from future literature teachers to be book lovers by nature. In practice, however, a central challenge teacher educators contend with is how to bring future teachers to read literature.

The scope of the present article is to present a teaching model that aspires to face the challenge and this by utilizing a Future Learning Space and incorporating digital tools. The model, developed for the course "Literature Teaching 3," was implemented in the 2018 and 2020 schoolyears.[1]

"Literature Teaching 3" is a didactic seminar that accompanies the practicum of third-year students specializing in elementary school literature teaching. The course's focal questions are, "What is literature teaching?" and "How to teach literature in elementary schools." Its central purposes include searching, testing, and experiencing new teaching-learning alternatives that leave behind the traditional frontal teaching the students had experienced themselves in school (see

[1] In developing the model, I worked in cooperation with Yael Yondler. Thanks go to Yochi Shelah, who guided us through the implementation process.

L. Glasner (✉)
Kibbutzim College of Education, Technology and Arts, Tel-Aviv, Israel
e-mail: Lily.glasner@smkb.ac.il

Y. Yondler et al. (eds.), *Cultivating Future-Oriented Learners*, Understanding Teaching-Learning Practice, https://doi.org/10.1007/978-3-031-63253-2_9

Shemer-Elkayam et al., 2021). One explored topic is how to motivate reading (reading for pleasure or leisure reading).

In training future literature teachers, reading for pleasure and becoming acquainted with a varied corpus go hand in hand with introducing the students to literature research and enhancing their literary skills, including writing texts in various genres and styles.

Finally, the didactic seminar and the practicum become spaces where the students are invited to form an inclusive, supportive, and empowering peer community. This component does not essentially reflect knowledge, indicating instead the emergence of a relatively new perception according to which the educational space functions as a place of collaboration, mutual enrichment, and as a source of support (Lieberman & Miller, 2016).

Observing the teaching model presented in this article through the prism of polyphonic wisdom will help us to shed light on how environment, technology, content, and pedagogy come together in creating a polyphonic community even when the basic activity is one that appears to be just an individual activity. Because, as illustrated so well in the poem by Nurit Zarhi I referred to in the beginning (*Esther*), literature reading for pleasure is perceived as a personal activity that the individual performs within her own private inner space, detaching the reader, be it for a short while, from the external reality occurring in the real world. Thus, even if the reader is in a public space in body, cognitively, she is immersed in a separate space where no communication exists with others. Moreover, sometimes book's reading provides the individual with a means of retreat that allows him to avoid complex, sometimes painful, social struggles (this is, for example, the solution of the banned girl in Lidar Harel's book (2023, p. 95). As mentioned, the polyphonic wisdom perspective will emphasis components that contribute to promoting agency, social interaction, attentiveness, and beneficial opinion exchange. It will show how an initially individual activity (reading alone) may evolve into an identity feature of future teachers as social change leaders.

Reading and Playing—Promoting Reading of Literature via a Digital Game: Model Description and Purposes

This section describes the purposes of the model and the four stages of performing it in the course. I begin by introducing the model's main activity—a digital role-play on TBE (To Be Education). TBE is a free Israeli educational enterprise for creating digital games which are centered around a dilemma or a controversial issue. Each participant assumes the role of one of the figures in the game. Over the game, the participants receive questions prepared in advance and write explanatory answers representing their assumed figures' viewpoints. The participants receive in advance the game's dilemma and figures (but not the role they are about to play). They can thus prepare their answers before the game begins. However, as the game progresses, they also have to react in real time to the answers of their co-players. The game ends with a digital vote on the presented dilemma. The vote reflects the participants' stands (which may differ from those of their assumed figures). The teacher takes the role of a figure that encourages the participating figures and urges them to react to each other.

In the model presented below, the students played a game I had devised especially for the course: "*The Double Lottie* vs. *Captain Underpants*: Canonic vs. popular literature in promoting reading in elementary schools." The dilemma is which of the two books fourth-graders should read. It is presented briefly at the beginning of the game: "Shir Cultura, the initiator of a reading promotion program, invites you to join the 4th-grade committee in taking a vote. Half of the committee members advocate choosing only classical books and propose *The Double Lottie*. The other half recommend contemporary books and propose *The Adventures of Captain Underpants*." The game figures comprise the four committee members: a male teacher, a female teacher, a girl-student, and a parent. Upon registration to the game, the digital platform opens parallel groups and randomly ascribes the students to them. The group members remain anonymous until the end of the game. However, the details and scripts of the group acts, including the students' answers and reactions, are saved on the system, and the teacher has access to them.

Let us return to the larger context. My initial purpose was to design a practice that will illustrate to my students how reading a book can be an enjoyable event the pupils associate with pleasant sensations of joy, curiosity, enthusiasm, and involvement. The very fact that reading in school is compulsory, entailing an assignment such as writing a book report or creating a product inspired by the book is a significant challenge to promoting *reading for pleasure*. Thus, a perk is required to counterbalance the mandatory work and highlight the pleasure. In the described model, that perk is the game (cf. Rafaeli & Segev, 2010).

Another significant dimension of the model is the social one. Although reading a book is usually perceived as an individual activity that offers the reader an esthetic, emotional, and cognitive experience, I wished to show my students it is possible to broaden the limits of that experience by setting up a reading community that in turn promotes reading for pleasure (see further elaboration below).

The productive collaboration with Yael Yondler, an expert on Assessment for Learning (AFL), has led to expanding the activity and consequently broadening the pedagogical goals in three fields: Knowledge (1–2 in Table 1), Assessment for Learning culture (3–4 in Table 1), and technology incorporation in teaching (5–8 in Table 1). Table 1 summarizes the meeting points between the course goals and the goals of the activity.

As the table shows, activity goals 1, 2, and 7 derive directly from the course goals namely reading motivation, reader identity development, literacy enhancement, and deepening knowledge in the relevant field of study. Activity goals 3, 4, 5, 6, and 8 correspond to the course goals of experiencing alternative teaching-learning and assessment modes. As to the social dimension, activity goal 8 supports creating a reading community by means of the digital sphere. Finally, activity goals 3, 4, and 8 support creating a collaborative space (peer community).

Table 1 Meeting points between the purposes of the course and the activity

Course goals / Activity goals	Motivate reading, develop reader identity, improve literacy and deepen knowledge in the field of study	Experience alternative teaching-learning and assessment modes	The social dimension: Create a reading community	Create a collaborative space
1.Motivate reading for pleasure to suite the MOE curriculum	✓			
2. Foster literacy[1]	✓			
3. Experience AFL culture		✓		✓
4.Understand AFL contribution.[2]		✓		✓
5. Familiarize with the TBE platform		✓		
6. Understand the value of technology as an alternative assessment tool		✓		
7. Understand the value of technology in supporting academic & creative writing	✓			
8. Understand the value of technology in creating a different learning experience		✓	✓	✓

[1]Including the ability to read referenced academic materials—identifying central arguments and ideas; writing well-established and relevant answers based on educated use of suitable materials; incorporating creative techniques in writing, such as using humor and puns
[2]Including learner participation in building the indicator, reflection on teaching-learning-assessment processes, peer learning and discussions to promote the learning process

The model implementation is conducted in four stages corresponding to four consecutive academic sessions. They follow an additional preliminary stage in which the students read the two mentioned books in their free time. The following is a description of the four model stages.

Session 1: Panoramic Overview

This stage introduced the students to the four stages of the planned activity, and the three perspectives of the activity goals: knowledge in the field of study (literature), assessment-for-learning, and technology incorporation into teaching. A screened presentation given jointly by the author and Yael Yondler accompanied the explanations. This session may be held in the classroom or on Zoom and it requires a computer and a shared screen.

Session 2: Presenting the Game and an Independent Learning

In the first part of the session, the students learned that the practice framework was a digital game. They received the script with the dilemma, the participating figures, and the questions the game figures would have to answer. They also received auxiliary academic materials to assist them in preparing answers in a thorough, educated manner.

The second and longer part of the session was dedicated to independent reading of the auxiliary materials and formulating the answers. The students had several options to choose from: Preparing for the game on their own, in pairs, or in a group; in the classroom or away from it; via group thinking and a discussion; writing down the answers or points for further development; highlighting the auxiliary materials or searching for additional references. They were told that they would be permitted to bring the auxiliary materials, and any other materials they prepared in advance, to the game itself. During the independent work, some students asked me to join their learning group and assist them. The session's duration was insufficient for the students to prepare all the required materials, and they completed the work later in the week. The second session, like the previous one, may be held in the classroom or on Zoom. It requires a computer and a shared screen.

Session 3: It's Game Time!

The session included two game rounds: a demonstration and the central game the students had prepared for. The demonstration, taken from the game gallery of the TBE platform, acquainted the students with the game's technicalities: registration, answer posting, reacting, etc. Its purpose was to reduce concerns that may arise upon encountering new technology.

The students played on their laptops, and most used earphones to disconnect from the surroundings and focus on the game. They had at their disposal the books and auxiliary materials prepared in advance. An extended team comprising, in addition to the two instructors, a representative of the TBE platform, and a technical support team from the college collaborated in conducting the session.

This session can be held in the classroom or on Zoom. In classroom sessions, each student must have an available laptop.

Session 4: Experiencing Assessment and Meta-cognitive Reflection

The session was held in an active learning classroom. At the beginning of the session, the students grouped as they did for the game. Each group received the script of another group and an assessment indicator prepared by the instructors. Their task was assessing the answers' quality and writing feedbacks on shared files (Google

Docs) prepared in advance by the instructors. Each group shared one of the active learning classroom's large screens.

Upon completing the group tasks, the whole class reassembled. A representative from each group presented the group feedback using the central screen in the front. The students shared their deliberations around writing the feedback and the professional opinion differences that emerged in the group. They were also invited to scrutinize the indicator's suitability and propose amendments, explaining why they were required.

The session ended in a sharing circle, in which the students shared at will their sensations and insights gained over the project. Finally, the instructors joined them in sharing their impressions and thoughts.

As mentioned, this model may be implemented in a classroom or online (Zoom). For implementation in the classroom, the model utilized a presentation (screened from the lecturer's stand), a digital platform (TBE), shared Google documents, laptops, and large screens. At the online implementation, zoom rooms and a shared screen replaced the large screens. The classroom used for the implementation was an *active learning classroom*: A spacious room equipped with a computerized lecturer stand, four large screens, and mobile table-chairs that enabled reorganizing speedily in different configurations: dispersed throughout the classroom, gathered in groups around a screen, or forming a full-class circle.

From Practice to Concept: Humanistic Foundations

The pedagogical rationale of the model presented in this article is complex and multi-faceted, considering that it covers three fields—content, AFL culture, and technology. I will expand here on one facet encompassing the core motivation for the activity and model: Promoting reading for pleasure with a view to developing future teachers' personal and professional identities. I will begin by presenting observations concerning the reading habits of in-service and pre-service literature teachers made in studies about reading motivation and note the existing link between these observations and elementary school curricula. Next, I will comment on the significance of literature reading in a humanistic educational worldview. The current gap between the actual situation and the educational outlook will shed light on the importance of reading motivation in training future literature teachers.

Research studies reveal a positive correlation between the reading habits of in-service and pre-service teachers and their use of optimal teaching practices to motivate reading for pleasure (McKool & Gespass, 2009). Moreover, a recurring claim is that regular reading and broad acquaintance with children's literature are directly associated with teachers' capability to arouse in their students a passion for reading (Applegate & Applegate, 2004; Burgess et al. 2011; Danielson & Roger, 2000). These are essential points given that one declared goal of the curriculum is to encourage making literature reading an integral part of students' daily routines, and to make them lifelong readers. The MOE promotes this goal through various venues, such as launching the website "The Joy of Reading for Elementary Schools," holding a "Book Parade," endorsing the "Pajama Library" project, publishing papers listing the principles of reading motivation, recommending reading and related activities arranged by age, and organizing meetings of authors with students (*Sal Tarbut Artzi*).

Considering the above, an additional goal of the course is developing literature reading as part of pre-service teachers' personal and professional identity. Although it seems self-evident that those who intend to become literature teachers should enjoy and regularly engage in reading, research on reading motivation indicates that a broad gap exists between this obvious assumption and the actual literature reading habits of in-service and pre-service literature teachers. In fact, studies made in recent decades reveal that while students recognize the importance of reading for pleasure, they do not read much, and some even never use their leisure time for reading (Levin, 2016; Nathanson et al., 2008; Skaar et al., 2018; Tohar, 2004).

From a humanistic perspective, being a lifelong reader is perceived as a central personality trait essential for promoting humanistic and democratic values. Rachel Elior acutely expresses this approach:

> A worthy person has broad horizons. [He] is educated, wise, and conversant in various fields of knowledge. Such a person is characterized by curiosity, education, knowledge, and criticism, [being] exposed to literature and poetry, art, and culture. [Such person] can independently form an opinion and consider matters that regard him and his family, community, and country based on thorough reading of varied literature. […] People who do not include reading in their daily routine—reading that broadens the horizons, teaches about the complexity of human nature, develops identification with difficulties and challenges, fosters curiosity and courage, tolerance, moderation and restraint, integrity, fairness, generosity, care and mutual responsibility, reveals the infinite expanses of the world and the multiculturality developed over thousands of years—are ignorant and complacent, poor and narrow minded, uncultured people. (Elior, 2013, p. 87)

Whilst one may contest her final conclusion (no less than the opposite assumption that avid readers are "cultured"), Elior's words represent an ideal that sees literature reading as essential for developing a worthy humanistic and civil consciousness (cf. Harpaz, 2018, p. 47).

Nimrod Aloni's words about cultural literacy (Aloni, 2005a) reveal a similar approach. Like Elior, Aloni believes that culturally literate people are a defense wall essential for the continued existence of an enlightened and democratic society (Ibid.) In another essay addressing the image of elementary school teachers, Aloni claims that nowadays when mass culture and post-modern worldviews that refute the existence of universal values and criteria are prevailing—teachers must consciously and fearlessly introduce their students to the greatest works of humanity (Aloni, 2005b).

The humanistic approach of Elior and Aloni maintains that worthy educators are lifelong readers who recognize the importance of literature and wish to introduce their students to the best canonic and contemporary world literature. Reading motivation is, therefore, a distinct goal deriving from this assumption (or ideal model). In "Literature Teaching 3", we act to achieve this goal by investigating and experiencing practices designed to this end, such as the role-playing game on the TBE platform.

Another aspect to dwell on is the forming of a *reading community* that potentially will help students develop an identity of a lifelong reader. Two models underlie this idea. The first relates to the sphere of schools (notwithstanding there are also strong ties to students' homes). The second takes place and is identified with the private sphere.

Let us consider the first model. In an article published in the early 1990s, Paul Baker and Kay Moss described U.S. elementary schools that act to promote reading for pleasure as a central educational value—shared by the school staff, the students, and their parents—by creating a reading community (Baker & Moss, 1993). The authors see this idea as part of a broader trend that aims to leave behind the school-as-a-factory model and the norm that regards the individual as an isolated autonomous unit, and replace it instead with a community approach. These schools translate the educational value of literature reading into a series of high-visibility acts on school premises as well as in the domestic sphere of each student. They promote this move by publishing an explicit declaration of intent and holding routine activities marked by peak events. The authors note that the "Shared Reading Program," where every age group reads two selected books followed by varied activities inspired by them, is an effective way of bringing home the message that reading can also be a social activity (Ibid., pp. 25–26).

Baker and Moss maintain that publishing a clear list of expectations from the student, the teaching staff, and the parents is crucial for instilling the educational value of this idea. The table annexed to their article, which indicates the project's breadth in U.S. schools, reveals an interesting detail: The column addressing the teaching staff notes the expectation that teachers keep professionalizing their reading strategies (Ibid., p. 26). Yet, it misses the most basic and significant point—encouraging book reading, included in the expectation list of students and their parents (Ibid.). Although the first expectation is that teachers regularly read to their students this is different from a teacher reading for her own pleasure. In comparison, the parents' column defines two distinct expectations. The first is that parents should read books to their children at least twice a week, and the second—that as role models, they engage themselves in book reading. The students, for their part, are expected to ask their parents to share their impressions of a book they (the parents) have recently read. Thus, the table highlights the reading experience of parents and students and their identity as avid readers while completely ignoring teachers' identity as lifelong readers. A table summarizing the authors' recommendations for creating a reading community mentions teachers' reading habits only implicitly (Ibid., p. 34).

Let us examine now how the idea of a reading community corresponds with the teaching model presented in this article. The purpose of the practice the students experienced (digital role play) was to illustrate an alternative teaching-learning mode they could later adjust for implementation in their elementary school classes.

This practice, combined with various others, may assist them in turning their classes into reading communities. They could possibly even venture a broader act, as Baker and Moss describe in their article, if the school management, teaching staff, and parents enlist in the effort. No less important—through this practice I sought to allow my students, if only for a short while, to feel an essential part of a reading community. Unlike the models Baker and Moss describe, underlying our model is the assumption that the reading habits of pre-service and in-service literature teachers should also be placed at the center. They too should be encouraged to identify themselves as readers of fine literature and to consciously cultivate this identity through various means, including those relevant to the current technological culture.

A second model the practice evokes is that of a *reading group*. A group of non-professional readers, i.e., ones that are not literature researchers, meet regularly for joint interpretive reading of literary texts. Each reader contributes to the joint reading her experiences and "the strategies she has been culturally exposed to " (Naishtat Bornstein, 2017, p. 188). In describing such a group and its characteristic dynamic, Lilach Naishtat Bornstein writes,

> Indeed, reading groups form a kind of 'textual communities' that empower their participants, assist in creating a community and a shared memory, challenge tradition, and give the readers authority against which they can consider their lives. [...] Joint reading and interpretation reveal the advantages of the group as a site of creativity and interpretation. [...] In such groups, reading becomes more shared and active, it explores the distance between public and private, and it allows room for critical deliberation that is vital for discussing ethical and ideological dimensions of social identity. (Ibid., pp. 189–199)

This model enables the individual as well as the group to grow internally (personal identity growth) and externally (critical examination of social identity and norms).

Indeed, an activity within an academic course will take place in a very different sphere, physically as well as mentally, than that which Naishtat-Bornstein described. In her model, readers meet privately, in their leisure time, free of grading. Yet, certain features of the proposed model create the right time-space conditions for setting up a reading group with its typical dynamic. They include the preliminary work on the game questions in the second session, where many students opted for working in a group over individual work, the dialogue between the game figures in the third session, and the non-formal post-game discussions during and after the third session.

Each student-reader brings to the joint interpretive reading her experiences, impressions, insights, and strategies she has come across in other classes and even in different life circumstances. Some also bring anxieties, memories of difficult past reading experiences, things they did not understand, and knowledge gaps. In the second session, they may choose to include the teacher in their discussions or create an intimate autonomic conversation circle, even away from the classroom. In the third session, group activity occurs in the digital space (the game), followed by face-to-face personal talks. The group events might also include the shared summary meeting that concluded the fourth session, even though it did not engage with literary texts (Fig. 1).

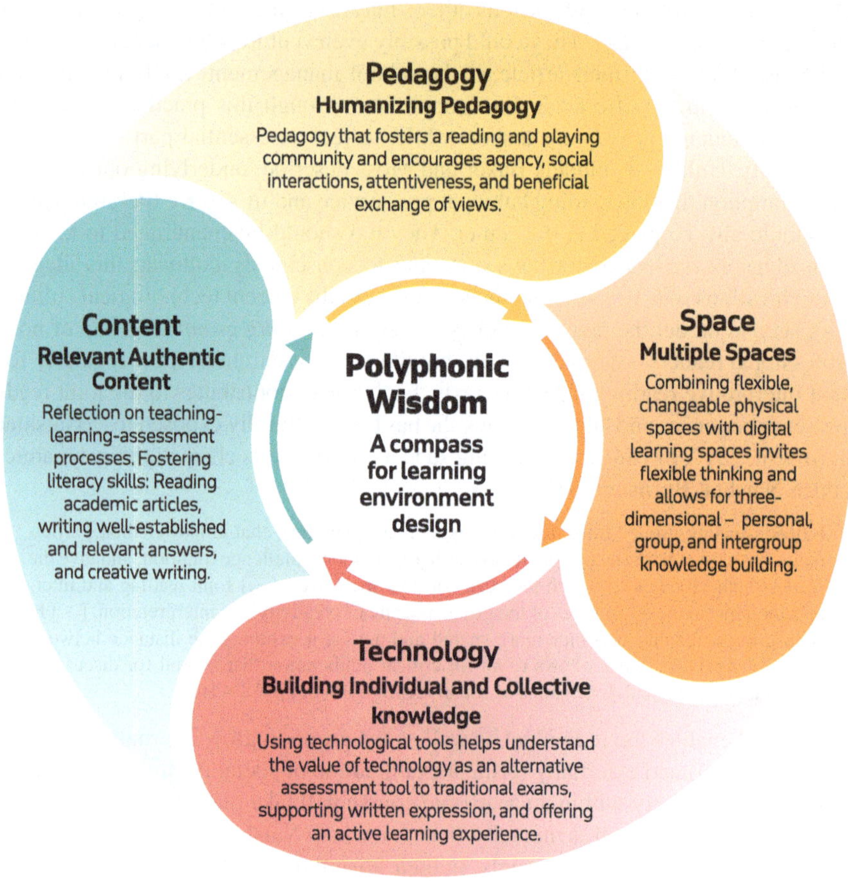

Fig. 1 The polyphonic wisdom model

Connection with the Polyphonic Wisdom Model

The polyphonic wisdom model described in the introduction to this book is unique in integrating conceptually and practically two educational approaches: The humanistic and the social-constructivist approaches. Both approaches aspire to motivate learners and generate a move from the personal to the socio-public domain. The "Reading and Playing" model invites students to identify themselves as literature readers. This is the initial personal perceptual change each student must undergo. It is a necessary—but not the only—condition for pre-service teacher to become in due course a leader of social change, given that the classroom and the school are distinct social spaces.

More on the Synergy Between Pedagogy, Learning Space, Technology, and Content

In the "Reading and Playing" model, students experience their literature reader identity in playful and communal ways. Using digital means—the TBE platform, computers, and large screens, and the flexibly changing environment of an active learning classroom turn reading, which is a challenging assignment for some, into a Happening and a multidimensional experience.[2]

Moreover, an important part of the learning experience is the narrative that the learner creates for herself (cf. Harpaz, 2018). The unique physical venue—an open space with chair-desks that allow for movement and advanced digital equipment—enabled students to visualize their experience as part of a pedagogical innovation. I was under the impression that this directly contributed to generating sensations of satisfaction and professional pride. Although some of the preparations for the game (reading the books, for example) did not occur in the active learning class, knowing that those preparations led to active participation in a digital game in a "class of the future" seemed an exciting incentive for the students.

In my opinion, the physical advantages of an active learning class, which enable organizing the given space in various structures and moving effortlessly between them, generated *a physically and mentally flexible learning experience*. Re'ut Gordon's article "A Place for Learning," which describes the architectural changes required in the school and classroom structure, confirms my sensations in a descriptive and theoretical way. It advocates abandoning the traditional disciplined classroom structure in the spirit of the *panopticon* and the nineteenth-century factories and replacing it with a flexible, weblike learning space that allows for configuration changes and corresponds to future-oriented pedagogy (Gordon, 2017). Yet, Gordon also mentions that a learning space using mobile seats has an essential disadvantage: "However, it is worth noting that although this method allows for considerable mobility within the classroom, it is a movement of chairs and not a movement of the children themselves that is vital for their development." (Ibid., p. 75).

"Reading and Playing" and Teacher Education

The teaching model presented in this article touches on several challenges teacher educators must handle in training future teachers. These challenges—emerging in disciplinary and pedagogical classes—constitute the core of the future teachers' personal and professional development in all fields of study. They form four categories, although this division is sometimes arbitrary, as the categories often interweave:

[2] This echoes the expansive approach that sees literature reading as a multidimensional experience encompassing, in addition to the reading itself, pre- and post-reading text-inspired activities (Cf. Bar-Hillel, 2012).

- **Developing intellectual curiosity**, namely, broadening one's horizons and developing literature reading habits.
- **Developing academic skills and abilities**, manifested in reading academic materials, using them and other sources in an educated manner (and distinguishing between them), and improving academic and creative writing skills.
- **Developing pedagogical knowledge**, i.e., replacing traditional teaching methods with innovative ones, including digital pedagogy and game-based learning, and replacing the grading method with the Assessment for Learning (AFL) culture.
- **Developing a socio-communal approach** that sees the individual as part of a community and promoting education spaces that follow the communality.

The presented model supports the development of these principles. Moreover, metacognitive discussions at relevant stages (in the first and fourth sessions) impart these principles explicitly to the learners (cf. Zohar, 2016).

Another advantage that emerged on the model's first implementation was that watching the two instructors exemplified to the students a **shared modular expanding teaching model**: Collaboration between the instructors, between them and the technical team, and with the students.

At the same time, the need arises for empirical studies that will examine the effectiveness of the model and its various components both in the short and long terms.

A Practical Tip

It is commonly assumed that the current generation of students, born into a reality where digital means make part of the daily routine, would be comfortable in a digital environment, and using digital tools would be second nature to them. Reality is, however, quite different. Many students do not possess digital literacy skills (Losh, 2021). In fact, despite using digital means routinely, some have concerns about using a new platform that make them shy away. We must be aware of this and address the difficulty in the teaching-learning process. Organizing the activity in stages, dedicating a session to acquaintance with the platform, peer instruction—are but some basic practices that could be integrated into a model such as the one presented here. They could help the students befriend the digital tool and bolster their self-efficacy. However, this requires allocating additional time while planning the activity.

On a Personal Note

Designing and implementing the described teaching model have opened a door for me to the new world of digital pedagogy. My enthusiasm, however, was mixed with genuine concern as I am not conversant with the technological world. "But," I told myself, "if I expect my students to challenge themselves, experience new ways and tools, and leave the familiar behind—I should also muster the courage to dive into this undertaking and practice what I preach."

References

Aloni, N. (2005a). *arba oryanuyot: Tarbutit, bikortit, academit upedagogit* [Four literacies: Cultural, critical, academic, and pedagogic]. In N. Aloni (Ed.), *kol shetzarich lihyot adam: Masa befilosofia hinuchit—Antologia* [Everything needed to be human: A journey in educational philosophy—Anthology] (pp. 275–282). Hakibutz Hame'uchad (In Hebrew).

Aloni, N. (2005b). *etgarav shel hamoreh hakolel beveit sefer humanisti* [Challenges of a General Teacher in a Humanistic School]. In N. Aloni (Ed.), *kol shetzarich lihyot adam: Masa befilosofia hinuchit—Antologia* [Everything needed to be human: A journey in educational philosophy—Anthology] (pp. 487–494). Hakibutz Hame'uchad (In Hebrew).

Applegate, A. J., & Applegate, M. D. (2004). The Peter effect: Reading habits and attitudes of preservice teachers. *The Reading Teacher, 57*(6), 554–563.

Baker, P. J., & Moss, K. (1993). Creating a community of readers. *School Community Journal, 3*(1), 23–36.

Bar-Hillel, G. (2012, December 21). *kvar lo kor'im kmo pa'am.* [They no longer read as before]. *od daf ehad vedie* [Just another page]. https://gilibarhillel.wordpress.com/2012/12/21. Accessed 12 July 2021. (In Hebrew).

Burgess, S. R., Sargent, M., Hill, N., & Morrison, S. (2011). Teachers' leisure reading habits and knowledge of children's books: Do they relate to the teaching practices of elementary school teachers? *Reading Improvement, 48*(2), 88–102.

Danielson, K., & Roger, S. E. (2000). You can't pass it on if you don't have it: Encouraging lifelong reading. *Reading Horizons: A Journal of Literacy and Language Arts, 41*(1), 35–45.

Elior, R. (2013). *lifrotz gvulot, likbo'a gvulot* [Breaking limits, setting limits]. *Hed Hahinuch, 87*(4), 86–90. (In Hebrew).

Gordon, R. (2017). *Makom lilmida* [A place for learning]. In I Ben Asher-Gitler, et al. (Eds.), *Timely teaching: Educational idealism and modern architecture* (pp. 63–78). Architects' House Gallery Edition (In Hebrew).

Har'el, L. (2023). *lo medabrot im Ana* [Not speaking with Anna]. Hakibbutz Hame'uchad. (In Hebrew).

Harpaz, Y. (2018). *eich letachnen sviva hinuchit beshisha tze'adim: Hamadrich* [How to plan an educational environment in six steps: A guide]. Bnei Brak: Sifriat Po'alim. (In Hebrew).

Levin, O. (2016). *Kri'a rishona besafa shniya: Thushat hamesugalut shel studentim umorim lehora'at genre haroman le'or hergelei hakri'a shelahem.* [First reading in a second language: Self-efficacy of in-service and pre-service teachers in teaching the novel genre, in light of their reading habits.] In Kliman, S. (Ed.), *Ivrit bekavana thila* [Hebrew First]: Articles from the international online conference on Hebrew as the second language of varied populations in Israel and around the world (pp. 35–46). Raanana: Mofet Institute (In Hebrew).

Lieberman, A., & Miller, L. (2016). *Kehilat lemida: Nekudat hazinuk lilmida miktzoit bevatei hasefer uvakitot.* [Learning Communities: The starting point for professional learning is in schools and classrooms.] (M. Kirsner, Trans.). *Hashkafa Mehkarit 2*, 6–8.

Losh, E. (2021). Universities must stop presuming that all students are tech-savvy. *Times Higher Education*. https://www.timeshighereducation.com/opinion/universities-must-stop-presuming-all-students-are-tech-savvy. Accessed 7 Dec 2021.

McKool, S., & Gespass, S. (2009). Does Johnny's reading teacher love to read? How teachers' personal reading habits affect instructional practices. *Literacy Research and Instruction, 48*(3), 264–276.

Michael, S. (1975) *Sufa bein dkalim* [Storm in the Palm Trees.] Am Oved.

Naishtat Bornstein, L. (2017). Mi mefahed miChristabel? Sipura shel kvutsat kria [Who's afraid of Christabel? A story of a reading group]. Tel Aviv: Gama. (In Hebrew).

Nathanson, S., Pruslow, J., & Levit, R. (2008). The reading habits and literacy attitudes of in-service and prospective teachers: Results of a questionnaire survey. *Journal of Teacher Education, 59*(4), 313–321.

Rafaeli, S., & Segev, L. (2010). *Mishakim retziniim: Ma lemis'hekei mahshev umaarechet hahinuch. Dugma leyisum* [Serious games: What do computer games have to do with the Education System. An example for implementation.] *Hed HaHinuch, 85*(3), 90–93. (In Hebrew).

Shemer-Elkayam, T., Shavit-Miller, A., & Arbiv-Elyashiv, R. (2021). *Havaya studentialit aheret behachshara lehora'ah: Nekudat hamabat shel morei hamorim.* [A different student experience in teacher training: The teacher trainers' perspective.] *Gilui Da'at, 18*, 23–36. (In Hebrew).

Skaar, H., Elvebakk, L., & Hegdal, N. J. (2018). Literature in decline? Differences in pre-service and in-service primary school teachers' reading experiences. *Teaching and Teacher Education, 69*, 312–323.

Tohar, V. (2004). *'Hirgashti sheha'olam niftah befanai'* [I felt the world opened before me]: A course on reading and reading encouragement for teachers specializing in literature teaching. *Dapei Yozma, 4*, 35–46. (In Hebrew).

Zarhi, N. (1976). Esther. In *Hanamer itahat laMita* [The tiger under the bed] (p. 42). Ramat Gan: Massada (In Hebrew).

Zohar, A. (2016). *Hashiva meta-cognitivit ulemida likrat havanah* [Meta-cognitive thinking and learning toward understanding]. In Y. Harpaz (Ed.), *Lehavin havana, lilmod lehavin: Musagim uma'asim* [Understand understanding, learn to understand] (pp. 162–171). Mofet Institute (In Hebrew).

Part IV
Self-Regulated Learning: Fostering Autonomous Learning Skills

'Learning How to Learn' in Light of the Universal Design for Learning Approach

Efrat Kotzer

One Size Does Not Fit All!

This statement is equally true for the field of teaching as for the field of clothing. Classes in the education system are characterized by great heterogeneity. In every class there are different students who learn in different ways and require different teaching and learning methods. The existing heterogeneity of a class often expands by inclusion of students with special needs, especially students with attention and learning disorders, who are integrated in high percentages in the regular education system (Weissblai, 2019). Aligning with the Polyphonic Wisdom Model that advocates a plurality of voices, the question arises as to how it is possible to respond to each unique voice in the class simultaneously and harmoniously with the teaching of the whole class? It follows that one of the greatest and most complex challenges in daily educational work is teaching in the heterogeneous class. At the same time, alongside the challenge there is also an opportunity—an opportunity to improve the teaching methods and learning means, while searching for creative solutions that will meet the needs of different learners (Barak-Medina, 2019).

So How Can One Handle the Heterogeneity in the Classroom?

The model proposed in this chapter relies on humanistic-collaborative pedagogy and offers a way to address the diversity of the students in a classroom through a differential response to each student, while utilizing the advantages of group work

E. Kotzer (✉)
Kibbutzim College of Education, Technology and Arts, Tel-Aviv, Israel
e-mail: Efrat.kotzer@smkb.ac.il

Y. Yondler et al. (eds.), *Cultivating Future-Oriented Learners*, Understanding Teaching-Learning Practice, https://doi.org/10.1007/978-3-031-63253-2_10

for cross-fertilization and exposure to different learning methods. This model was communicated as part of an annual course on learning disabilities and attention deficit hyperactivity disorder (ADHD). The course objectives are to expose the students to **theory** and current research in the field, to understand what learning disabilities are and what ADHD is, what underlies them, how it **feels** to live with them, and no less important, to equip the students with a **'toolbox'** that will assist them in teaching when they go out to the field. Aligning with the course objectives, the proposed model features a demonstration of connecting between theory (what—content), practice (how—teaching and learning strategies) and emotion (feelings following the activity, the motivation to carry it out), while emphasizing the importance of using a wide variety of teaching techniques, methods and means according to the **Universal Design for Learning**.

Before outlining the model, a few words about the **Universal Design for Learning (UDL)** approach. The concept of UDL was developed at the USA Center for Applied Special Technology (CAST) in the early 1990's (Hitchcock et al., 2002). Corresponding with the polyphonic approach advocating a plurality of voices and diversity among people, the UDL approach is based on the understanding that the human mind is different from one individual to another. Each of us learns differently and this variance is the norm, not the exception (Peretz, 2017). Therefore, there is no reason to expect that the same teaching and learning methods would fit all learners (Hall et al., 2012). The approach was born out of the world of architecture and assumes that the designed world is not suited for every person (Israeli Ministry of Education, Pedagogical Administration, 2015). A person in a wheelchair will only be able to go up if there is a ramp, but the same ramp also serves people with strollers, cargo carts, cyclists, and more. In the context of education, the corresponding premise is that different adaptations of teaching methods intended for students with certain difficulties may address many students in the class who learn optimally in diverse ways. According to the UDL approach, flexibility and diversity in teaching methods and learning means will help remove various learning barriers, making learning accessible and possible for all students in the class (Hitchcock et al., 2002; Israeli Ministry of Education, Pedagogical Administration, 2015). The UDL approach comprises three main principles (Hall et al., 2012). These principles are detailed in Fig. 1.

For more information about the UDL approach from the CAST website, scan the barcode

In recent years, the Universal Design for Learning has become a popular pedagogic tool among teachers across the world (Griful-Freixenet et al., 2021). The

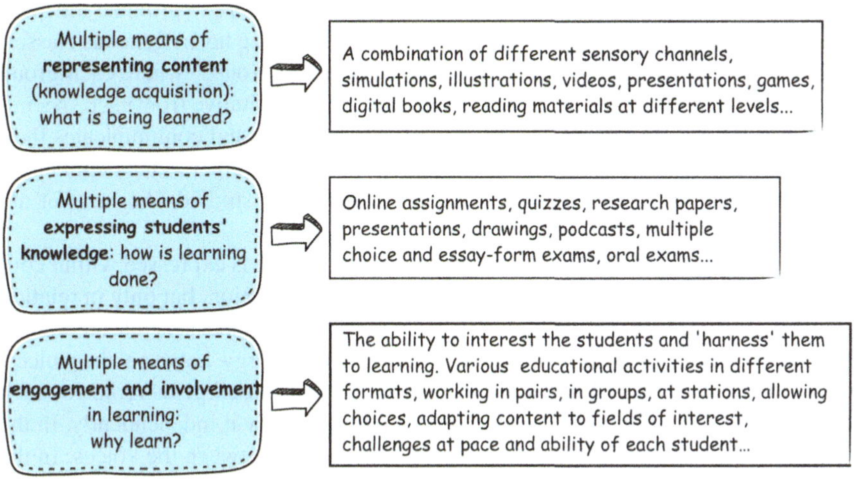

Fig. 1 Three main principles underlying the Universal Design approach to learning

growing number of students coming from different backgrounds and cultures, with and without disabilities, who study in the regular education system, increases the need for teachers to develop flexible lesson plans that will address the diverse learners in the classroom (Unluol Unal et al., 2020). In this context, it was found that even a short training focused on the principles of UDL helped teachers to develop more flexible and varied lesson plans (Lee & Griffin, 2021; Scott et al., 2019; Spooner et al., 2007) that met the needs of different learners with varied capabilities (Hitchcock et al., 2002). Moreover, the integration of technological tools in teaching allows for even greater flexibility in the development of learning materials and the diversification of learning environments (Hall et al., 2012; Hitchcock & Stahl, 2003).

Studies that examined the effectiveness of teaching according to the principles of UDL found an improvement in the learning process among all learners, including students with learning disabilities who are integrated into regular education (Dewi & Dalimunthe, 2019; King-Sears & Johnson, 2020). The students reported a reduction in stress and an increase in self-confidence and self-efficacy (He, 2014; Kumar & Widerman, 2014). Their interest in learning grew and so did the motivation to continue researching the topics learned (Davies et al., 2013). Beyond the improvement in learning ability, an improvement in teacher-student relations, cooperation and interaction between learners was also observed (Dewi & Dalimunthe, 2019).

Model Description: 'Learning How to Learn' in Light of the Universal Design for Learning Approach

The activity the model establishes is based on structured collaborative learning according to the Jigsaw method. The Jigsaw Method is based on the assembly game "jigsaw puzzle", in which the players assemble and put together different pieces to a complete picture. This method was developed out of a desire to promote independent learning of students and to answer the needs of teaching heterogeneous classes. According to it, the class is divided into 'specialization groups' where each group 'specializes' in a certain subject. In the next step, a representative from each specialization group joins a new group called the 'mother group' and communicates their topic to the other group members. The puzzle is thus put together as the members of the mother group are being introduced to all the topics studied (Aronson et al., 1978; Costouros, 2020).

According to the polyphonic wisdom model, difference is expressed within context, i.e.: the difference of a person is not expressed in isolation, but only in relation to others (Naot-Ofarim & Solomonic, 2016). Therefore, emphasis is placed both on each voice on its own and on the collectivity, the synergy between the voices. Accordingly, the Jigsaw Method on which the model is based gives room for each learner to choose the topic he wants to delve into and study it independently. In the next step the focus shifts to group learning, for synergy between the voices. In the last step each voice gets a stage, empowered and responsible to explain the part it was entrusted with. Each (voice) part of the puzzle plays a role! Without it the puzzle will not be complete. Moreover, the whole, in this case, is greater than the sum of its parts.

Working According to the Proposed Model Comprises Four Stages

Step 1: Independent Learning of the Chosen Topic by the Specialization Groups

At this step the study material is divided into topics. According to the number of topics, the students receive a collaborative file (Google Sheet) in which they are asked to place themselves in specialization groups (about 5–6 groups). This way they are given the ability to choose the topic and/or their teammates. Each group specializes in a certain topic. The students are asked to independently study the topic they have chosen thoroughly before the first meeting.

Step 2: Working in Specialization Groups—Processing the Material Using Thinking Maps (Visual Representation)

In the first meeting, each group is asked to prepare thinking maps that represent the main ideas (and the connections between them) of its topic. The students receive an outline of a collaborative presentation (Google Slides), into which each group uploads its maps. The material processing is done **from the general to the**

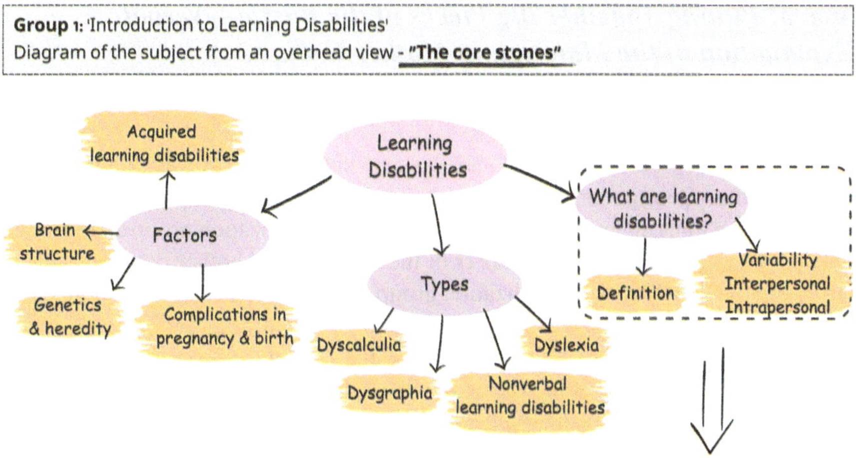

Fig. 2 'From the general to the particular'—examples of the mind maps built in step 2, **'The core stones'**

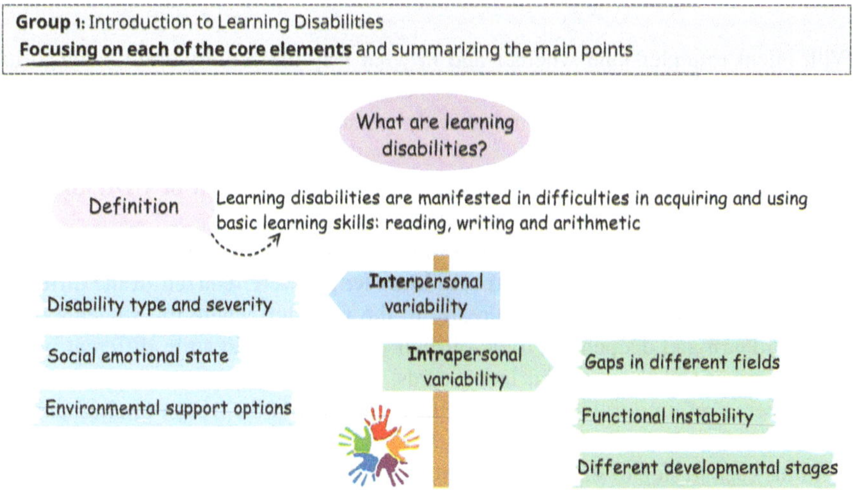

Fig. 3 'From the general to the particular'—examples of the mind maps built in step 2, **'The breakdown of each sub-topic'**

particular: an overview chart of the 'core stones' of the topic, followed by a clear and concise breakdown of each sub-topic within the thinking maps. See an example in Figs. 2 and 3. On the last slide, the students are asked to add 2–3 applied questions in a multiple-choice format addressing the topic. For the purpose of building the maps, it is recommended to use collaborative technological tools that allow continued work asynchronously after class, without time or place limitations. The students respond to each other in groups, so feedback and peer evaluation are carried out as well.

Step 3: Putting Together the Pieces of the Puzzle—Verbal Explanation of the Material, in Mother Groups, in a Peer-Teaching Format

At this step, a representative from each specialization group moves to a **heterogeneous Mother Group** that includes representatives from all groups. Each representative uses the thinking maps they have built in the specialization group and explains (orally) their sub-topic to the members of the new group. Another option is to have representatives from each specialization group explain their part to the whole class. Whether in groups or in plenary, the process of peer teaching and tutoring others results in higher levels of understanding of the material (Aronson et al., 1978; Costouros, 2020). At this point, the assembly of the puzzle takes place: the students receive a consecutive explanation of all the material, as well as the complete collaborative presentation that includes the thinking maps of all the groups.

Step 4: Reflection and Feedback at the End of the Activity

With intent to understand whether and in what way the activity contributed to its participants, a feedback conversation is held in the class at the end. Afterwards, students will be sent a link to provide personal (anonymous) feedback via Google Form.

As mentioned, the proposed model was built in the spirit of UDL and corresponds to the three principles underlining it:

The first two principles according to UDL, which refer to multiple means to represent the material and to express knowledge, were realized in the different steps of the model. For starters, already in the first step where the students were asked to learn and deepen the topic of their choice, they did so in different ways: some summarized the material using cards, some wrote important points on the side, others preferred to listen again to the recordings of the lesson or alternatively read the summaries.

In the second step of the model, the students are asked to use technological tools to represent the material through visual thinking maps. This strategy is an alternative to a verbal summary of the material, as a way of representing content and expressing knowledge. Moreover, they are given freedom of choice in everything related to the construction of the maps: they choose which platform to build them on (each group according to its convenience), whether to integrate photos, videos or different means of illustration, and whatever comes to their mind, with the help of their good imagination. Evidence of this can be seen in the creative and diverse products obtained from this activity. To this it should be added that writing multiple-choice questions on a subject is another way for learners to express their knowledge, as the very act of writing the questions and thinking about suitable distractions involves further processing of the material and requires a thorough understanding of it.

In the third stage of the model, the principles of UDL gain a new validity when another channel is added to the representation of material and the expression of knowledge—the auditory channel. In the process of peer teaching, the participants teach each other the material so those who prefer learning through hearing can benefit from its continuous elucidation and alternatively, those who need to 'photograph' the content and thus understand and remember it better can use the visual maps. Furthermore, it was found that many learners benefit from multi-channel learning. The combination between the visual and auditory channels promotes optimal learning, while improving the efficiency of perception, the processing of content and its assimilation into memory (Hillyard et al., 2016). Also in this context, it should be noted that throughout the activity, there is strict adherence to clear instructions presented in writing (visually) and orally (auditorily).

The third principle of UDL, which refers to multiple means of engaging and participating in learning, is already reflected in the first step of the model where learners are given the opportunity to choose the subject they want to delve into and/or their group mates. Furthermore, unlike a regular class in which relatively few students actually participate, in working according to the Jigsaw Method, everyone participates! Each of the participants play a part in completing the puzzle. In step 2, of building the maps, the students divided the work between them after class. In step 3, of oral explaining in mother groups, if for some reason one of the participants is missing, **a piece of the puzzle is missing and the picture is incomplete**: there is no one to teach the group the sub-topic on which he was entrusted. According to the third UDL principle, being aware of this and experiencing group responsibility also contribute to the 'harnessing' and the involvement of learners. On top of that, the additional circulation between the groups ('station rotation' practicing) also diversifies the learning with changing the composition of the groups and adds interest and motivation to participate in the activity.

The activity was held at the ending of the first semester as part of a course for first-year students, prior to their first exam period. At this stage, they still haven't had time to develop strategies for learning and summarizing the material and have not yet experienced exams at the academy. In this sense, it was held at the right time and in the right place. Moreover, it was based on the learning material that they had to study for the exam anyway and participation in it also included a grade reward; thus, the activity was relevant for the participants and served a current need, which increased the motivation to perform it.

Hybrid Space

The proposed model is an example of hybrid learning in different spaces: physical and digital, synchronous and asynchronous. First, it can be implemented in synchronous teaching, both in the classroom and via online Zoom meetings (See Figs. 4 and 5). It was first delivered face to face in one of the Kibbutzim College 'future classrooms'. These classrooms are relatively large and equipped with many screens that enable work in small groups, as well as caster chairs that facilitate easy and

Fig. 4 The activity in face-to-face format

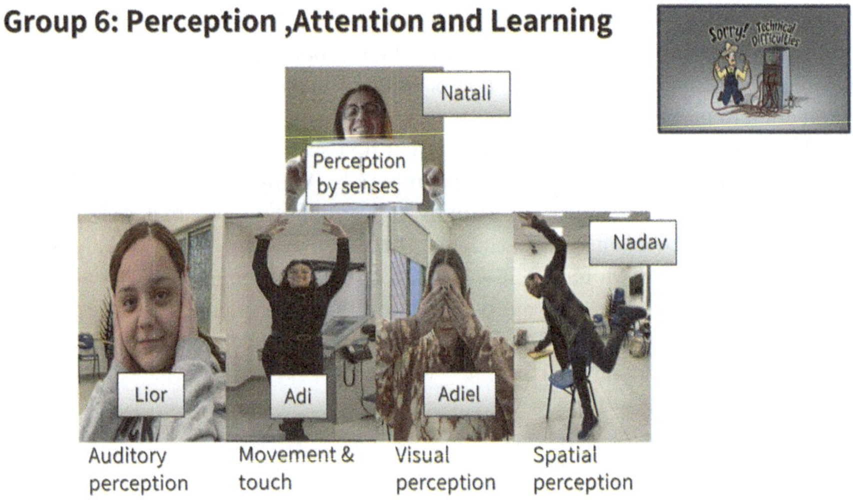

Fig. 5 The activity in online zoom format

quick mobility in the room space. However, one of the disadvantages that accompanied group work in the classroom was the noise that disturbed some of the learners and especially those with ADHD, who have difficulties concentrating in noisy situations. A solution to this issue was actually found in the online format. During the work in Zoom's breakout rooms each group worked alone, in its own room—which neutralized background noises coming from the other groups. Finally, the asynchronous part of the model was reflected in continuing the work on the thinking maps online after class—both by the students who responded to each other and by the lecturer. The lecturer throughout the activity functions as a guide: his role is to review the products, listen to the explanations, and if necessary to clarify things, direct, reassure, remind, and highlight. The activity thus includes a formative assessment, both on the part of the group mates and on the part of the lecturer. This way, the learners are the producers of knowledge and as such they are required to think critically. Moreover, they actively build their personal knowledge, and at the same time they build collective knowledge through teamwork and collaboration.

Another added value of the model is reflected in the combination of skills with areas of knowledge and in the practice of skills essential for optimal coping in the twenty-first century:

One of the most significant gifts that can be given to all students, and in particular to students with ADHD and learning disabilities, is 'how-to-learn' strategies. One can go a step further and combine the learning of skills (learning strategies) with areas of knowledge that the students currently study (Levi-Shimon, 2015). This way we gain twice: a more significant processing of the learning material and "deep learning"—the ability to transfer what we learned in a certain situation and apply it in another, new situation (National Research Council, 2012). After several times a child implements a certain strategy and understands in what way it helps him, it is likely to be assimilated into his toolbox and applied in other situations and areas of knowledge. The current activity is based on this concept. **The combination of knowledge and skills is part of the twenty-first century skillset**. Further to this and as an added value, the model comprises skills that will help learners face the demands of the twenty-first century: **executive functions** (mental flexibility, planning, order and organization, monitoring; Jurado & Rosselli, 2007) are thus required for separating the wheat from the chaff and organizing the mind maps, as well as for **standing in front of an audience**, while organizing the verbal message in a coherent and clear manner. In this respect, the students gained a kind of a 'dry run' experience, standing in front of a sympathetic audience; an important skill (especially for preservice teachers) that was made possible by group work and strengthened their sense of competence. Also, **independent work** is required to repeat the material on the one hand, and on the other, **teamwork, communication and cooperation** to work in groups and assemble all the puzzle pieces into one whole. **Critical thinking** is necessary for peer evaluation as well as for self-monitoring during the map making. Since several technological tools are used, **digital literacy** is also required to become familiar with the tools and use them. Finally, the ability to **reflect** and understand to what extent and in which ways the activity has contributed to each one—is also part of the twenty-first century skillset. The integration between independent and active learner (the humanistic educational approach) together with social interactions (co-agency) meets what is required from a learner to operate successfully in a global world in the twenty-first century.

In conclusion, the learning process according to the proposed model, in all steps, is done through **experimentation and experience**. The diverse learning strategies proposed in the model (summarizing and organizing the material in thinking maps, group learning, verbal explanation of the material) as well as the diverse teaching methods through which they are taught (collaborative work and peer teaching based on the Jigsaw Method, formative assessment, combination of synchronous and asynchronous activity, and integration of technology in a hybrid space (both face-to-face and online), are in harmony with the Polyphonic Wisdom model and with the UDL approach, which variability in teaching and learning methods is one of its cornerstones.

The described model can be applied within different areas of knowledge. It was originally developed for students in higher education institutions, but it is also suitable for teachers in regular schools and in particular for teachers whose classes include students with attention and learning disorders. Likewise, special education teachers will benefit from it as well. As added value, the model is a fertile ground for developing skills necessary for optimal functioning in the twenty-first century and it goes hand in hand with the principles of humanistic-collaborative pedagogy, as detailed in the next chapter.

Polyphonic Wisdom is the ability of a teacher to create an empowering synergy between the four components: space, pedagogy, technology and content, while promoting the values of humanism and collaboration. This section reviews how the proposed model corresponds with these principles. Figure 6 presented above visually summarizes the elements of polyphonic wisdom, at the base of the model, as a compass for designing a learning environment.

First, besides the stated goal of imparting strategies for effective learning, another goal of the activity is to promote **independent and collaborative learning in the online space**, while **cultivating self-efficacy** of learners as providers of knowledge. The teacher, in this teaching model, takes a guiding position and does not operate as the exclusive knowledge transmitter; he provides the initial framework and direction, but the **responsibility** for organizing, processing and delivering the knowledge lies with the learners! These characteristics are the **basis of humanistic pedagogy**. Further to this, as described in detail above, the model is based on the UDL approach which places the **student at the center**, while allowing room for interpersonal variation and diverse learning styles. Everyone can find in it the **differential solution** that suits them, **both in terms of content representation and knowledge expression (the first two principles of UDL).** The students were provided a structured framework through which they built and expressed their knowledge **independently** and collaboratively, while socially constructing collective knowledge. In addition, during the group sessions they discovered different study methods of their group mates. This exposure has also enriched the variety of learning strategies accessible to them. Moreover, in learning by the Jigsaw Method, **everyone** takes an **active part** in the process, as everyone has an essential role in completing the puzzle—the final product. Active learning has been found to lead to significant improvements in the academic achievements and motivation of all learners (Freeman et al., 2014) and in particular of learners with attention and learning disorders (Minskoff & Allsopp, 2003). Active learning in different formats, personal and group responsibility, encouraging creativity along with choice and a grade reward—all together assisted

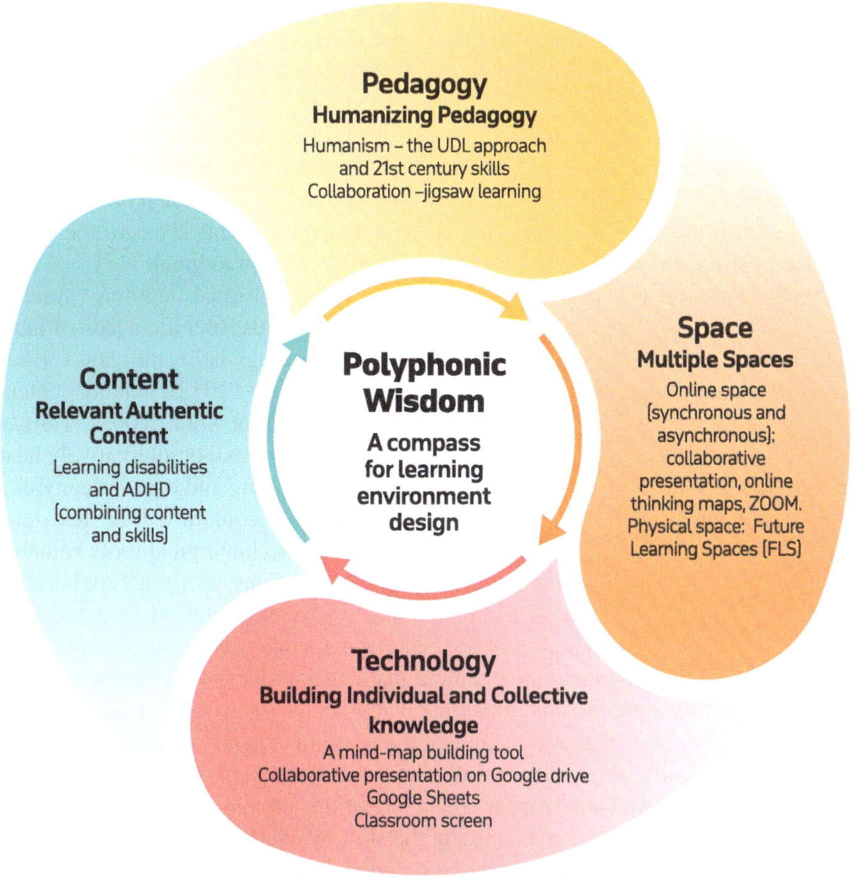

Fig. 6 Polyphonic Wisdom as a compass for designing a learning environment: multi-spatiality, technology, pedagogy, and content in the light of humanism and collaboration

in 'mobilizing' the learners and engaging them in learning—in congruence with the third UDL principle and the principles of humanistic pedagogy. Furthermore, at the end of the process the participants were given an opportunity to **speak up** and evaluate if and how they have benefited from the activity, via two types of feedback: an open discussion in class and an anonymous Google Form.

Likewise, **cooperation** is a major key factor in the activity: the Jigsaw Method itself is based on collaborative work in specialized groups and heterogeneous mother groups. Each individual contributes to his group and each group contributes to the complete, class product. The whole is thus greater than the sum of its parts. According to the Polyphonic Wisdom model, each voice is a whole and contributes to the group synergy. Similarly, group work drives **cross-fertilization**. For example, a student who is knowledgeable in a certain subject can contribute to another student who may be less knowledgeable in that subject. The use of **collaborative technological tools** (i.e. Google Slides, Cacoo mind maps) enables **active collaborative**

learning unlimited by time and place, for continuing the work after class. Each contributed their share on their free time and each could see what the other was doing. Working with the collaborative tools promoted **collaborative knowledge construction within a continuous dialogue**, during which the group members responded to and reviewed each other, exercising judgment and critical thinking. Alongside that there was also a dialogue with the lecturer in the process of formative assessment. The comments could be viewed online to correct and modify by, in order to refine the final product. Just as importantly, the students also saw the praise and the positive and reinforcing responses that were written to them.

Technology is a complementary factor in the universal learning system. Supporting the principles of humanism, it is set to meet the specific needs of individuals, to allow them to express their abilities. Technology helps mitigate various learning barriers and opens ways to bypass them (Hall et al., 2012), making content and activities accessible to different learners (Hitchcock & Stahl, 2003). Thus, a child who has difficulty reading can enlarge and space the text, or alternatively hear the content; a child who has difficulty writing can use typing and even voice typing or alternatively summarize content in mind maps that contain a little text, etc. Following the above, the outlined model used several technological tools valuable in the context of collaborative-humanistic pedagogy. Thus, using a collaborative **google sheet** allowed students to choose the topic they preferred to delve into, divide tasks between them and see who their group members are. Today's age where everyone has a smartphone with a camera made it possible to ask the members of each group to take a picture and immediately upload it to the collaborative presentation—which enhanced the enjoyment and the sense of group belonging.

More specifically, the **online mind maps** were a means of implementing the learned strategy: they offered visual organizing of the learning material in a friendly and simplified way, as well as practicing the skill of separating the wheat from the chaff (since there is only room in the diagrams for the gist—key words or a main statement). **Google Slides** made it possible to upload an outline of a collaborative presentation that provided a structured, organized framework for all the groups. This collaborative presentation slowly took shape and eventually included an accurate recap of all the material and had become a significant aid in preparing for the exam. Last but not least, the synchronous format in the classroom had also applied **Classroom Screen**—a lesson management tool for structuring an activity: setting schedules and work format. The explicit and structured workflow reduced ambiguity and helped conduct during the activity for all students and especially for students with ADHD, so even if they experienced lapses of attention during the lesson, the visual anchor of the classroom board helped them find their place in the lesson.

Finally, and as added value, working by the proposed model also included exercising skills essential for optimal performing in the twenty-first century. In the spirit of humanism, in the era we live in, the cultivation of these skills among students is known to be of great importance to empower them and prepare them for their adult lives (Aloni, 2020; National Research Council, 2012). In line with this, the proposed model features practicing of executive skills (planning, organization, mental flexibility, monitoring, taking the wheat from the chaff and reflection). twenty-first century skillset goes hand in hand with collaborative pedagogy, while also including teamwork, communication and cooperation. The ability to integrate technological tools and make appropriate use of them requires an additional skill of digital literacy (Larson, & Miller, 2011).

A Theoretical and Practical Contribution of the Teaching Model

The proposed model has several pedagogical objectives, both on theoretical and practical levels. First, the model is based on Polyphonic Wisdom and the UDL approach and exercises important skills required for optimal functioning in the twenty-first century, in the spirit of humanism and cooperation. The model was delivered as part of a course dealing with learning disabilities and attention deficit disorder. Throughout the course, emphasis was placed on the importance of combining theory (learning material) with practice (tools, learning skills). The teaching model was developed in congruence with this, offering a variety of ways to engage with the learning process thus addressing the diversity existing in the education system and opening doors for different learners: it includes learning activities in different forms (visual maps, oral explanations), in different platforms (face-to-face and online teaching, synchronous and asynchronous) using different teaching techniques (self and group learning, formative assessment, peer assessment, station rotation) and appropriate technological tools. Teaching according to the proposed model is expected to improve the efficiency of information processing and its assimilation into memory for all students. Beyond that, the model is generic and can be applied in different areas of knowledge and at different ages.

Since these are preservice teachers, the benefits of the proposed activity are manifested in two hats: the student's hat and the future teacher's hat. The students not only **learned about** the UDL approach and the importance of combining knowledge and skills as teaching techniques, but also **experienced them** in practice themselves. The personal experience and the sense of utility resulting from the activity are highly important in terms of its likelihood of being implemented in the future. We usually make use of something that we ourselves have benefited from. Moreover, through experience, the connection between what is learned in theory and its application in practice is reinforced. The preservice teachers who underwent the activity felt the sense of usefulness and enjoyment from the final product they have produced. The experience of success at the end of the activity and the satisfaction of the joint creation establish the emotional connection in our triangle. In addition, the activity illustrated to the students how important are the planning, diversifying and adjustments that we as teachers apply in class, for all students and for students with ADHD and learning disabilities, in particular. For these students, teaching according to the proposed principles often opens a door to the learning circle, which was otherwise closed to them (Rao et al., 2014). Through explicit meta-cognitive teaching, the students understood the principles behind each step of the activity they underwent and made the connection between theory, practice and emotion. This connection will serve them in the future in building further teaching models and lesson plans, adapted to the needs of different learners.

Important Practical Recommendations

Below are some important tips that may contribute to the successful implementation of this specific model and other models similar to it.

1. **Clear and targeted instructions**: What helped successful collaborative work was clear instructions, given in writing and orally, and a defined time frame for completing the activity. Everyone knew what they had to do and what the schedules were.
2. **Preparation in advance**: Since this is an activity that requires preparation in advance, it should be announced ahead of time so the participants can prepare in terms of their schedules and not stress at the last minute.
3. **Incentives**: the activity should be weighed in the final grade. This activity accounted for 10% of the annual grade—which enhanced the motivation to perform it well.
4. **Acquittance with the digital tools**: the participants should be given time to become familiar with the digital tools before working with them so that the technical tinkering does not take up unnecessary time and become an obstacle.
5. **Face-to-face format**: if you do the activity face-to-face in class, it is better that during the oral explanation phase, the presentations will be delivered in the class forum and not in groups. This way, a representative from each specialization group will indeed present only part of the subject and not all of it, but the noises caused by talking at the same time will be avoided.

Finally, **on a personal note**, as a lecturer, I gained much satisfaction and gratification from the students, the seriousness they worked with and the depth they have reached. They put thought, were creative, took seriously all aspects of the activity. Moreover, their feedback indicated that they have even enjoyed and benefited from the process and not only from the outcome (product). For me, too, the pieces of the puzzle connected in some way, as the triple rationale of theory-practice-emotion took shape. The highlight for me was when I moved between the groups as a bystander and heard them explain the material in their own words. It was an amazing feeling of contentment!

A 'quote tasting' from the feedback:

- 'I think this is an amazing idea. Helps and improves learning for the exam, sets things in order and focuses on the important things for those who have attention disorders like mine.'
- 'Until today I have not found a method that will help me study appropriately for exams. The order and organization created by the graphs helped me to sort each topic and its subtopics in my head.'

- 'The diversity between the students allowed each one to take the lead in the field they are strong at; to benefit to, and to benefit from where they have difficulty.'
- The collaboration contributed to the creation of a complete piece and gave everyone a place to express themselves and enriched the basic level of understanding of the material, that we had to communicate to the other classmates.
- 'This way of learning can be applied in any content area.'

References

Aloni, N. (2020). *The skills of the 21st century are functional skills, but no less principled orientation, critical awareness and social activism*. The Kibbutzim Seminar—College of Education and Arts, Institute for Advanced Education, UNESCO Chair for Humanistic Education. (in Hebrew).

Aronson, E., Stephen, C., Sikes, J., Blaney, N., & Snapp, M. (1978). *The jigsaw classroom*. Sage.

Barak-Medina, A. (2019). *Heterogeneous education—How to do excellent education in a reality of diversity?* Ministry of Education, Pedagogical Administration, R&D Division, Experiments and Initiatives, Primary Education Division. (in Hebrew).

Costouros, T. (2020). Jigsaw cooperative learning versus traditional lectures: Impact on student grades and learning experience. *Teaching & Learning Inquiry, 8*(1), 154–172. https://doi.org/10.20343/teachlearninqu.8.1.11

Davies, P. L., Schelly, C. L., & Spooner, C. L. (2013). Measuring the effectiveness of universal design for learning intervention in postsecondary education. *Journal of Postsecondary Education and Disability, 26*(3), 195–220.

Dewi, S. S., & Dalimunthe, H. A. (2019). The effectiveness of universal design for learning. *Journal of Social Science Studies, 6*(1), 112–123.

Freeman, S., Eddy, S. L., McDonough, M., Smith, M. K., Okoroafor, N., Jordt, H., & Wenderoth, M. P. (2014). Active learning increases student performance in science, engineering, and mathematics. *Proceedings of the National Academy of Sciences, 111*, 8410–8415.

Griful-Freixenet, J., Struyven, K., & Vantieghem, W. (2021). Toward more inclusive education: an empirical test of the universal design for learning conceptual model among preservice teachers. *Journal of Teacher Education, 72*(3), 381–395.

Hall, T. E., Meyer, A., & Rose, D. H. (Eds.). (2012). *Universal design for learning in the classroom: Practical applications*. Guilford Press.

He, Y. (2014). Universal design for learning in an online teacher education course: Enhancing learners' confidence to teach online. *MERLOT Journal of Online Learning and Teaching, 10*(2), 283–298.

Hillyard, S. A., Störmer, V. S., Feng, W., Martinez, A., & McDonald, J. J. (2016). Cross-modal orienting of visual attention. *Neuropsychologia, 83*, 170–178.

Hitchcock, C., & Stahl, S. (2003). Assistive technology, universal design, universal design for learning: Improved learning opportunities. *Journal of Special Education Technology, 18*(4), 45–52.

Hitchcock, C., Meyer, A., Rose, D., & Jackson, R. (2002). Providing new access to the general curriculum: Universal design for learning. *Teaching Exceptional Children, 35*(2), 8–17.

Jurado, M. B., & Rosselli, M. (2007). The elusive nature of executive functions: a review of our current understanding. *Neuropsychology Review, 17*(3), 213–233.

King-Sears, M. E., & Johnson, T. M. (2020). Universal design for learning chemistry instruction for students with and without learning disabilities. *Remedial and Special Education, 41*(4), 207–218.

Kumar, K. L., & Wideman, M. (2014). Accessible by design: Applying UDL principles in a first year undergraduate course. *Canadian Journal of Higher Education, 44*(1), 125–147.

Larson, L. C., & Miller, T. N. (2011). 21st century skills: Prepare students for the future. *Kappa Delta Pi Record, 47*(3), 121–123.

Lee, A., & Griffin, C. C. (2021). Exploring online learning modules for teaching universal design for learning (UDL): Preservice teachers' lesson plan development and implementation [Article]. *Journal of Education for Teaching, 47*(3), 411–425. https://doi.org/10.1080/02607476.2021.1884494

Levy-Shimon, S. (2015). *Overlap: The art of teaching classes that integrate students with difficulties and learning disabilities overlapping with areas of knowledge. Ministry of Education and Culture.* The psychological advisory service. The unit for learning disabilities. (in Hebrew).

Ministry of Education, Pedagogical Administration. (2015). *Universal design for learning*, in: Inclusion in fact—Newsletter for inclusion guides, bulletin number 3, the Division of Elementary Education. (in Hebrew).

Minskoff, E., & Allsopp, D. (2003). *Academic success strategies for adolescents with learning disabilities and ADHD* (pp. 21285–20624). Brookes Publishing Co.

Naot-Ofarim, Y., & Solomonic, S. (2016). Educational polyphony. *Studies in Philosophy and Education, 35*(4), 385–397.

National Research Council. (2012). *Education for life and work: Developing transferable knowledge and skills in the 21st century.* The National Academies Press. https://doi.org/10.17226/13398

Peretz, H. (2017). *Universal design for learning—UDL.* Beit Izzi Shapira. (in Hebrew).

Rao, K., Ok, M. W., & Bryant, B. R. (2014). A review of research on universal design educational models. *Remedial and Special Education, 35*(3), 153–166.

Scott, L., Bruno, L., Gokita, T., & Thoma, C. A. (2019). Teacher candidates' abilities to develop universal design for learning and universal design for transition lesson plans. *International Journal of Inclusive Education, 26*, 1–15. https://doi.org/10.1080/13603116.2019.1651910

Spooner, F., Baker, J. N., Harris, A. A., Ahlgrim-Delzell, L., & Browder, D. M. (2007). Effects of training in universal design for learning on lesson plan development. *Remedial and Special Education, 28*(2), 108–116.

Unluol Unal, N., Karal, M. A., & Tan, S. (2020). Developing accessible lesson plans with universal design for learning (UDL). *International Journal of Disability, Development and Education, 69*, 1–15. https://doi.org/10.1080/1034912X.2020.1812539

Weissblai, A. (2019). *The special education system.* The Knesset Research and Information Center. (in Hebrew).

The Challenge: How to Preserve the Human Values Embedded in a Pedagogical Course During the Transition from the Physical Environment to the Online Environment

Adva Margaliot and Dvora Gorev

Background

The instructional model described in this chapter reflects a collaborative online pedagogical course, the result of over a decade of thought and development. The pedagogical course was carefully designed; we experimented with its teaching, explored the instruction/learning, and the evaluation that took place during its course, continuously improving it. Its inception marked a transition from frontal teaching to distance learning, which occurred in the winter of 2008 during Operation "Cast Lead". At that time, the teaching staff at Achva Academic College received guidance to continue and teach remotely due to the security situation that required the suspension of frontal studies. The intention of transferring the course to the online space so that learning could continue from the same place where it was stopped, was communicated to the students through a shared email. The response letters from the students, including some who were under significant missile attacks, expressed an inability to continue their learning. This prompted each of us to act in accordance with the values of our humanity. These include dialogue, collaboration, mutual assistance, addressing events, adjusting activities and learning to events, listening to students, and building an engaged and supportive learning community.

The research we conducted on the discourse that accumulated on the online learning platforms revealed that both discourse and learning were successful, and a strong camaraderie was formed among the learning partners. In the process of the online course construction which aimed at promoting collaborative learning in online environments, we sought ideas and methods that would guide course participants to create mutual sharing among themselves. This was done after realizing that collaboration, which naturally occurs in a physical classroom, is challenging in

---

A. Margaliot · D. Gorev (✉)
Achva Academic College, Arugot, Israel
e-mail: adva.margaliot@live.achva.ac.il

Y. Yondler et al. (eds.), *Cultivating Future-Oriented Learners*, Understanding Teaching-Learning Practice, https://doi.org/10.1007/978-3-031-63253-2_11

online environments. The reason for this is that in these environments, each of the learning participants is secluded in their own home in front of their personal computer. In this situation, collaborative learning does not naturally occur as it would otherwise happen in face-to-face encounters.

From our initial experience with online teaching, we realized that its added value lies in its lack of limitations of space and time, allowing it to be carried out independently of physical constraints. Due to anticipation of further crises, it is evident that online learning is here to stay. The pedagogical challenge we faced was to construct a teaching model in virtual environments that incorporates the human values guiding our work.

From this perspective, we approached the planning of an online pedagogical course. Human values include recognition of the importance of a learning group also in the online space, so that group members are familiar with each other and can take responsibility for advancing learning. This responsibility implies that they can be partners in the processes of knowledge construction, building skills while supporting personal and professional development. These processes include developing the ability to identify the strengths of group members so that during the collaborative knowledge-building, each expresses their abilities and worldview, giving space and value to different positions and recognizing their importance.

During the collaborative work, challenges arise that require a renewed definition of the instructor's role, who builds the course according to a polyphonic wisdom and promotes the learning processes taking place in it. In order to construct a course whose conduct aligns with these values; we relied on the theory of Online Collaborative Learning (OCL) as a foundation for building learning tasks in the course. A special emphasis was placed on the dynamics of online dialogue that took place during the execution of learning tasks between the instructor and the students, as well as among the students themselves.

Course Model: From Cooperative to Collaboration Learning in an Online Pedagogical Course

The teaching practice of OCL refers to an instructional model that emphasizes collaborative discourse and knowledge construction through technology. This practice is conducive to creating proactive communication that leads to collaborative outcomes. According to this model, learners work together to define and promote a shared understanding of topics, analyze concepts, solve problems, and articulate explanations on a phenomenon (Fu & Hwang, 2018; Harasim, 2002, 2012; Scardamalia & Bereiter, 2006; Shonfeld & Weinberger, 2018). Collaborative learning is guided by an educator and is based on online texts and discourse (Scardamalia & Bereiter, 2006).

The course is structured as a sequence of tasks that involve a transition from individual sharing to collaborative activities (see in Fig. 1). Lotan (2011)

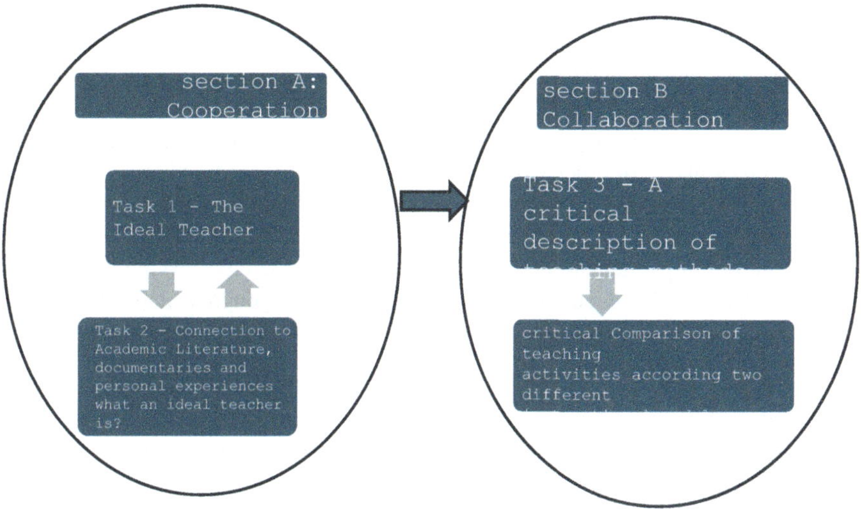

Fig. 1 Course structure

distinguishes between cooperative learning and collaborative learning, where cooperation involves individuals sharing their knowledge without interdependent actions, meaning separate actions that lead to a shared outcome (such as building a shared database). Whereas collaboration represents a collection of actions performed collaboratively during the process, leading to a shared outcome.

The rationale for planning an online course based on a gradual process of collaboration and partnership arises from the professional need to set and achieve multiple goals simultaneously: deepening familiarity with various teaching models, providing students with the opportunity to experiment with collaborative online learning, and acquainting them with future teaching suitable for the evolving nature of work in the twenty-first century.

The course took place on the Moodle platform, mostly asynchronously. During the course, participants were required to complete four major tasks. Two collaborative tasks involved each participant uploading content to the course website according to instructions (as detailed below) and sharing their work in a collaborative forum and a database. Afterward, participants were divided into groups and collectively created collaborative documents while the online learning discourse took place. The collaborative document prepared in the third task was exposed to other participants and served as part of the learning content required for the fourth task. Grades for the first two tasks given individually while for last two tasks, grades were given based on both individual contributions and the quality of collaborative outcomes.

Humanistic education refers to the holistic approach to the individual. As instructors that embody the values of humanistic education, we based the learning and teaching processes in the course on the following principles: personal growth, relevance, autonomy, interpersonal closeness, diversity, creativity, dialogue, and partnership (Darom, 2005). Another principle that guided us was the principle of innovation derived from the transition to learning in the digital environment, while respecting the personal voice of each learner when addressing relevant content. In reality, the course was designed to create synergy between the digital learning environment, the values guiding humanistic learning, and the pedagogy through which learning takes place. In other words, we sought to maintain the humanistic values that guided the pedagogical courses we conducted in the physical environment when transitioning to digital learning. These are constructed and manifested throughout the implementation of online course tasks while preserving the leading values of the course content, as well as the processes through which the learning outcomes are constructed and evaluated.

Task One: Online Familiarization with the Content Area and Participants

In the first task, which serves as the foundation for the course's context, the instructor introduced herself in the forum and described a meaningful experience with a teacher who left a significant impression on her. Course participants were then asked to do the same. This task, fostering interpersonal connection, was conducted in an asynchronous online forum. The connection to a meaningful learning experience is intended to ignite the learning process so that despite being primarily asynchronous, participants can engage with the course content from a personal, authentic, and sometimes emotional perspective. This is done to ensure that the handling of the course materials in the following tasks is based on an understanding of the personal significance to the participants and the connection between their professional choice and personal experiences.

Task Two: Developing Active Dialogue in Online Communication

The second task initiates a dialogue among learners, as each student is required to read two articles on the topic of significant teaching or learning. They are then asked to upload a successful teaching tip to a shared table in the course forum (one that has not been previously uploaded by another participant). Following this, participants are instructed to "like" one of the tips uploaded to the course website. In the next stage, they are invited to upload a segment from a movie relevant to one of the tips on the website and explain the connection between the tip and the chosen movie segment. Additionally, they are asked to relate the chosen movie segment to one of the descriptions of meaningful teacher-student learning experiences shared in the first task. The humanistic values embedded here include relevance, autonomy, and choice in both the selection of movie segments and the connection to responses provided by other participants in both tasks. This task involves a cooperation, deepening the familiarity process among participants. The use of technology begins with the uploading of two articles to the course forum. The requirement to write a successful teaching tip necessitates reading the articles and focusing on one meaningful tip among them. Furthermore, participants are instructed not to repeat tips that had already been given and as such, participants are required to read the materials uploaded by other participants to the forum. The requirement to "like" one of the tips encourages positive acknowledgment of contributions from other participants, recognizing their importance as resources that can be utilized as guides.

The subsequent part, which involves connecting a segment from a movie about teachers to one participant's tip, demanded technological knowledge in addition to metacognitive skills. Participants had to identify the relevant segment from the movie, edit it, upload it to the database being built on the website, and specify the connection to it. This task appears to be a personal task, but it requires the ability to deeply understand the meaning behind the tip provided by another participant. A meta-cognitive ability is also needed at this stage in order to connect a specific movie segment to the chosen tip and to describe a link between the selected movie segment and a participant's description of a significant learning experience with an educational figure. This connection also demanded a thorough understanding of the experience through empathy for the shared description and an attempt to identify an experience (usually emotional) to which the student connected. The ability to find meaningful connections between the movie, personal experiences, and tips for future teaching involves openness, identification with the experience, and the discovery of personal relevance.

The following two tasks are collaborative tasks. The pedagogy of collaborative online learning is aimed at creating perceptual change in learners. In the first stage, learners generate ideas; in the next stage, they organize them, and finally, they converge to formulate a focused statement (Harasim, 2012). The creation of a shared language among group participants is required so that they can express divergent opinions and emotions arising during learning, towards the attainment of shared agreements. The humanistic values included in the third task encompass autonomy, relevance, and strengthening the relationship among learning partners, while managing online discourse necessary for preparing the collaborative output required in this task. Harasim (2012) emphasizes the central role of the instructor as a link between learners and the knowledge community in the field. According to her, learning activities need to be well-defined and guided by the norms of the discipline, as well as by managing discourse that promotes learning and encourages knowledge construction.

Stage Three: Building a Collaborative Product Through Online Critical Discourse

The third task designed in accordance with the pedagogy of OCL. participants were asked to form groups on the course website and choose one of the following instructional models: frontal instruction, extracurricular instruction, lab-based instruction, instruction through class discussions, group work-based instruction, instruction through games, and instruction integrating digital tools. They were asked to create a collaborative academic product presenting the instructional model and the pedagogical principles it is based on, with a critical analysis of the model's advantages and disadvantages. The groups uploaded their products to the course website. The course website included the option to enroll in a learning group, and each participant registered to their chosen group. Subsequently, a forum was opened for each group.

Participants were required to conduct the online discourse accompanying the product preparation, and upon completing the preparation process, they were asked to upload the collaborative document as an assignment. Concurrently, they were also required to upload this document to a database. The document uploaded as an assignment was reviewed by the instructor, and a grade was given. That document also uploaded to the database and served the other groups in preparing the fourth task.

The instructor facilitated and guided the process of collaborative learning through the task structures, and by focusing on communication between herself and the students, as well as among the students themselves. We chose to manage the dynamics of online discourse in the manner described by Xin and Feenberg (2006). They emphasize the importance of the lecturer as a forum moderator in mediating and managing communication among participants, outlining the instructor's roles in three areas:

(a) *Context Building:* The instructor is responsible for initiating discussions with stimulating topics, establishing communication norms, providing explicit guidelines for collaborative discourse, setting examples through personal experiences, determining communication content and learning topics, and referring to relevant learning materials.
(b) *Monitoring:* The lecturer, as the discussion manager, should directly address participants, respond to their comments, promote constructive contributions, and correct where necessary. The lecturer should seek feedback from individual participants or the entire group and acknowledge participants' achievements.
(c) *Management:* The lecturer should provide "meta-comments", summarize the discussion's status, identify threads connecting participants' contributions, and delegate some responsibilities to group members. Referencing to participants' statements can inspire them to explore directions that advance the conversation's goals.

In addition to managing learning in the online course, Robinson et al. (2017), highlight the need to develop teaching approaches that incorporate effective online communication. Their research emphasizes that caring (for others) forms the basis for collaborative learning support. They found that for successful online collaborative learning to occur, time should be given for building relationships using user-friendly interfaces for meticulous instructional planning. It is highlighted that emotional and social experiences influence students, emphasizing the importance of learning how to integrate them effectively (Darling-Hammond et al., 2019).

Stage Four: Creating Learning Activities as Synergy Between Humanistic Values, Technology, Pedagogy, and Content Knowledge

The fourth task took place in the same groups that were engaged in the third task. They were asked to create two instructional activities using two different instructional models of which one was taken from another group, created in the previous task. Subsequently, they were required to conduct a critical comparison between the activities they prepared based on jointly formulated comparison criteria. A synergy occurred in this task between humanistic values, technology, pedagogy, and the content area. The leading humanistic values were personal growth, motivation and effective learning, relevance, autonomy, creativity, innovation, and collaboration. These were achieved through the freedom given to groups to familiarize themselves with the writing products of other groups and use them as part of the course content itself. This was done while leading the creation of new collaborative documents and choosing relevant learning activities for them. In this fourth task, participants were able to recognize the reason for the nature of learning and the understanding that there is a real contribution for them when they will be teachers in online environments in the future.

As such, the course structure according to the sequence of tasks, can be seen as a process of the development of collaborative learning. A learning that began with initial acquaintance, progressed through a personal experience of meaningful learning to familiarization with theoretical definitions of meaningful learning from articles, and developed into a deep theoretical and practical understanding of various and diverse instructional models. Learning in the course required participants to move from individual learning to collaborative learning and from there to collaborative academic writing according to standards set by the instructor. This process required groups to organize for collaborative work under time constraints while maintaining a level of appropriate academic learning and discourse, as the instructor who managed the course was involved in preparing the tasks and, when learning did not progress, took care to advance it and create a connection between students while responding sensitively and empathetically to difficulties that arose in the writing process.

Course Development According to the Research Model

This instructional model was initially implemented in the academic year 2013–2014. During this year, evaluation research of the instruction in the course was conducted (Margaliot, 2018). The evaluation framework of Pozzi and colleagues (Pozzi et al. 2007) was used for the assessment. This framework was selected because it focuses on evaluating knowledge-building processes based on online group discussions. The social and cognitive processes involved in learning were evaluated according to five dimensions: (1) participation, (2) interaction, (3) sociability, (4) cognition and metacognition, and (5) instruction.

In the research by Margaliot (2018), it was found that there is a need to involve course participants in the pedagogical rationale that led to the development of a model based on collaborative online learning. This is explained through an overview of the learning process in the course and how the learning model is adapted to the challenges of online collaboration. An additional conclusion from the research was that a synchronous meeting should be added, during which the principles of OCL, will be presented to students along with the reason for choosing this instructional model as the one that will guide learning throughout the course. This model is based on students taking responsibility for their learning so they can experience the process of building academic-pedagogical knowledge. A synchronous meeting will emphasize not only the connection between collaborative and cooperative learning and the skills required in the twenty-first century but also the way grades are given in the course. Namely, grades are derived from the evaluation of the collaborative output and the individual contribution to building this output, as reflected in the collaborative discourse that took place in the forum.

There is a need to address the emotional dimension that arises from the transition to online learning. Therefore, it was decided to add a number of synchronous meetings throughout the course designed to address students' concerns regarding the grading process and the collaborative task-writing process. Additional improvements included enhancing the accuracy of the instructions guiding the learning tasks in the course and improving the visual presentation of the learning platform where the course took place.

Theoretical and Practical Contributions Concerning Challenges in the Course

Course Design

In the process of creating a synergistic learning experience that integrates humanistic values, technological environment, pedagogy, and course content, there is a need for meticulous course planning. The course construction process begins with creating the context in which learning takes place. This involves designing tasks that allow learners to operate autonomously and choose the content they engage with. Familiarity with technological tools suitable for collaborative online learning is required to tailor them to the tasks.

A clear structure for the course website and the progression of learning throughout the course is essential, transitioning from individual learning to collaborative learning. This structure includes integrated thinking and planning of technological tools, adapting them to the required tasks, establishing clear communication channels at the beginning of the course, throughout its duration, and towards the submission of the final product. Preparation of content available to learners and a clear description of the expected outcomes are also part of this structure.

A study conducted by Margaliot et al. (2018) in an enhanced course measured the satisfaction of students who experienced it. The research findings suggests that as the efficiency, variety, and user-friendliness of the online learning platform increase, so does the satisfaction of students with collaborative online learning.

Course Management

During the course's learning management, regular attendance of the instructor on the course site is required, paying attention to the progress of the learning discourse. The instructor should provide assistance to participants in dealing with emerging difficulties, aiming to encourage, support, and promote learning. It is also necessary to adapt technological tools so that the instructor can monitor learning, provide feedback on writing processes, and link them to the academic content on and beyond the course site. The instructor's involvement is particularly crucial when participants do not contribute as expected and leave the main workload to others. Active involvement, timely and context-specific, can help group members collaborate and respond to the academic writing challenge while recognizing the unique value each participant contributes to the collaborative outcome.

In the aforementioned study by Margaliot et al. (2018), it was found that the instructor's availability and engaged presence contributed to advancing collaborative learning. It was also identified that there is a need for exposure and transparency regarding difficulties encountered in the process of forming an effective writing process, while highlighting possible coping strategies. Exposure to the principles of the OCL teaching model encouraged peer dialogue and assisted in constructing metacognitive discourse. The instructor's transparency, while managing a discourse about difficulties and providing clarity regarding requirements and grading methods, helps participants join the learning process and develop trust in its management.

Course Assessment

In this model, tasks should be constructed in conjunction with their evaluation method so that participants understand how the assessment (both individual and group) is built starting from when they engage in their tasks. This is because students are required to rely on the work of their peers in the group, listen openly to different perspectives, and contribute to the academic writing process of the final product. Therefore, they need to understand the criteria by which the assessment for learning is given and conduct themselves in a way that allows them to receive the maximum personal grade, as well as contribute to and promote both their own and their group members' learning and collective assessment to maximize the group grade. In the working process, they were required to engage in proactive communication with other learning partners.

The Added Value of Collaborative and Cooperative Learning

In the research conducted by Margaliot et al. (2018) it was found that students identified the importance of experiencing the process of reaching agreement on how to prepare the task and the topics to be included in the final product as a source of professional development for them. Constructing learning materials allowed them to compare different teaching approaches and align teaching methods with instructional goals. Most of them noted that the experience of collaborative *and cooperative* learning contributed to their personal learning as a result of success in building group discourse that included proposing writing, discussing proposals, making decisions, and overcoming disagreements. Participants mentioned that they were able to collaborate despite difficulties that arose in the initial stages of working on the task, during the division of work among group members, in agreement on how to prepare the task, and on the topics to be included in it. They also noted that the need to construct materials themselves, without frontal instruction, required them to develop the ability to compare various teaching approaches they were familiar with, especially when adapting teaching approaches to the teaching situation, all within a group learning context.

This ability developed as they independently sought relevant materials for the teaching approach they wrote about, selected relevant information from them, and critically reviewed the information presented in group discussions, deciding what to include and what to omit. In addition, they organized the academic writing of a coherent document. According to them, this task deepened their familiarity with the principles of the teaching approach they learned in the group, clarified its advantages and disadvantages. This experience deepened their understanding of their future ability to plan learning activities in different approaches and contributed to understanding the importance of instructional diversity, linking theories of learning/teaching to learning activities. These findings support the research of Akyol and

Garrison (2014) who found that collaborative learning activities increased the sense of belonging to a group, helped learners transition from an individual to a group perspective, and contributed significantly to academic learning and understanding of the processes of collaborative work construction. Furthermore, it is found that experiential collaborative learning has contributed to the preparation of education students as future teachers in the following aspects: developing the ability to cope with teaching situations; gaining experience in building a database of materials suitable for teaching, along with tips for effective teaching and the construction of a teaching vision; learning through observing and reading about teachers' experiences in complex teaching situations. They also testified that the databases they created during the course, which included teaching tips, detailed descriptions of teaching approaches, their advantages and disadvantages, and learning activities based on teaching approaches, will serve them as future teachers. Participants also noted that collaboration and reading their peers' contributions to the course encouraged them to think about the transformation a teacher must undergo to become an effective educator, essentially prompting them to build their own educational vision. Adopting a learning model in which students experience online collaborative *and cooperative* learning can assist future teachers in creating an effective learning environment that connects practice to theory and prepares the next generation to use contemporary practices.

Reflecting on the common challenge faced by both instructors and students when transitioning to this learning model, it is emphasized that a polyphonic wisdom must be created based on the new agreements regarding the nature of learning and its promotion. This type of learning is inherently more egalitarian, involving shared responsibility and each partner's contribution to the product they are collectively producing. Participants need the ability to be open to the opinions and contributions of other group members. They also require the instructor to be proficient in and recognize suitable technological tools for their work. Additionally, they need to be proactive and innovative in leaving the secure space where "the instructor teaches, and we learn." They are required to be active, plan their writing, find times for group meetings, deeply understand the expected outcome, and how it will be evaluated. Only when the connections between technology, learning promotion methods, and the content they produce are clear, and when it is evident who manages the learning and what role each participant individually and collectively assumes, suitable conditions are created to produce a collaborative academic product that meets the task requirements.

Summary

The transition from physical space to online space necessitates a systematic approach to the adjustments required for both the instructor and students to achieve collaborative learning in an online course. In terms of humanistic values, we had to build familiarity and trust among learning partners. We succeeded in this direction as we were convinced of the advantages and additional values of an online course—something that helped participants overcome difficulties that arose when learning was interrupted or deviated from the set goals. We found that course graduates were surprised by its contribution and even stated that this experience would help them as future educators to implement online learning, free from the constraints of time and place.

Figure 2 presents the theoretical framework, content, and technological tools on which the course described in this chapter is built:

This model exposes the transition from frontal collaborative learning to online collaborative *and cooperative* learning. It was implemented thanks to the connection between the humanistic values we believe in, familiarity with technological tools, and their integration into the course. It also involves an understanding of the instructor's role in building, guiding, routing, and managing the processes of teaching, learning, and evaluation. In the course, we connected the pedagogical models

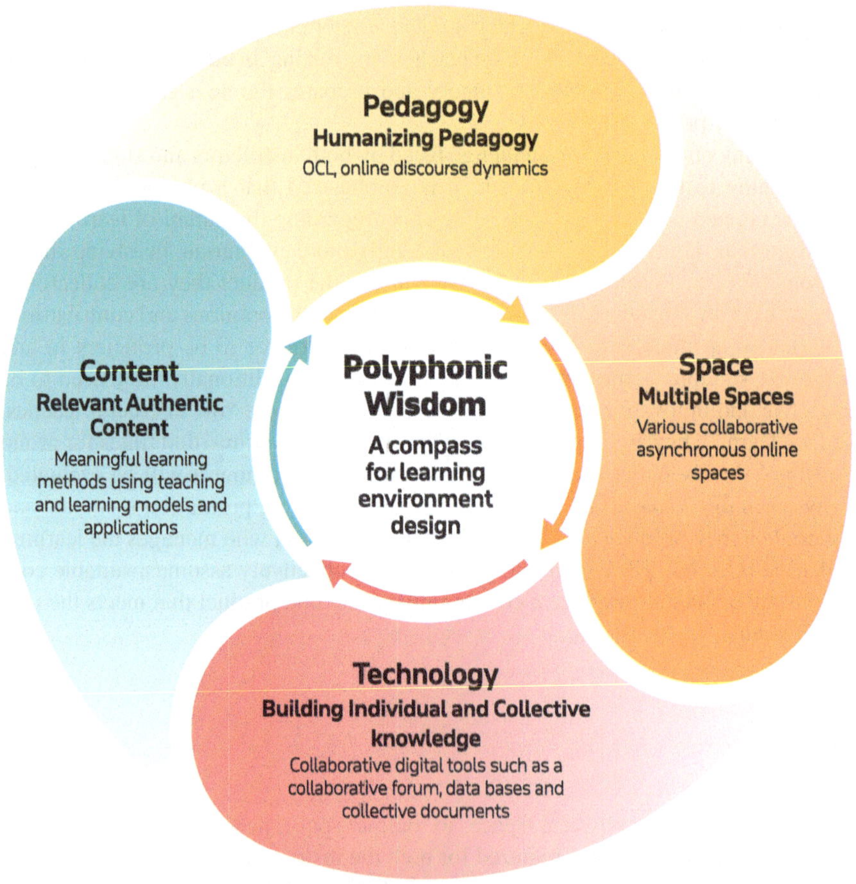

Fig. 2 Course model

learned with the academic content of the course to the participants' self-identity as learners and future educators. This was achieved by creating a connection between their learning experiences and the recognition of the need to use various models of instruction to maintain the relevance of the content. As such, it reflects the connection between the technological environment and humanistic values and the course content.

On a Personal Note

As instructors leading the transition from physical to online instruction, it was important for us to maintain the principle of collaborative learning, which is the foundation of our pedagogical approach. This is based on our deep belief that optimal learning is inherently dialogical. The role of the online course instructor is to transfer the responsibility for learning to the participants while maintaining active presence and involvement, ensuring that participants experience the instructor's close guidance in various groups. The learners' role on the other hand, is to take responsibility for advancing learning, maintaining academic standards in the writing process, and participating in discussions with course materials.

The role of all partners is to actively and dynamically recognize and explore a new learning model suitable for twenty-first-century skills, identifying difficulties and benefits that arise during the learning process, enabling them to promote learning in this model in the future. To achieve all this, we familiarized ourselves with relevant theories, explored satisfaction, and later examined the factors influencing it and the ability to commit to the effort through an investigation of learners' readiness and beliefs influencing it.

Our Thanks

First and foremost, we would like to express our gratitude to Dr. Tami Wiseman, who contributed her knowledge, experience and writing talent, and dedication to course planning and improvement over the years.

We thank Sarit Shamai for her close technological guidance, tailoring technological tools to various tasks, and her encouraging us to use up-to-date technological tools.

Special thanks to Jay Horowitz for technological support and endless discussions on technology and education.

Our gratitude is extended to the MOFET Institute for supporting our research over the years.

References

Akyol, Z., & Garrison, D. R. (2014). The development of a community of inquiry over time in an online course: Understanding the progression and integration of social, cognitive and teaching presence. *Journal of Asynchronous Learning Networks, 12*(3–4), 3–19.

Darling-Hammond, L., Oakes, J., Wojcikiewicz, S. K., Hyler, M. E., Guha, R., Podolsky, A., Kini, T., Cook-Harvey, C. M., Mercer, C. N. J., & Harrell, A. (2019). *Preparing teachers for deeper learning*. Harvard Education Press.

Darom, D. (2005). Integration of the progressive approach and humanistic psychology into humanistic education. In N. Aloni (Ed.), *Everything one needs to be a person—A journey in educational philosophy—An anthology*. Mofet Institute, Hakibbutz Hameuchad. [Hebrew].

Fu, Q.-K., & Hwang, G.-J. (2018). Trends in mobile technology-supported collaborative learning: A systematic review of journal publications from 2007 to 2016. *Computers & Education, 119*, 129–143.

Harasim, L. M. (2002). What makes online learning communities successful? The role of collaborative learning in social and intellectual development. In C. Vrasidas & G. V. Glass (Eds.), *Distance education and distributed learning* (pp. 181–200). Information Age Publishers.

Harasim, L. M. (2012). *Learning theory and online technologies*. Routledge, Taylor & Francis Group.

Lotan, C. (2011). *Online collaborative learning—What models do we know?* http://shluvim.macam.ac.il/blog/view/35894/ [Hebrew].

Margaliot, A. (2018). Step into online collaborative learning: What teacher educators can learn from the initial online collaborative experience? *Ubiquitous Learning: An International Journal, 11*(4), 51–63.

Margaliot, A., Gorev, D., & Vaisman, T. (2018). How student teachers describe the online collaborative learning experience and evaluate its contribution to their learning and their future work as teachers. *Journal of Digital Learning in Teacher Education, 34*(2), 88–102.

Pozzi, F., Manca, S., Persico, D., & Sarti, L. (2007). A general framework for tracking and analyzing learning processes in computer-supported collaborative learning environments. *Innovationsin Education and Teaching Internationa, 44*(2), 169–179.

Robinson, H., Kilgore, W., & Warren, S. (2017). Care, communication, support: Core for designing meaningful online collaborative learning. *Online Learning Journal, 21*(4) Retrieved June 3, 2021, from https://www.learntechlib.org/p/183775/

Scardamalia, M., & Bereiter, C. (2006). Knowledge building: Theory, pedagogy, and technology. In K. Sawyer (Ed.), *Cambridge handbook of the learning sciences* (pp. 97–118). Cambridge University Press.

Shonfeld, M., & Weinberger, Y. (2018). What influences teacher educator's use of collaborative learning? In M. Shonfeld & D. Gibson (Eds.), *Collaborative learning in a global world*. IAP.

Xin, C., & Feenberg, A. (2006). Pedagogy in cyberspace: The dynamics of online discourse. *Journal of Distance Education Review De L'eduction À Distance, 21*(2), 1–25.

Space Education: Training Teachers to Face Challenges in an Era of Uncertainty

Ayelet Weizman

Background

The field of education has been undergoing an upheaval in recent years, the main characteristic of which is uncertainty (Zohar & Bushurian, 2020). The reality we live in is changing in a variety of aspects—from technological aspects to health, employment, transportation & economy aspects. The rapid development of new technologies causes major changes in our living habits and, as a result, also changes in the work options in the future. Students who enter the education system today do not know what the required subjects will be, and which subjects will disappear or change when they finish their studies (Lake, 2018, 2019).

In view of the rapidly changing needs and the uncertainty that accompanies them, the demands from the future graduates of the education system are being reshaped, and accordingly the expectations from the system, represented by the teachers. In the past, the education system was mainly required to transfer agreed bodies of knowledge and develop basic skills, whereas today it must also take care of the students' mental resilience, increase the motivation to learn, and focus on skills and qualifications that will enable students to face changing challenges in an environment of uncertainty and rapidly changing technology (OECD, 2018).

Computational Thinking

One of the recommendations following these changes is to integrate the field of Computational Thinking (CT) in the current curriculum (Acevedo-Borrega et al., 2022; Barr & Stephenson, 2011).

A. Weizman (✉)
Kibbutzim College of Education, Technology and Arts, Tel-Aviv, Israel
e-mail: ayelet.weizman@smkb.ac.il

Y. Yondler et al. (eds.), *Cultivating Future-Oriented Learners*, Understanding Teaching-Learning Practice, https://doi.org/10.1007/978-3-031-63253-2_12

Computational thinking is defined as a systematic approach to solving technology-integrated problems. It is a thinking process that includes formulating problems and solving them, in such a way that the solution is presented as an algorithm that can be executed by a computerized tool (Tang et al., 2020, Wing, 2006). This approach to problem solving can be implemented in many fields of knowledge, even without the final step of creating the code (Barr & Stephenson, 2011), and therefore this is an approach that can be suitable for solving problems in all fields of knowledge. The systematic thinking prepares the learners to understand processes and actions that include the use of computer-based devices, such as sensor-based systems or robots. When a representation of the solution in the form of an algorithm is added to the thinking process, the process can form a basis for creating projects that include code, and even for learning programming. Many countries in the world have introduced computational thinking into the basic school curricula, from elementary school to high school (OECD, 2018).

The awareness of the possibility of using "Computational thinking" in a variety of disciplines began with the publication of Wing (2006), who stated that computational thinking is a basic ability that must be imparted to every child, just like the ability to write and read. Later, Wing defined computational thinking as a process of problem solving, which allows for the most efficient processing of the problem, breaking it down into factors and arriving at the best solution (Wing, 2011). Wing defined 11 stages of thinking in a strategy for solving problems through computational thinking, of which the most commonly used are decomposition, pattern recognition, abstraction, and writing algorithms. The computational thinking approach corresponds with the idea of polyphonic wisdom, since both approaches enable the development of a variety of twenty-first century skills. Computational thinking is also suitable for integration within a model for teacher training and professionalization, to allow better coping with contemporary and future educational challenges (Dvir and Pinto, 2020, Hsu et al., 2018).

Characteristics of the Computational Thinking Approach as a Response to the Need

What are the skills and abilities required to face the challenges of the future?

Position papers such as (OECD, 2018) and the report of Morgenstern et al. (2019) define required qualifications and skills and formulate recommendations to deal with the increasing characteristics of uncertainty, complexity, and ambiguity in our lives. In this document OECD refers to three categories of skills:

1. Cognitive and metacognitive skills, including critical thinking, creative thinking, learning how to learn and self-regulation.
2. Social and emotional skills SEL, including empathy, self-efficacy, responsibility, and cooperation.

3. Practical and technical skills, such as using information and communication technology applications.

Morgenstern et al. (2019) indicate six general fundamental principles, which are influenced by future trends, and are applied holistically in pedagogical and organizational aspects, while taking advantage of opportunities, technologies and enabling environments. The principles include personal, collaborative, informal, glocal, transformative and inclusion of identity and personal vocation.

Of the above six principles, in the computational thinking approach the following principles are mainly expressed:

(a) Personality—Learning in a digital code environment allows for the personalization of learning, when each student progresses at his own pace, and can use digital training materials. This principle promotes humanistic values of giving expression to the realization of personal ambitions and strengths, and personal cultivation of the learners.
(b) Cooperative—The approach based on problem solving encourages working in teams while cooperating between them. Cooperative learning fundamentally promotes humanistic values of social cultivation
(c) A-formality—Since physical-digital technology is used (i.e. there is no dependence on connection to a screen or a specific location), learning becomes hybrid, including face-to-face, online learning, learning in the classroom and outdoors. In addition, since learning is fun and experiential for the students, many of them continue to experience it beyond the classroom.

As for the categories of required skills, studies show that computational thinking encourages learners as creators in the digital environment, as opposed to acting as consumers only (Resnick & Robinson, 2017). Furthermore, activities that make use of computational thinking principles through innovative technology are encouraging creative thinking, which is one of the key skills in preparing current learners to face the challenges of the future (Glăveanu & de Saint Laurent, 2020, Henriksen, & Mishra, 2016, Deschryber & Yadav, 2015). Also, Resnick and Robinson (2017) showed in their research that digital coding environments, such as Scratch, develop problem-solving and critical thinking skills, as well as digital literacy skills.

The learning compass 2030 according to OECD (2018) refers to holistic knowledge, which includes central ideas and theoretical concepts along with practical understanding based on experience. Knowledge and skills are interrelated and mutually reinforcing. The ability to understand, interpret and apply knowledge and skills in changing situations is of increasing importance. Therefore, the tendency in the world is to focus on teaching and learning in interdisciplinary connections and connections around big issues and questions, instead of studying each field of thought separately.

Therefore, an innovative approach to teacher training, designed to train them for teaching that prepares students to face the challenges of the future, must be interdisciplinary, deal with generic issues, and combine content teaching with skills and competencies.

The Field of Space as a Context for Interdisciplinary Issues That Integrate Technology

A field that is particularly suitable for such an approach is the field of space, which includes a variety of issues that require interdisciplinary learning while applying skills and qualifications that have been characterized as being required to deal with the future. For example: the issue of how to prepare for a future settlement on Mars summons a problem-solving process with a computational thinking approach, while referring to interdisciplinary aspects and solutions involving technology.

Furthermore, space on its diverse aspects is one of the most intriguing areas for children and adults alike. The mystery, the challenges and the unknown arouses motivation to learn, explore and create, also during leisure time and beyond the school framework. Dealing with challenges in the context of space requires a systemic understanding, and familiarity with many and varied fields, but is no longer considered the exclusive domain of STEM—Science, technology, engineering and mathematics–(Knezek et al., 2020).

Israel's involvement in the "new space" trends and systemic decisions recently accepted for investment in this field generate educational opportunities, such as those developed by the Ramon Foundation and the Israel Space Agency around "Rakia mission" –Israeli launch to the space station, and even before that around the first Israeli spacecraft mission "Bereshit 1" Today, high school students in Israel are already participating in the construction of nanosatellites and sending experiments to the space station. Hence, that educators. There is an opportunity take advantage of the space domain and the Israeli connection to space, in order to challenge their students and arouse interest, while focusing on acquiring required skills and connecting space connections to a variety of tangential fields—not necessarily from the fields of science and technology, but also from fields such as behavioral sciences, environmental sciences, architecture, languages, art and literature, and more. As written in the report of the Knesset's research institute already in 2012,The field of space is considered a field that excites the imagination of children and teenagers and can be an incentive for them to invest in general studies.

Uncertainty is an integral element in the field of space, due to the different conditions in space compared to Earth, which create many challenges for man. That is why elements of uncertainty, risk management and future thinking underlie the planning of all space missions. Space missions require close cooperation and teamwork. In addition, the challenges of the space missions incorporate innovative and ground-breaking technologies, both in the field of space exploration, and in the quest to allow humans to survive in space and on other planets. Many of the technological developments we are familiar with were developed as part of the development of space missions (starting with baby food, through clothing details, water purifiers, thermal blankets, sensors, safety measures, satellite communication, cyber protection and much more). These technologies are integrated into all areas of life, therefore the occupation in the field of space can connect to all areas of thought. Furthermore, the "new space" era (referring to the entry of private and commercial entities into the field of space, which resulted in the lowering of launch costs and, as a result, the expansion of the possibilities for connecting a variety of professions to space contexts, such as design, psychology, economics, law, tourism, and education) makes it possible to connect through space to the interests and aspirations of the learners.

Training to Deal with Situations of Uncertainty

Solving problems from the field of space requires the integration of advanced technology and digital literacy, and provides teachers with plenty of opportunities to apply constructivist teaching approaches, the same approaches that are also used in teaching computational thinking (Hsu et al., 2018). Therefore, the connection between computing thinking and the field of space is natural. The reference to challenges from the field of space with a computational thinking approach creates the technical basis for a model to deal with situations of uncertainty. This is because these are problems of a type "Ill-defined problems" That is, problems that are not well defined, that have more than one solution, and that need to be researched and studied in order to reach their solution. The problems presented to the students in the learning process form a basis for their training in the future to deal with other problems during their work, problems relevant to education and teaching. Dealing with this type of tasks requires the learners to have transformative skills, which is defined as "the learner's ability to adapt, thrive and act optimally in a complex reality that is rapidly changing towards uncertain future directions-certainty" (Morgenstern et al., 2019).

The acquisition of such an ability is built gradually and cannot be taught by traditional methods. The method of coping chosen in the model described in this chapter is the scaffolding method, which is implemented through a modeling strategy. The scaffolding method is attributed to Vygotsky's socio-cultural theory. The intention is to gradually decrease the support provided by the teacher (similar to lowering the scaffolding of a building), at the same time as gradually increasing the responsibility given to the learner (Dominguez & Svihla, 2023, Van the Pol et al., 2010). In this way, along with learning the content, the learner develops and internalizes humanistic values, such as self-sufficiency, responsibility, and cooperation, which are included in the second category of required skills according to the OECD.

The literature describes a variety of strategies for building and taking down scaffolding, one of the most common of which is modeling (Van the Pol et al., 2010). In the context of teacher training, this refers to a strategy in which the lecturer/mentor intentionally uses a certain teaching method to promote the professionalism of the learners, who are teaching staff. (Lunenberg et al., 2007).

The advantage of this strategy is the ability to understanding metacognitive activities at the same time as cognitive activities, as well as explaining the rationale for learning. In this way, it is possible to reduce possible feelings of frustration of the learners, who are faced with complex tasks. Modeling is a recommended approach in teacher training, so as not to create a gap between learning innovative teaching approaches and the way these approaches are taught. This is how we demonstrate to the teacher what is the way we expect him to teach his students (Hogg & Yates, 2013).

Enabling Environments

The complexity of the tasks facing the learners is amplified due to the need to know and master innovative technologies. Therefore, it is necessary to create enabling environments (Morgenstern et al., 2019), in such a way that learning is on the one hand appropriately challenging, and on the other hand appropriately supportive. The use of scaffolding that is gradually removed as the learners acquire knowledge and experience NMakes it possible to gradually teach the programmatic, pedagogical and technological goals. In addition, in the learning process the teacher accompanies the students when they experience challenges and crises but does not prevent them from the feeling of difficulty, which in the end may also lead to feelings of satisfaction and success. In this way, learning is also a strengthening and promoting emotional experience. Enabling environments also include the type of learning space appropriate for each stage: physical, digital or extracurricular space.

Following the challenges we have experienced since the outbreak of Covid19 Insights have changed and developed regarding the suitability of each type of learning space for the purposes of teaching, and for the specific combination of content, pedagogy and technology. Therefore, in the model described here, an effort is made to utilize the added value of each of the possible learning spaces and to match each of the learning stages with the most suitable space.

(a) Classroom physical space—Used to experiment with physical technology: microbit cards, sensors, robots, as well as to demonstrate classroom activities that involve face-to-face learning. Such learning includes, for example, working in groups, a prolonged workshop, presenting products to colleagues.
(b) Online space—used both in synchronous learning, when joint or group discussions in zoom rooms are important, and in asynchronous learning, when learning is individual, learning using the "flipped classroom" method, or learning that requires more than the time of a class.
(c) Outdoor environment—Used for going on tours, visiting an informal learning site, a laboratory, or a unique site like the Ramon Machtesh.

Description of the Model: Training to Face Challenges in an Era of Uncertainty

The model proposed in this chapter is intended for the training of educators (mainly teachers) in an academic setting, to deal with challenges in a changing environment. The model is based on the use of space as an example and the context for learning, combined with the computational thinking approach to solving technology-integrated problems. This combination enables learning and experience in a variety of skills and abilities required to deal with changing challenges in an environment of uncertainty. The technological applications integrated in learning are of the type known as "physical-digital" (Torres et al., 2021), such as sensors, controllers, and robots. The training process is based on the scaffolding method, implemented through a modeling strategy.

This model is the basis of the teaching in a new path called "Tomorrow's Technologies: Mixed Reality, Space and Robots" in the master's degree program in technology in education at the kibbutz seminary. The model is intended for a heterogeneous target audience of learners who have a bachelor's degree in various fields of knowledge, with diverse backgrounds and interests, who teach at all age levels from kindergarten to high school. They participate in a weekly learning day over the course of 2 years as part of the Master's in Technology in Education program.

The learning process combines advanced technologies with innovative pedagogies in education and space contexts, during which skills and abilities are promoted that will allow them to successfully face challenges in an environment of uncertainty.

The tasks presented to students in many cases are not well defined, or require research and learning of new topics, thus allowing those who experience them to go through a process that combines "failures", or feelings of frustration and difficulty, and to face changing challenges. The role of the supervisor/teacher is to accompany the student/pupil, to encourage or focus him, but not to prevent him from these feelings. The ambition is that at the end of the learning process the student-teachers who participate in it will be able to successfully face challenges that combine content, pedagogy and innovative technology, and beyond–will be able to teach their students in the same way and prepare them to face challenges in an age of uncertainty.

The model described here expresses the polyphonic wisdom, since it represents inclusion of diversity, integration of multiple voices, promoting dialogue and recognizing the value of different perspectives and positions in the educational framework (Naot-Ofarim & Solomonic, 2016; Schwarz-Franco, 2018). These aspects are reflected throughout the whole learning and instruction process. Since the students come with diverse previous backgrounds both in terms of fields of knowledge and in terms of teaching experience, heterogeneous groups are created that represent a variety of voices and points of view. The tasks that require cooperative problem solving allow each individual to contribute and be contributed, and thus humanistic values of personal cultivation on the one hand and the promotion of the individual's social responsibility as a contributing member within the group are expressed on the other hand.

The stages described here (Fig. 1) are spread over 2 years and are intended for older learners. At the same time, the model can also be adapted to young students and for a shorter period of time, by shortening and adjusting the tasks, as will be explained later.

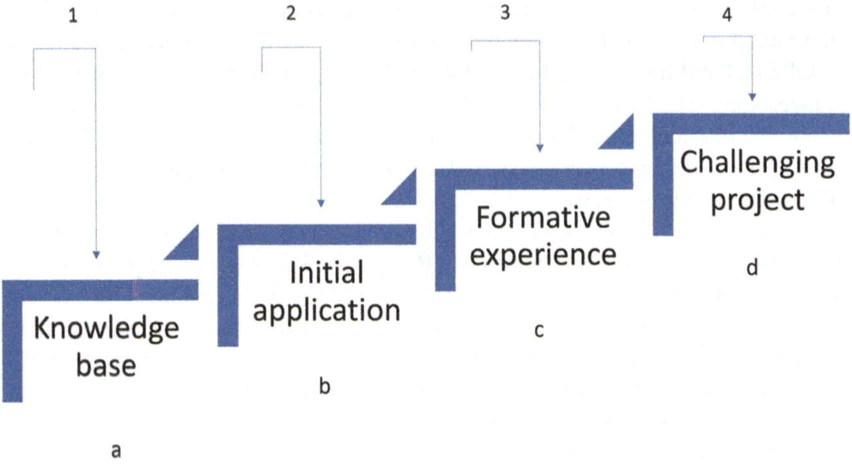

Fig. 1 The structure of the model: the numbers represent scaffolds; the letters represent pedagogical stages

Model Goals

- Teacher training for teaching in a changing environment and innovative technology
- Familiarity with the principles of computational thinking and their application in teaching through physical-digital technology
- Acquiring skills and abilities to deal with challenges and situations of uncertainty in teaching (at the teacher level)
- Making the field of space accessible as a context for experiences with students in all fields of knowledge and age levels

The Stages of the Learning Process

Diagram 1 depicts a representation of the structure of the model, including the stages of learning, in which the level of the tasks increases, and at the same time the scaffolding provided to the learners decreases. In the content aspect, a combination of content from different fields of opinion and examples from the field of space is made. In the pedagogical aspect, a computational thinking approach is used, and in the technological aspect, the emphasis in this model is on physical-digital technology applications, and in particular the microbit card, which is operated through the digital code environments MakeCode or Scratch. In more advanced stages, several types of educational robots are also used. Other digital tools used in the learning process include tools for collaborative learning and creation (such as Google documents, mind maps, Miro), digital code environments like Scratch, and digital environments for product development, like Genially and Canva.

Phase A—The Knowledge Base Building the principles of computational thinking while experiencing as learners.

The assumption is that the group of learners is heterogeneous, and most of them have no prior knowledge of computational thinking and not in the field of space. Therefore, the purpose of the first stage is first of all to build a knowledge base that will allow the continuation of learning. Principles of computational thinking are learned while experimenting in a digital code environment. The teaching strategies combine short lectures, tasks for building knowledge, practice activities, hands-on experience in digital code environments, and experience in independent learning in activities from an online course. The learning is accompanied by an assessment of the understanding of the principles on the one hand and application in the digital environment on the other hand.

Digital code environments like Scratch and MakeCode are used at this stage (Fig. 2)—These environments have been found to be particularly suitable for learners who have no previous background in STEM fields.

At this stage the learning environment is Hybrid. It is desirable to combine online and physical meetings since the experience with the code simulator is digital and personal. Progressing at a personal pace is important from a humanistic point of view, to strengthen the sense of each student's ability, as well as for the purpose of bringing the learners who come from different backgrounds and with different knowledge to a state of being able to work together later.

The use of scaffolds helps to overcome the initial fear of new technologies, since it allows students to experience success already at the beginning of the learning process. They experience applications in contexts relevant to their teaching areas, and work both individually and in groups. This experience is important from the humanistic aspect and also promotes the acquisition of technological skills.

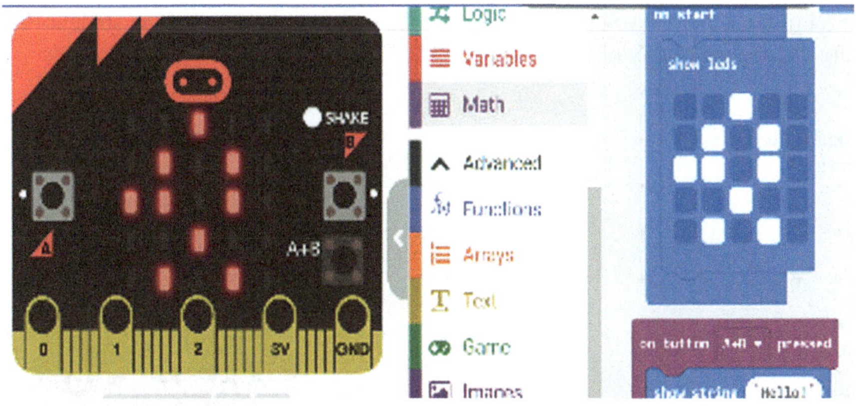

Fig. 2 The MakeCode digital environment

With the help of the code environments, you can easily learn the principles of computational thinking, experiment with a simulator that displays an indication of the code, and use them from the very first step as a means of expression and creation, while connecting to any topic that the learner is interested in. For example, students are asked to propose algorithms for solving problems from everyday life. Suggested examples: arranging clothes in the closet, choosing a school, finding a match, and more.

Learning at this stage is mostly guided, with the tasks being relatively short. The introduction to the code language is done gradually at a level that allows participants to use several basic commands to create simple projects. At the same time, content, and contexts from the field of space are studied and students who show interest can progress and study independently in their free time. The learning is hybrid and includes meetings in a physical classroom space and in a synchronous and asynchronous online space. In most meetings, a combination of personal and collaborative learning is made. During problem solving practice the tasks will always be collaborative as brainstorming and joint thinking about solutions is very important.

Phase B: Application in Teaching Planning and delivering a computational thinking activity to students at teacher level.

At this stage the students are familiar with the Micro:bit (Fig. 3). It is a computerized card that contains a number of sensors built into it (light sensor, temperature, acceleration), and the possibility of connecting additional sensors. The microbit makes it possible to move from a digital space to a physical space, therefore it is an excellent basis for creating physical projects based on computational thinking. At the content level, the students passed the stage of establishing knowledge and moved to the stage of application. Now they are asked to plan in groups a short activity for their students, including code development in one of the digital environments studied, on a topic related to the field of space. For example, in 2015 we made a connection to the "Rakia" mission–The first Israeli to stay on the space station, and thus the students are asked to integrate computing thinking in the field of space both at the level of a teacher (development of the mission) and at the level of the student (the target audience of the mission).

Fig. 3 The Microbit device

The task is not closed and has elements of uncertainty. At the same time the level of scaffolding and guidance decreases. As a result, there is a decrease in the level of confidence that may cause a feeling of frustration since the learners do not yet feel confident in their skills. Here the mentors' role is important, as well as the use of teamwork, division of duties and successful cooperation. Covid19 challenges added difficulty at the level of application with students and cooperative learning, but such real-life difficulties may serve as an opportunity to practice using the tools of computational thinking that have been learned.

Learning is still Hybrid at this stage: The first experience with the microbit controller must be done in a physical classroom space to demonstrate to learners the physical elements of using a computerized device. As part of their studies at the college, the students can get Microbit cards for the duration of the semester, so they can continue to study and practice online as well. The online component of the learning is expressed during the planning stage, when students collaborate online, as well as during their digital presentations.

After experimenting with teaching the activity they developed to the students, each group presents the activity and the insights from its delivery at a peer meeting. The meeting also includes discussion, feedback and reflection on all the stages of the work and the insights following the process. The experience at the teacher level requires the learners to deepen their understanding of the knowledge base, and to evaluate the product they have developed. At this stage the emphasis is on values like collaboration, teamwork, and creating joint products.

An example of the product in step b which combines computational thinking with the field of space– A friend from another planet

Phase C—A Formative Experience Applying the principles learned in an unfamiliar environment and under conditions of uncertainty—as a student.

This stage is one-time and important to maintain in a different and challenging outdoor environment. This is an opportunity to connect with the space context, by choosing a site where the physical and emotional feelings will be of a new and unfamiliar environment with many elements of uncertainty. At this stage it is important to choose a unique site that will allow a shared experience that combines physical and emotional aspects.

The environment we chose is Makhtesh Ramon (Fig. 4), at the Mars simulation facility of DMars, which is used to carry out analog missions for the exploration of Mars, in preparation for the establishment of a human settlement in the future. The tour includes a variety of tasks involving the use of sensors and application of the principles of computational thinking. The goal here is for the learners to experience dealing with challenges that involve uncertainty in an environment that is outside of their comfort zone. The challenges combine existing knowledge (principles of computational thinking, use of sensors or other learned technological tools) with new knowledge, in an unfamiliar context. This combination allows learners to experience feelings of frustration, difficulty, fear, and on the other hand to overcome them and experience success and achievement, all in a relatively short time. Going outside the classroom invites a connection to new dimensions—social and emotional.

Fig. 4 A formative experience at the Ramon Makhtesh

The combination of challenging learning in a different environment (and preferably the view is impressive and unique) invites meaningful learning—a combination of a cognitive and an emotional experience, accompanied by group formation. At the level of values this stage allows combination of values of Humanism and cooperation. On the one hand students go through a personal experience that connects to their background, and on the other hand, the tasks in the field emphasize the importance of teamwork in order to cope successfully with challenges.

The tour is a formative experience for the participants. The learning experience in an outdoor environment has an added value to the entire process. It is used both to apply previous learning, and as an inspiration for further learning.

Phase D—A Challenging Project Construction/design of educational projects from the student world.

The last stage is the application and evaluation of the integration of all the skills, competencies and content learned in the past. The students carry out an open project, in which they must refer to both the teacher perspective and the student perspective. At this stage, most of the scaffolding has been removed, and the component of choice is significant: the students choose a topic from their teaching field, develop the idea for a computational thinking activity, write the algorithm and the code, and implement it with their students at school. The learning is done in stages, with the supervisor acting as a mentor, and in combination with peer learning at a number of stages in the process. At this stage the learning is again hybrid and involve physical-digital tools. Students use physical devices such as robots and engage in online meetings to share and learn with colleagues. The process is accompanied by reflection and students who chose this can also accompany it with action research around the teaching unit they developed.

The previous three stages prepare the participants for the last and most challenging stage, in which they will apply the knowledge and skills they have learned to meet an educational need in their field of teaching. At this stage, the participants go through an independent research process, where the lecturer acts as a mentor, and if necessary, additional mentors are recruited. Each participant defines a problem or educational need that she wants to investigate and formulates a research question. The process lasts several months and includes all stages of research—from literature review, the formulation of the questions, the research outline and the development of the research tools, experimenting with the target audience and collecting findings, analyzing the findings and writing the conclusions and insights. The entire process is accompanied by reflection, and in particular emphasis is placed on reflection during the experience with students.

The solution to the defined problem must include physical-digital technology, such as robots, sensors, controllers, or digital computational thinking environments, in such a way that the technology will have an added value to solving the problem. In this project, computational thinking principles are applied at two levels: at the level of the student who plans the project, and at the level of the students who will carry out the activity in class. During the project dimensions of Humanism are expressed, since the project begins with a personal-educational need that connects to the learner's world.

The foundation built in the previous steps, including content, pedagogy, and technology in combination with strengthening emotional skills, allows the students to be challenged with more complex and open-ended tasks. Additionally, at this stage the students combine experience with their students and gain confidence in teaching that integrates physical-digital technology.

An Example for a Product from Phase D

The problem from the world of education: How to increase the level of involvement of students in science classes? The student who researched this question teaches sixth grade students in an elementary school as part of a project for gifted students. She carried out action research in order to answer the question: To what extent does a teaching unit that integrates robots in space exploration influence and encourage involvement, interest and motivation for science and technology studies among sixth grade students in my class?

Fig. 5 Experiential learning: students building a robot from Lego bricks

The solution: Using a robot EV3 that the students build from Lego parts and program by themselves to solve problems presented to them (Fig. 5). The framework is a teaching unit developed by the student, in which the robot represents a space vehicle exploring the surface of Mars and identifying morphological structures.

Product description (The learning duration is two semesters): The student developed a physical product as part of a project seminar, and at the same time, as part of the final workshop, she performed action research around a teaching unit she developed. In the teaching unit, teaching strategies were incorporated similar to those that were incorporated in the courses studied during the master's degree. The students were given tasks to perform using the robot they built and performed them in groups in a problem-solving process using a computational thinking approach.

The student's learning process in the project seminar included formulating the need and searching for a solution in an iterative process accompanied by a mentor. The initial solution was presented to colleagues and tested with a group of students, and following the feedback it went through a further improvement and design process until it was presented on the project presentation day. The learning process in the thesis was guided by a lecturer-mentor, and included submitting a research proposal, developing a teaching unit and research tools, collecting data, analyzing, and processing data, and writing an academic paper. During the work, meetings of student groups were held for sharing, presentations, and peer evaluation.

The polyphonic wisdom model (Fig. 6) represents the synergy between all components of the paradigm that form the polyphonic environment.

The multiple-spaces component in the model represents a combination of diverse learning spaces (physical, digital, outdoor) that provide enabling environments adapted to the learning phases.

The technology component in the model includes the technological applications studied in the program, all from the physical-digital field. The physical devices

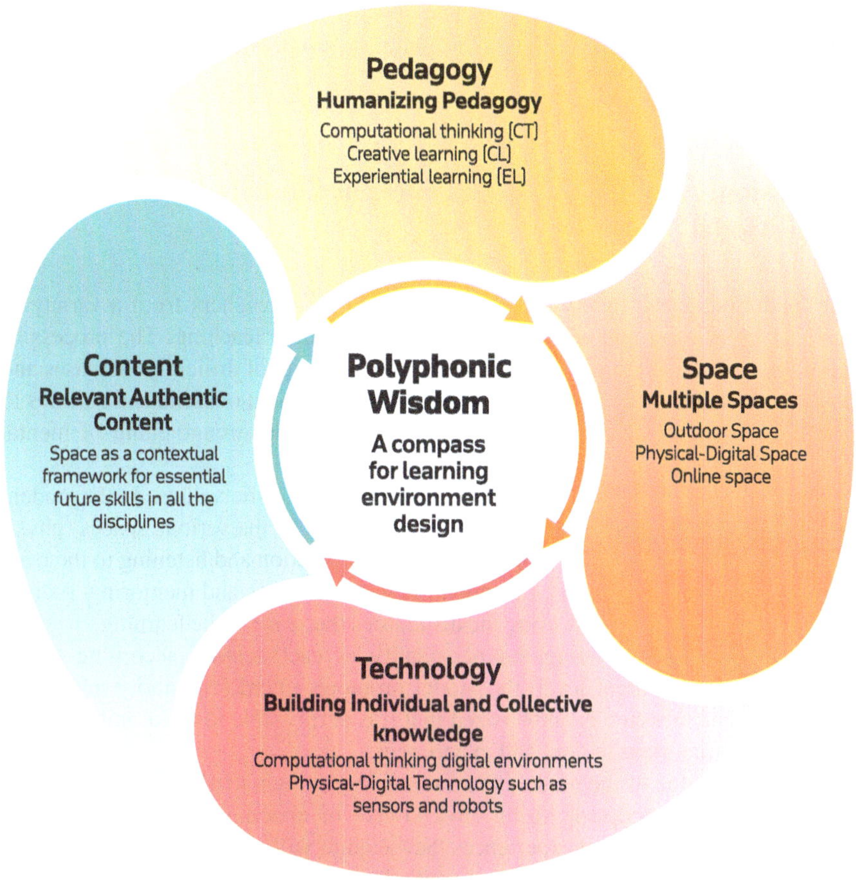

Fig. 6 The polyphonic wisdom model

combine also digital editing when part of learning is independent in personal spaces, and part of it is done in teams in collaborative spaces.

The pedagogy component combines in this model humanistic and future oriented pedagogy, centered around the computational thinking approach. The components of personality and cooperation are expressed side by side, when the moderator-lecturer allows each learner to progress independently and express her voice in the group. The tasks require a combination of personal and interpersonal skills for solving complex problems.

The content component is fundamentally interdisciplinary, in accordance with the population of students who have bachelor's degrees in a variety of fields of knowledge, and the futuristic context of the track. There is a reference to the most innovative technologies such as artificial intelligence, immersive spaces and educational robots. The context of Space makes it possible to refer to complex interdisciplinary issues and ways of dealing with conditions of uncertainty.

The four components together create a synergy that allows a student-teacher to consolidate polyphonic wisdom and through it to design learning environments for her learners.

Discussion: A Theoretical and Practical Contribution of the Model

The model described here can be suitable for training teachers from a variety of fields of knowledge and age groups for future-oriented teaching. The process of progressing through the stages described, when the level of difficulty increases and the level of scaffolding decreases, enables the development of skills and abilities to deal with changing challenges in combination with the strengthening of mental resilience.

In the training process, emphasis is placed on humanistic values. At the student level, the process requires cooperation and teamwork in the various spaces (physical, digital, classroom and extra-classroom), consideration and listening to the team members. At the teacher level, the emphasis is on guidance and mentoring, accompanying the learner and answering the difficulties that arise while learning, listening and dialogue and cultivating the personality of each learner according to his strengths. At the content level, the model promotes interdisciplinarity and at the value level, the message is emphasized that it is permissible to make mistakes and fail, and it is important to dare and experiment.

The added value of the model is in training the learners to deal with challenging teaching-learning processes, in an environment of uncertainty, regardless of the content area. The tools and experiences they acquire will serve them in the future in their practice, and especially in dealing with the integration of technologies in innovative teaching, in a changing and challenging environment. The students' feedback testifies to the significant experience they had in the learning process, and their belief that they will be able to implement a similar process with their students:

(a) Impact on self-efficacy

- *"I am proud of myself that I went with the idea to the end, I left my "comfort zone" and created an experiential activity that proves to the students and the teaching staff that it is possible to learn in a different way and that there is no need to avoid or fear the integration of technology in teaching"*
- *"We learned that not always everything works but when we succeeded we were certainly happy and it made us ac*t vigorously in favor of implement the project in the classroom to see the reactions of the students in the classroom"

(b) Developing skills for dealing with challenges

- *"I saw the students go through the same process that I went through in class and its essence in my view is actually learning while failing and understanding that failure is a significant part of a process of meaningful learning"*

- *"Then Covid19 started, which changed the rules for all of us... everyone is in isolation and there is absolutely no possibility of meeting. We didn't say we were desperate, and we worked very well in remote cooperation, when I try the experiments on the robot and he gives support and watches on video. We could have given up, but we managed to overcome a very big obstacle and for that I am very proud of us as a team."*
- *"A little more thinking and brain cell ventilation made me understand as someone who deals with pedagogical development that it is not the content of the learning that is important but the process that happens during the activity of the learners"*

(c) Cultivating mental resilience

- *"Every fear, apprehension, failure, we turned them into hope and success along the way until we reached our final destination. The road was really long and full of challenges, but all the knowledge, tools, learning and creativity will serve us along the way in our work as teachers in the technological age."*

The model can be used by teachers and lecturers, and maybe even form the basis for a new, interdisciplinary model for teacher training (with a bachelor's degree). Learning spaces often change between physical and online, and therefore a Hybrid and flexible model is required. In this model, the disadvantage is also the advantage, where every challenge is an opportunity to experiment and improve intrapersonal skills. One of the important messages is that failure is part of learning, and even a necessary part of it. In the field of space there are many examples for learning from failures. For example—the spaceship mission Bereshit 1—Apparently, the spacecraft did not achieve the defined goal: a soft landing on the surface of the moon, but it achieved a variety of other goals: a successful launch, successful maneuvers that led the spacecraft to the moon, and above all, the mission affected tens of thousands of children and young people in Israel, and proved that it is possible to launch a spacecraft to the moon with relatively limited means.

Practical Tips

By shortening the duration of each stage and adapting the contents to the curriculum, the model intended for students from the field of education can also be adapted to a target audience of students in the education system. The model can be applied in school teaching, provided there is flexibility in teaching hours, in the application of interdisciplinary learning and project-based learning (Table 1).

Table 1 A possible model for school students

Phase	Title	Method	Pedagogy	Learning space	Contents
A	Knowledge base	Personal & Group work	Creative learning	Physical + online (simulator)	Computational thinking
B	Initial application	Group work	Peer learning Problem-based learning	Physical + online	Tasks in space contexts
C	Formative experience	Group work	Application in an environment of uncertainty	Extracurricular physical	Outdoor learning combined with technological applications
D	Challenging project	Group work	Design based learning	Physical + online	Product design

Summary

The model described in the chapter is intended to help teachers formulate a polyphonic understanding for themselves. That is, to train teachers to deal with changing challenges in teaching, and to be able to teach their students in a process that will strengthen their skills to deal with changing challenges themselves. The model combines tasks of increasing difficulty with decreasing scaffolds, in a hybrid learning environment and a supportive and enabling atmosphere.

It is important to emphasize that the model developed at the kibbutzim seminar is still in its initial stages. The number of students participating in the Technologies of Tomorrow path is relatively small, therefore the findings and conclusions refer to a small group. Research regarding the long-term effects is still required.

Finally, on a personal note: The lecturer and mentor also goes through a learning process during the teaching of the model. At the level of the lecturer, the course contains elements of uncertainty that include the composition of the group, the previous knowledge and the participants' areas of expertise, which influence the choice of content in the open projects. Over the last few years I coped, like the students, with unexpected challenges during the outbreak of Covid 19 and the war in Israel in 2023. I experienced frustration on the one hand due to changing constraints along the way, the need to deal with the objections and claims of the participants, and on the other hand the feeling of satisfaction when problems are solved, and despite the challenges, the students achieve impressive results. Therefore, I believe that this model can be defined as a joint learning journey of the teacher/facilitator and the students-teachers, where all participants develop knowledge and skills on a cognitive and emotional level and strengthen their ability to face the challenges of the future.

For more information about the "Technologies of Tomorrow" track and viewing examples of products see this link.

Sources in Hebrew

Dvir, K., & Pinto, A. (2020). *Computational thinking report—Challenges and recommendations in designing a desirable future based on the study of future trends*. R&D, Experiments and Entrepreneurship Division, Ministry of Education.

Morgenstern, A., Pinto, A., Vegerhoff, E., Hoffman, T., & Lottie, S. (2019). *Future-oriented pedagogy—Trends, principles, implications and applications*. R&D Division, Experiments and Initiatives, Pedagogical Administration, Ministry of Education.

Zohar, P., & Busharian, P. (2020). *Adapting the curricula and study materials to the 21st century: Summary of the expert committee's work, situational picture and recommendations*. Initiative—Center for Knowledge and Research in Education, Israel National Academy of Sciences.

References

Acevedo-Borrega, J., Valverde-Berrocoso, J., & Garrido-Arroyo, M. (2022). Computational thinking and educational technology: A scoping review of the literature. *Education Sciences, 12*, 39.

Barr, V., & Stephenson, C. (2011). Bringing computational thinking to K-12: What is involved, and what is the role of the computer science education community? *ACM Inroads, 2*(1), 48–54.

DeSchryver, M. D., & Yadav, A. (2015). Creative and computational thinking in the context of new literacies: Working with teachers to scaffold complex technology-mediated approaches to teaching and learning. *Journal of Technology and Teacher Education, 23*(3), 411–431.

Dominguez, S., & Svihla, V. (2023). A review of teacher implemented scaffolding in K-12. *Social Sciences and Humanities Open, 8*(1), 1–12.

Glăveanu, Ness, I. J., & de Saint Laurent, C. (2020). *Creative learning in digital and virtual environments: Opportunities and challenges of technology-enabled learning and creativity*. Taylor & Francis.

Henriksen, D., & Mishra, P. (Eds.). (2016). *Creativity, technology & teacher education*. Association for the Advancement of Computing in Education (AACE).

Hogg, L., & Yates, Y. (2013). Walking the talk in initial teacher education: Making teacher educator modeling effective. *Studying Teacher Education, 9*(3), 311.

Hsu, T.-C., Chang, S.-C., & Hung, Y.-T. (2018). How to learn and how to teach computational thinking: Suggestions based on a review of the literature. *Computers and Education, 126*, 296–310.

Knezek, G., Christensen, R., & Carolyn, Y. N. G. (2020). Inspiring STEM engagement: Space science education in the 21st century. *Journal of Computers in Mathematics and Science Teaching, 39*(4), 285–290.

Lake, R. (2018). *Thinking forward: New ideas for a new era of public education. A collection of essays celebrating CRPE's 25th anniversary*. Center on Reinventing Public Education. Link

Lake, R. (2019). Preparing students for the uncertain future: why America's educators are ready to innovate—But their education systems are not. *Thinking Forward: New Ideas for a New Era of Public Education*. Link

Lunenberg, M., Korthagen, F., & Swennen, A. (2007). The teacher educator as a role model. *Teaching and Teacher Education, 23*(5), 586–601. https://doi.org/10.1016/j.tate.2006.11.001

Naot-Ofarim, Y., & Solomonic, S. (2016). Educational polyphony. *Studies in Philosophy and Education, 35*, 385–397.

OECD. (2018). *Future of education and skills 2030: OECD Learning Compass 2030. A series of concept notes*.

Resnick, M., & Robinson, K. (2017). *Lifelong kindergarten: Cultivating creativity through projects, passion, peers, and play*. MIT.

Schwarz-Franco, O. (2018). Polyphonic teaching: The ability to facilitate multiple voices as a crucial teaching skill. *Educational Studies, 54*(4), 429–447.

Tang, X., Yin, Y., Lin, Q., Hada, R., & Zhai, X. (2020). Assessing computational thinking: A systematic review of empirical studies. *Computers & Education, 148*, 1–22.

Torres, et al. (2021). A systematic review of physical-digital play technology and developmentally relevant child behavior. *International Journal of Child-Computer Interaction, 30.*

Van the Pol, J., Volman, M., & Beishuizen, J. (2010). Scaffolding in teacher–student interaction: A decade of research scaffolding. *Educational Psychology Review, 22*, 271–296.

Wing, J. (2006). Computational thinking. *Communications of the ACM, 49*(3), 33–35.

Wing, J. M. (2011). Research notebook: Computational thinking—What and why. *The Link Magazine, 6*, 20–23.

Multiple Intelligences and PBL in the Digital Space: Students Design and Create an Applicative Product in a Collaborative Environment

Tal Shemer-Elkayam

Introduction

In the past few years, the education system has undergone changes to meet the need for educational innovation and prepare learners for a future mobile and vague workplace (Czerniawski et al., 2018; Debs et al., 2018; OECD, 2018). The International Economic Forum has recently listed the central skills required for the future job market, including creativity, flexible thinking, critical thinking, active learning capacity, complex problem-solving, and collaboration (The Future of Jobs Reports, 2020). To remain relevant, schools and higher education institutes must provide students with a personally adjusted learning experience to develop these skills and help maximize individual potential (Shemesh, 2017). The current era, where knowledge is easily accessible to everyone, challenges teachers and teacher educators. In these circumstances, teachers who do not encourage active participation in learning and knowledge construction independently and in groups may become irrelevant to the students. Additionally, teaching designed to develop collaborative learning and conflict-resolution skills must consider class heterogeneity and student differences. The Israeli education system, characterized by social, national, and cultural heterogeneity, bears responsibility for acknowledging each learner's uniqueness and allowing space for individual needs, capabilities, and wishes (Harkavi & Mendel-Levy, 2014).

As role models for teachers-to-be, teacher educators play an important role in designing new teaching-learning models that place the learners at the center (Poyas, 2016; Avidov-Ungar & Forkosh-Baruch, 2018). Such models offer flexible learning environments that foster creativity and peer learning and encourage learners to own their learning, become knowledge generators, and apply learning and assessment modes that produce expertise (Nurfaradilla, 2017; Shemesh,

T. Shemer-Elkayam (✉)
Kibbutzim College of Education, Technology and Arts, Tel-Aviv, Israel
e-mail: tal.elkayam@smkb.ac.il

Y. Yondler et al. (eds.), *Cultivating Future-Oriented Learners*, Understanding Teaching-Learning Practice, https://doi.org/10.1007/978-3-031-63253-2_13

2017; Shemer-Elkayam, Shavit-Miller, & Arbiv-Elyashiv, 2020; Uiboleht et al., 2019; Richter et al., 2021).

The present chapter describes a teaching model implemented in the past 3 years in the course "Adolescent Psychology" at Kibbutzim College of Education. The model offers future teachers the necessary tools for collaborative learning within the class in a way that emphasizes learner diversity and heterogeneity and allows them to assert themselves for what they are. The chapter illustrates how choice-making and thorough collective knowledge-building can result in a significant humanizing learning experience and facilitate knowledge acquisition in content fields and skills defined by the World Economic Forum as crucial for the future workplace.

Multiple Intelligences and PBL in the Digital Space: The Theories Behind the Discussed Teaching Model

The discussed teaching model derives its rationale and pedagogical principles from combining the Multiple Intelligences Theory and Project Based Learning (PBL). This fused theoretical approach translates into an applicative pedagogical practice via varied learning spaces and technological and pedagogical tools that express the learners' heterogeneity and strengths.

Multiple Intelligences in Teaching

Gardner's multiple intelligences theory contests using a single index to measure intelligence. It maintains that every person has eight intelligences: Linguistic, logical-mathematical, musical, bodily-kinesthetic, spatial-visual, interpersonal, intrapersonal and naturalist, and each of us has a characteristic individual intelligence profile. Gardner defines intelligence as the ability to solve problems in the "real" world by creating products that have value (Gardner, 1996; Wellizker, 2003). Learning based on the Multiple Intelligences Theory identifies the individual profiles of learners, allowing them to study fields that arouse their curiosity and interest (for example, allowing students with high bodily-kinesthetic intelligence to expand their theater studies). Such learning also encourages applying one's strongest intelligences to study any knowledge area (for example, students with high musical intelligence may learn a new language via music). In teaching, this theory advocates regarding each student individually and urges them to design learning products that represent their intelligence profile. Gardner recommends learning through projects that express individual abilities combined with group work. Such learning requires learning skills and acquaintance with relevant content worlds while emphasizing innovation, creativity, and imagination in realizing a project (Gardner, 1996).

Project Based Learning (PBL)

In project- based learning (PBL), learners plan and carry out a project that yields a product they present to an audience in a summary event. The learning trigger is a question that interests the students. As such, it can expand their horizons and orient toward a product that would eventually benefit others (Patton, 2012). This learning mode engenders active personal or group exploration relevant to the learner's life (Welicker, 2003). Group learning leans on collaborative learning principles, including teamwork, interpersonal communication, collaboration, and conflict resolution (Zohar & Busharian, 2020). Such learning is differential by nature as it allows the learners in the group to display their diverse capacities and skills, find different connecting points to a project, and discover different pathways to pave their way to success (Patton, 2012). Implemented in a digital environment using collaborative platforms, PBL enables achieving pedagogical goals such as developing digital literacy and bolstering learning processes (Zohar & Busharian, 2020). It boosts twenty-first-century skills in schoolchildren and teachers-to-be, advancing critical thinking, problem-solving, interpersonal communication, active information searches, teamwork, innovation, and creativity (Mettas & Constantinou, 2008; Abdullatif, 2020).

Description of the Teaching Model

The following section explores how the multiple intelligences theory and PBL come together.

Background

The teaching model described below—research for a product applicable in a shared digital space—was developed for the course "Adolescent Psychology." It aimed to acquaint students with the adolescent world, their behavior, and their interaction with their surroundings. The course participants were undergraduate trainee teachers and post-graduate education students. The course content and thoroughness, adjusted to the different groups, had three pedagogical goals: Creating a learning experience adjusted to the learners, associating theory and research toward school teaching, and encouraging learning that involves interpersonal communication. The teaching model corresponded to these three goals. The learners had to design collaboratively a digital product whose point of departure was a question that interested them and aroused their curiosity. In realizing this, they had to apply the strengths of different group members. The product had to be applicative and usable by teachers or parents of adolescent children. The model was both content-oriented and related to pedagogy. From the content perspective, it aimed to deepen the learners' acquaintance with typical dilemmas in adolescent relationships and let them experience humanizing social and personality values. On the pedagogical side, the learners experienced PBL, which allowed them to assert their strengths and utilize their differences to connect and jointly design a product. The resultant teaching model leaned on humanizing active learning where the learners experience personal and professional involvement. The group takes charge of the learning under the teacher's guidance. The following sections describe the process in detail.

The Beginning: Introduction to the Learning Process

The learning process begins with a frontal class on multiple intelligences intended to arouse interest and curiosity. At its beginning, the learners fill out a questionnaire on multiple intelligences that confronts them with whether the questionnaire results agree with who they are and the strengths they identify in themselves. Over the lesson, they hear explanations about the theory with numerous examples of teaching modes deriving from each of Gardner's eight intelligences. Over the following weeks, the learners divide into 3–5 person groups and decide on a question they are curious about in the broad field of adolescent relationships with their parents or peers.

The PBL learning has four stages described in Fig. 1.

Stage 1: Formulating Interest-Driven Research Question

In contemplating their research question, learners use the knowledge they acquired in the course and materials the teacher proposes for joint interactive presentations (such as Pear Deck or Nearpod), with their curiosity as their primary guide. At this stage, the teacher and each group discuss the contemplated research question to narrow it down and formulate an effective, connected, practical, comprehensive, and complex question. The teacher may open at this point a shared table where each

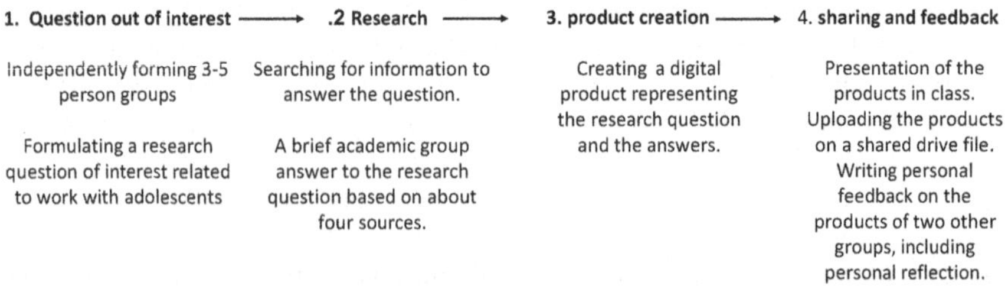

Fig. 1 PBL Learning Stages

group inserts its research question to facilitate communication with the learner groups, react to the questions, and propose guiding questions. The learners thus become aware of the other groups' questions and feedback. This table will remain utile in the following stages.

Stage 2: Research

Once the teacher approves the research question, each group searches independently for related information to enable the preparation of a sophisticated answer. This preliminary theoretical search should lean on academic sources. Although the products eventually represent the answers, the groups will also have to upload a short document on a shared digital space describing the research question, the main conclusions drawn from the literature review, and the sources used. Thus, the second stage combines joint information search and group learning of relevant theories and previous research results to enable the preparation of a focused, sophisticated response in the form of a product.

Stage 3: Product Creation

Having prepared an information-based theoretical answer to the research question, the students must devise a practical response and share it in a digital space with the whole study group. Each group conceptualizes and constructs a digital product that reflects and answers their research question. The product must meet two conditions: Be suitable for peer learning and potentially implementation-worthy in its specific field. Thus, the group knowledge and messages must be transmitted to a specific target audience via a digital tool that suits that audience. The learners choose the preferred platforms for their products, such as a digital poster, a playacting clip of a scene, a digital exhibition, a Facebook page, or a podcast. The ideas derive from the knowledge acquired in the Multiple Intelligences session. For example, learners with high linguistic intelligence may choose a poetry slam as their product; ones with high logical-mathematical intelligence may choose to run a survey and present its findings, and learners with high bodily-kinesthetic intelligence may choose to produce and record a short act describing their topic for all the course participants. While they work, the groups maintain contact with the teachers in various ways. One of them is inserting a short description of their product into the shared table mentioned in Stage 1. The advantages of the table for stages 1 and 2 are, obviously, also relevant to this stage. In the semester's last two or three classes, the groups have 20-min work meetings with the teacher. The learners use the remaining time to work in groups and continue their research. Once they complete their work, each group uploads its product on the shared digital space. The created learning environment with the various products is accessible to all the course participants, facilitating collaborative knowledge construction with contents and work materials that remain available for later use.

Example of a student product[1]:

An information site for adolescents, in response to the question "How to make appropriate comprehensive information on sexual development accessible to adolescents?" The following pictures appear on the site (Millan & Hadar, 2021).

An information site for adolescents

Stage 4: Sharing and Feedback

The learners give feedback to the different groups in two ways: Face-to-face, shared by the whole group, and to the teacher alone. The semester's last class is dedicated to product presentation. It may take place in one of the following modes: Online on Zoom, frontally in the classroom, or as a product exhibition in one of the colleges "classrooms of the future." After every presentation, the class gives feedback to the presenters to allow for product improvement. Once the products are uploaded on a shared file, each class member chooses the products of two other groups and writes feedback that comments on the knowledge gained by the products, the significance of its content to the feedback giver, and the presentation mode. Learning through multiple products exposes the participants to answers related to various angles of the relevant content field and different learning products. To give feedback, the learners must contemplate their peers' products critically. Finally, learners reflect and comment on the collaborative group work and their contribution to the process, considering their strengths and how they assisted in creating the joint product. Feedbacks are sent to the teacher who has exclusive access to them.

The following section presents the theoretical model corresponding to the four described stages of the learning process.

[1] The involved students have signed their informed consent for using this example.

Polyphonic Wisdom: A Humanizing, Active, Collaborative Learning Space, the Multiple Intelligences Theory, and PBL Learning

The presented teaching model reflects a humanizing collaborative theoretical approach that combines pedagogy and content and uses various technological tools in individual and group learning spaces. Together, these synergized components create a polyphonic environment that allows for hearing the distinctive voices of individual learners and bringing them together to create new shared knowledge. The following model summarizes this approach (Fig. 2).

The basis of the pedagogical part is, as mentioned, applying the multiple intelligence theory in teaching with the purpose of promoting the learners' intelligence

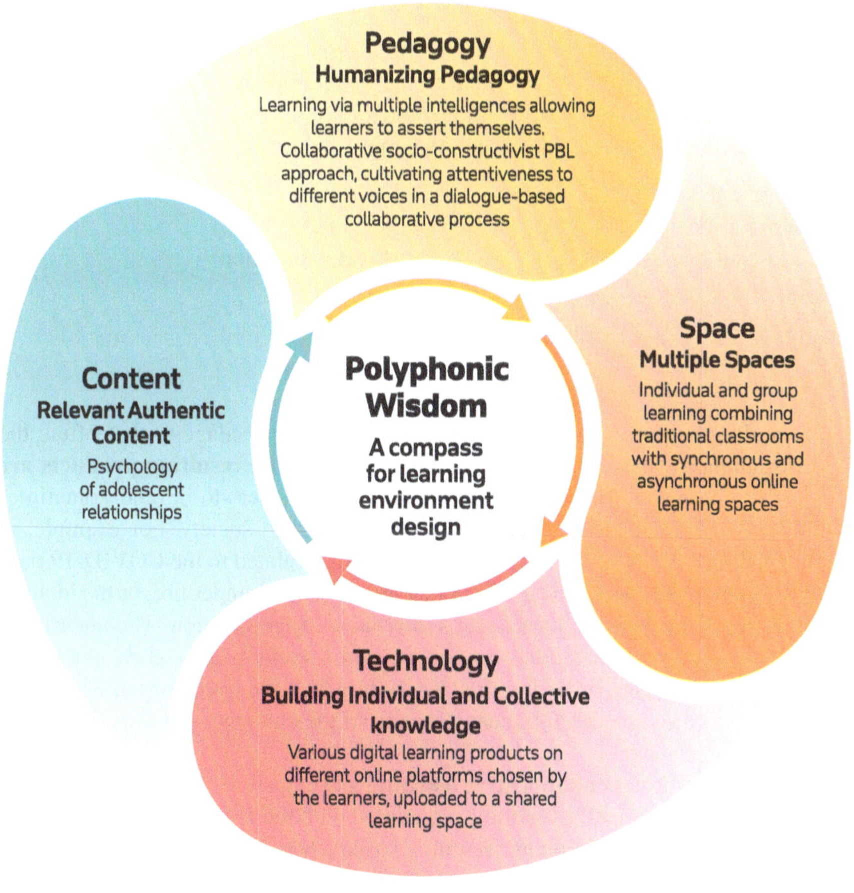

Fig. 2 Polyphonic wisdom model: A theoretical approach translates into applicative pedagogical practice

profiles and assessing them in ways that do justice to those profiles by observing them in action (Armstrong, 1996). Project-based learning (PBL) is central to the multiple intelligence approach, allowing teachers to thoroughly assess the learners as they display their understanding of the learned field through choice-making and personal expression (Armstrong, 1996). The presented model is unique in synergizing four central aspects: **Shedding light on learners' strengths, thorough learning through choice and interest, emphasis on applicable learning, and profound collaboration.**

PBL in a group, both face-to-face and via digital communication, builds shared knowledge by allowing individual learners to **demonstrate their strengths and unique capacities**. In this sense, this is a humanizing model, where learners assert themselves optimally for what they are in a process that gives the group's different voices an equal place. Optimal assertion of oneself primarily means fully utilizing the strong intelligences of each group member. Secondly, it means a positive learning experience that engenders a sense of self-value (contributing one's capacities to the group), joyful learning, relevance, and a sense of belonging. Thirdly, it advocates aspiring for excellence and developing a product that meets high-level academic criteria, is potentially beneficial to the target audience, and makes the best use of the chosen digital tool's specific features.

The model involves multiple choice-making:

- Choose one's group members
- Choose a specific topic from a broader general field
- Choose an interesting curiosity-arousing research question
- Choose the product type and its target audience
- Choose a digital space for the product
- Choose how to divide the tasks in the group
- Choose the learning times

These multiple choices epitomize an active humanizing pedagogy that offers the learners autonomy and active constructivist learning. **The resulting products are applicable**, deriving from the experiences of the teachers-to-be and sometimes from current affairs or central issues challenging Israeli society. For example, in 2021, some of the chosen products touched on issues related to the COVID-19 pandemic, the lives of adolescents in towns that are constantly under fire, or the identity issue of Arab adolescents, given Israel's internal security situation. The underlying rationale is that academic studies do not occur in a vacuum and tightly connect to the fields of knowledge related to the society in which we live. Consequently, it is not possible to disconnect adolescent issues from the challenges of the educational profession and society.

Most learners prefer **collaborative learning** and engage in group PBL. The process begins, as mentioned, by getting acquainted with the individual strengths, thus allowing for creating a polyphonic learning space where the group's various voices are heard, engendering a collaborative connection. The participants interact in hybrid ways they choose themselves. Achieving all the projects purposes requires applying interpersonal communication skills, decision-making, and sometimes handling conflict. To display their knowledge and introduce the product, the learners must fully understand the answer to their research question, discuss their insights together before presenting them to the class, and jointly find a way to impart the knowledge they acquired concisely and to the point. In this sense, the learning also comprises understanding-oriented performances that eventually allow the learners to act in the real world and use their acquired knowledge in a relevant, flexible way (Perkins, 1997). Finally, the collaboration circle expands from the research group to the whole class by creating a joint digital learning space containing all the class products.

The **content** part combines personal and group learning of the broader sense of multiple intelligences and adolescent relationships. Getting to know oneself and one's strengths and reflecting on one's unique contribution to the collaborative work promotes self-efficacy, self-appreciation, and self-confidence. Additionally, beyond acquiring new relevant knowledge, the contents of the different research questions offer the learners an opportunity to practice humanizing values involving socio-emotional skills. Being curiosity-driven, such skills combine care for the teenage students, genuine interest in adolescents' struggles in various relationships, and a wish to understand different aspects of their lives. Another element this experience includes is responsibility. Responsibility for the target adolescents but no less so for translating group knowledge into a potentially applicative product that could be useful for all the class members.

The **space** and **technology** parts combine individual and group learning with thorough collaboration. The learning process reaches its peak when the newly created shared digital learning space allows for building group knowledge. Yet, learning occurs in varied spaces using multiple technological and pedagogical tools, most of which the learners choose themselves. In implementing the model, we used a shared file drive that enables each group to create its own sub-directory for its product or a link to reach it and the accompanying file. Using a drive for joint knowledge building has the advantages of secure information storage, easy access from any end-device, and a space where all the products are kept in the same work environment. Over the work process, group members can prepare documents together in real time, and store their work products in a shared location rather than on their personal computers. They also decide the stage at which they should open the file to their co-learners (before the submission date). Moreover, they choose the technological tool for the product on their own. This underscores the significance of choosing a technological tool that suits the group members, one that they like and displays their strengths. The selected technological tool must not necessarily be highly innovative but should integrate well with other choices they make over the learning and work process. Let me give an example of how a group of learners, one of whom was an actor in a playback theater, used the popular Zoom application. The group's research topic was the body image of adolescent girls. Given this strength of one group member, they chose as their product a playback theater evening on Zoom with an invited audience, in which they introduced the subject by leaning on guests' stories. Their work illustrates that working in different learning spaces with various technological tools allows for breaching time and place regularities, enabling the participants to learn, meet, and work together or separately at their convenience rather than within the limits of a fixed curricular lesson.

The described synergy between the different parts of the flower model creates a polyphonic environment that encompasses personal and group work in an active collaborative process where the various strengths of the group members co-exist in a non-hierarchic space. Diversity becomes, in fact, a source for building new shared knowledge. Synergy underlies the model's theoretical and practical contribution to the field of education, as described next.

Theoretical and Practical Contribution of the Teaching Model

Theoretical Contribution: The Multiple Intelligences Theory Translated into Practical Training of Teachers-to-Be

At this time, when the education system works to adapt teaching, learning, and assessment to twenty-first-century challenges, educational institutions contend with numerous questions: How to remain relevant and stimulate interest, curiosity, and learning motivation? What is the best way to strengthen the learners' self-efficacy? How can they acquire significant and relevant current and future skills? The training of future teachers is central to answering these questions. Designing training models that put the learners at the center (Avidov-Ungar & Forkosh-Baruch, 2018) and using flexible learning environments that encourage problem-solving and entrepreneurship would spur the learners to become knowledge producers (Darling-Hammond et al., 2017). The presented teaching model leans on numerous twenty-first-century skills, including active learning that fosters curiosity, creativity, innovation, and responsibility. It also promotes skills such as teamwork and problem-solving through technology use and joint knowledge building. The model enables learners to generate a group narrative that relates to and manifests the members' strengths, with the teacher as a guide accompanying the process. The theoretical challenge in designing the model regarded translating the multiple intelligences theory into practice in student training in a way that follows the principle that a single method does not suffice to achieve fair teaching and assessment of many students. Such practice should be a platform for the learners to display their best intelligences and realize Gardner's (1996) combination of adapting the learning to each individual learner while allowing space for multiple intelligences in the classroom. Coupling the multiple intelligences theory with the PBL model has met all these requirements, creating a collaborative learning space in keeping with humanistic values that synergizes content and pedagogy, and allows for breaking learning regularities via varied technological tools.

Practical Contribution: Active Learning that Maximizes the Learners' Potential and Results in Expertise

Implementing the model with its multi-dimensional hybrid learning environments in teaching creates mobility between collaborative teamwork and role distribution where members offer their talents to the group. In a teacher-training college, its implementation aspires to see trainee teachers using it with their future students. Pedagogically, this would require active collaborative PBL that relies on varied learning environments. From a human perspective, it would be attentive to the learners' multiple intelligences and encourage them to work collaboratively in a team where they can manifest their strengths. Teachers who adopt this model would promote active learning in their classes in a way that combines humanism with collaborative work and enables assessing the students according to their unique capacities. Such teachers would cross the limits of frontal teaching and experience student creativity and motivation. In this learning process, the teachers are not exclusive sources of knowledge and may learn from their students other angles of their content fields and new digital ways to display their knowledge. These learning and teaching processes are, of course, not devoid of challenges. I will briefly describe the three central ones:

1. **The challenge of personalized learning**: As mentioned, a central goal of the model is maximizing the personal potential of each learner. The question arises whether this purpose contradicts the principle of collaboration. Undoubtedly, individual wishes and interests would clash at some points with those of the group, and the end product would reflect the compromises the group members had to make. However, we should remember that personal learning processes include collaborative work and do not contradict it as long as selecting the group members and the learning process are flexible (Shemesh, 2017). Although the reflective final part of the work enables some extent of individual learning and self-expression, most of it occurs collaboratively in a group. Note that in the specific course described in this chapter, the learning model applied only constituted part of the learning, complemented by independent and whole-class learning.
2. **The challenge of time division**: Thorough group learning of one content unit necessitates prioritizing the curricular material and deciding what content students must complete independently rather than learn in the course. Dedicating several weeks to one broad topic necessarily comes at the expense of other ones. The meaning of each group thoroughly learning part of that broad topic would be giving up learning the complete topic frontally in the classroom. I therefore recommend that in planning a course, the teacher should decide which part necessitates frontal teaching, which can be part of group learning, and which should be omitted, trusting the students to complete it on their own. Note that while collaborative work is encouraged, students also have the option of learning individually, acknowledging that in every class, there are students for whom working

independently is more suitable than in a group (although my experience shows that no more than 1–2 students in every learning group wish to work on their own).

3. **The assessment challenge**: While displaying knowledge via varied products involves students in the learning process, offers choices, and increases motivation, it also complicates the teachers' assessment, given the variety of products. To address this challenge, I devised a detailed indicator covering general aspects of the products that allows examining each product through its unique features. The question remains to what extent the group grade reflects the effort of each group member and what additional elements could determine and assess the work and effort of individuals within the group work.

On a personal note…

> *It's not how smart you are that matters; what really counts is how you are smart.* (Howard Gardner Gardner)

This quote has accompanied my teaching and spurred me to seek a teaching and assessment mode whose focus is maximizing the learners' capabilities. In building the model discussed in this chapter, I aimed to view learner diversity as a group resource and organize the teaching and learning accordingly. My premise was that individual learners deserve an opportunity to develop and learn by applying their strengths and using them to connect to the group and contribute to it.

We live in an age of uncertainty and frequent changes, an information age where students have theoretically independent access to the learned material. As a teacher, I would sooner emphasize increasing the learners' curiosity and involvement and let them acquire and practice collaborative teamwork skills while recruiting individual resources to complete a group task. I prefer offering them an opportunity to thoroughly learn one relevant subject close to their hearts to encompassing a curriculum. I assume this kind of learning would equip them with sufficient skills to search for reliable information, learn individually and in groups, and use these skills later in life. Finally, as a teacher educator, I consider it my mission to be a model of teaching where students learn to know themselves and express themselves individually and in a group. All these feelings and thoughts have guided me in building and refining the teaching model presented in this chapter. In implementing it, my task was to be a mentor rather than a teacher and help the students navigate the learning. I was not the learners' chief source of knowledge but a guide that worked to arouse their curiosity, help them find their inner spark and burning questions, and guide them in searching for up-to-date, relevant information and optimal technological tools to apply their acquired knowledge optimally. I find this role highly interesting, engendering diversified teaching that is rewarding to the students but no less so to myself. In such teaching, I learn from my students and deepen our acquaintance through group meetings and doubt-sharing. Their varied products and gushing creativity keep exciting me. At the end of the process, even checking and grading the products is considerably more interesting than checking tests or papers, where the answers keep repeating themselves. The learners, for their part, noted verbally and in their feedback that although challenging and significantly time-consuming, this learning experience was enriching, engaging, relevant, and practical and had the added value of understanding and familiarizing with various digital tools. I am confident that this model can be adopted and adapted to many courses in different fields of knowledge. After deciding what the learners should learn in-depth and what he is ready to omit, the teacher could select one broad subject from the curriculum, let the learners find out first what their strong intelligences are, and based on this personal learning, create collectively products on various digital learning spaces that synergize between individual and group work.

References

Abdullatif, A. M. (2020). The effectiveness of the project-based learning (PBL) approach as a way to engage students in learning. *SAGE Open, 10*(3). https://doi.org/10.1177/2158244020938702

Armstrong, T. (1996). *Inteligentziot merubot bakita* [Multiple intelligences in the classroom] (A. Zuckerman, Trans.). Branco Weiss Institute.

Avidov-Ungar, O., & Forkosh-Baruch, A. (2018). Professional identity of teacher educators in the digital era in light of demands of pedagogical innovation. *Teaching and Teacher Education, 73*(1), 183–191.

Czerniawski, G., Donalf, G., MacPhail, A., Bain, Y., Conway, P., & Guberman, A. (2018). The professional learning needs and priorities of higher-education-based teacher educators in England, Ireland and Scotland. *Journal of Education for Teaching, 44*(2), 133–148.

Darling-Hammond, L., Hyler, M. E., & Gardner, M. (2017). *Effective teacher professional development.* Learning Policy Institute.

Debs, L., Miller, K. D., Ashby, I., & Exter, M. (2018). Students' perspectives on different teaching methods: Comparing innovative and traditional courses in a technology program. *Research in Science & Technological Education, 37*(3), 297–323.

Future of Jobs Survey. (2020). World Economic Forum.

Gardner H. (1996). *Inteligentziot merubot: Hateoria halacha lema'aseh* [Multiple intelligences: The theory in practice] (A. Zuckerman, Trans.). Branco Weiss Institute.

Harkavi, A., & Mendel-Levi, N. (2014). *Hinuch lakol ulekol ehad bema'arechet hahinuch beyisrael.* [Education for one and all in Israel's education system]. Jerusalem: Center for Knowledge and Research in Education, The Israel Academy of Sciences and Humanities. (In Hebrew).

Mettas, A. C., & Constantinou, C. C. (2008). The technology fair: A project-based learning approach for enhancing problem solving skills and interest in design and technology education. *International Journal of Technology and Design Education, 18*(1), 79–100.

Millan, A., & Hadar, N. (2021). *Everything you want to know about sex: Sexual education for teens.* https://sites.google.com/view/sexualeducationforteens/home

Nurfaradilla, M. N. (2017). Self-directed learning through the eyes of teacher educators. *Kasetsart Journal of Social Sciences.* https://doi.org/10.1016/j.kjss.2017.08.006

OECD. (2018). *The future of education and skills education 2030.* OECD Publishing.

Patton, A. (2012). *Ma'aseh hoshev, lemida mevuseset proyektim: Madrich lamoreh* [Work that matters: The teacher's guide to project-based learning] (A. Peleg & A. Sadowski, Trans.). The Hebrew University Secondary School.

Perkins D. (1997). *Bitzuei Havana* [Understanding performances]. *Hinuch Hahashiva 10*, 13–14. In Hebrew.

Poyas, Y. (2016). *Hachsharat morim bemavoch hahadshanut hapedagogit* [Teacher training in the labyrinth of pedagogical innovation]. Mofet Institute. In Hebrew.

Richter, E., Brunner, M., & Richter, D. (2021). Teacher educators' task perception and its relationship to professional identity and teaching practice. *Teaching and Teacher Education, 101*(3), 103–303. https://doi.org/10.1016/j.tate.2021.103303

Shemer-Elkayam, T., Shavit-Miller, A., & Arbiv-Elyashiv R. (2020). *Havaya studentialit aheret bahachshara lehora'a: Nekudat hamabat shel morei hamorim.* [A different student experience in teacher training: The perspective of teacher educators]. *Gilui Da'at 18*, 59–85. In Hebrew.

Shemesh, A. (2017). *Skirat sifrut—Personalizatzia shel halemida* [Literature review—Learning personalization] https://meyda.education.gov.il/files/MadaTech/MadeayHatechnologia/hishtalmut/personalization.pdf

Uiboleht, K., Karm, M., & Postareff, L. (2019). Relations between students' perceptions of the teaching-learning environment and teachers' approaches to teaching: A qualitative study. *Journal of Further and Higher Education, 43*(10), 1456–1475.

Welicker M. (2003). *Teoriat ha'inteligentziot hamerubot—Hatvayat derech leshitot hora'a-lemida veha'aracha halufiot.* [The multiple intelligences theory—Alternative teaching-learning-assessment ways in science and technology in society]. *Notice of the Science and Technology in Society Supervisor*, 2, 94–107. In Hebrew.

Zohar, A., & Busharian, O. (2020). *Hat'amat tochniot halimudim vehomrei halimud lame'ah ha-21.* [Adjusting the curricula and learning materials to the 21st century]. Center for Knowledge and Research in Education, The Israel Academy of Sciences and Humanities. (In Hebrew).

Active Viewing: Multiple-Screen Learning in a Future Learning Space

Miki Kritz

Introduction: The Need for Multiple Screens in Teaching and Learning

In teaching courses such as Integrating Technological Applications in Class, an inherent difficulty emerges due to the need to present at least three perspectives of the learned subject. For example, when teaching students how to use learning-enhancing software (an educational "platform," "tool," or "application"), teachers often lean on a presentation that offers a single perspective. Educational applications usually have a teacher's interface used by teachers to build a learning unit and a student interface the students use to carry out the unit's assignments. The need arises to teach the students how to use both interfaces, offering two additional perspectives. By displaying them simultaneously, learners can notice how they interrelate, enriching their polyphonic wisdom in the learned subject. Polyphonic wisdom stems from an empowering synergy between the four components of a learning environment: a pedagogy that agrees with the content and the learning space, physical and online learning space, the learned content, and technology selected to support the pedagogy. With the constitutive values of humanism and socio-constructivism that underly all the teaching models proposed in this book, all these result in an ability to apply polyphonic wisdom.

The theoretical and practical aspects of the mentioned difficulty exist in education, specifically in teacher education, waiting for a solution. A Future Learning Space (FLS), where several television screens display side-by-side different aspects of a learned subject, illustrates how a change in one interface (e.g., the displayed teacher's interface) affects another (e.g., the students' interface, displayed on

M. Kritz (✉)
Kibbutzim College of Education, Technology and Arts, Tel-Aviv, Israel
e-mail: miki.kritz@smkb.ac.il

Y. Yondler et al. (eds.), *Cultivating Future-Oriented Learners*, Understanding Teaching-Learning Practice, https://doi.org/10.1007/978-3-031-63253-2_14

another screen). A third screen displaying the lesson's outline presentation offers a broader context of the lesson's progress. Illustrating the interconnection between the learned subject's components deepens understanding and yields an empowering synergy between the learning space components and the humanizing and socio-constructivist values discussed below.

This unique teaching model promises to improve the learners' understanding, offering a tool to meet the difficulty of simultaneously illustrating various aspects of a learned subject. The present chapter describes the model's use in FLS teaching, the added value of using three screens simultaneously in class, and the insights gained from this experience. This chapter aims to assist teachers in advancing the ongoing pedagogical need for humanizing collaborative teaching by using this multiple-screen teaching model.

Background

Technological Personalized Learning Models in Hybrid Learning Environments

In Hybrid learning, education shifts from teacher-focused to student-focused environments (Alamri et al., 2021). In this chapter and throughout the book, the term "hybrid learning spaces" refers to teaching in a technology-rich face-to-face and online learning space. This teaching combines a humanizing approach, encouraging active involvement of the learner in an individually optimal learning mode (Aloni 2014a, b) with a socio-constructivist approach (Vygotsky, 2004), encouraging knowledge building through social interaction (OECD, 2018).

Learning Environment Development

Technology has become an irreversible force generating changes in teaching and learning methods. Teaching and learning increasingly employ cloud computing, learning analytics, big data, and artificial intelligence. Education researchers have been looking for ways to integrate innovative means into traditional learning modes to enrich the learning experience and make it more effective. Pedagogical and technological innovations have enhanced and empowered the learning spaces, now collectively known as "smart learning spaces" or "future learning spaces." They incorporate various terms such as "flexible learning," "personalized learning," "mobile learning," "adaptive learning" (using computer algorithms to adapt the learned content to the needs and abilities of individual learners), and "mixed learning." New terms and definitions related to smart learning spaces keep emerging (Cheung et al., 2021). Some have assimilated into the accelerated hybrid teaching and learning that accompanied the COVID-19 pandemic (Núñez-Canal et al., 2022).

Smart Learning Spaces

Smart learning spaces aim to make the learning more flexible and efficient, involve the learners, and enhance the learners' capacity to contend with learning challenges and reflect on the learned subjects (Gambo & Shakir, 2023; Spector, 2014). To this end they combine formal and informal learning (Gros, 2016). They are designed as an adaptive system that improves the learning experience by meeting students' learning abilities, preferences, and progress, increasing student involvement, access to knowledge, feedback, and guidance. To achieve these ends, they use rich media with access to information relevant to real life, harnessing technology to keep improving the learning environment (Singh & Hassan, 2017). Academic researchers have been exploring smart learning environments. A simple Google Scholar search of "Smart learning environment" yielded in October 2023 about 24,000 articles.

Numerous studies have researched the impact of digital technology on education, highlighting the complexity involved in teaching and learning. Technological developments and AI applications present educational communities with numerous possible resolutions of varied academic challenges (Dimitriadou & Lanitis, 2023). They ultimately intend to integrate digital technologies in learning spaces to complement face-to-face teaching and learning. A classroom can become a smart teaching and learning space by integrating technology to make curricular teaching more efficient and respond to individual learning needs. Turning traditional classes into technology-rich smart learning spaces has several advantages: Automated distribution of educational resources makes it more time-effective, improves teaching and learning by blurring the boundaries between physical and digital spaces, boosts flexibility and mobility thus creating more learning opportunities, frees teaching time to respond to individual needs, adds time to completing assignments, improves students' focus on the learning purposes, and encourages students to regulate their learning according to their abilities and needs (Bogiannidis et al., 2022). This chapter demonstrates how to turn a traditional classroom into a smart teaching and learning space.

Future Learning Spaces (FLS)

The ongoing development of science, technology, economy, and society has diversified the learning spaces and their functioning (Abdelshiheed et al., 2023). In 2020, the COVID-19 pandemic has significantly accelerated the development of online learning spaces. A comprehensive study conducted in 2022 (170 universities and 960 faculty members in Europe and North America) revealed that in many learning programs, students have access to innovative interactive learning spaces (ILS) and active learning spaces (a sub-category of ILS). Room design, enabling technology, flexible teaming and seating in class, and lack of opportunity for practical experience are a challenge in implementing active learning in full (Ben Farrow & Wetzel, 2022).

The following example, a 2020 description of an innovative learning space in an elementary school in central Israel, illustrates this point:

> The planning of the physical space epitomizes physical, esthetical, and, of course, virtual architectural innovation. The space offers a dynamic response to varied instruction-learning-assessment frameworks on the class, group, and individual level (including students with ADHD) and to students' diverse preferences, such as learning styles (standing desks, floor desks, interpersonal space, quiet corners, group tables). The space features desktop computers, laptops, 3D binoculars, tablets, and a creative art corner connecting directly to informal out-of-class areas such as lawns, pet corners, and a library. The traditional classroom board is replaced by a projector and mobile erasable whiteboards that move between the learning spots. The physical space design is flexible, multi-purpose, and readily changed to suit the changing needs. It allows for varied interactions between teaching-learning and active experiences adjusted to the present and future needs. (Rotary-Saban, 2020)

An innovative learning space is not necessarily physical. A study of formal learning via social media describes the advantages of such learning: It is a significant hub of learning, motivation, and involvement, facilitating intercultural adaptation and boosting communication skills and global intercultural interaction. Additional advantages mentioned were convenience, collaboration, and connections across geographical boundaries. Among its mentioned disadvantages were being distractive, time-consuming, and interpersonally challenging. Resource and source reliability could also be a problem. The improvements suggested in using social media as learning spaces included recommendations to offer guidance by integrating educators into social media and devising means and methods to manage students' social media (Alesia, 2022).

New hybrid learning space models emerged during the emergency distance learning the COVID-19 pandemic imposed on education systems and academic institutions. While it became clear that combining classroom and online teaching was possible, these models also revealed the critical value of integrating technology into education (Shohel et al., 2022).

Despite this, research on innovative learning spaces has not been sufficiently thorough yet (Abdelshiheed et al., 2023; Shi et al., 2021). The present chapter describes how teachers-to-be have used a Future Learning Space in a teachers' education college and offers additional suggestions based on insights gained.

Description of the Course Implementing the Multiple-Screen Learning Model

Integrating Technological Applications in Class is a course that explores ways of using digital tools in class to activate learners in various matters, provide real-time feedback and assessment of the learning status, and facilitate personalized learning. These advantages make the learners more involved and active and enhance their learning. The COVID-19 pandemic has upended our world and compelled us to reinvent education and other life aspects. The previously recommended creativity and entrepreneurship in preparation for the twenty-first century have become essential survival means. This state of affairs has turned the digital world into an increasingly significant success factor in every area of life. The primary purpose of the course was to instruct teachers-to-be on integrating digital tools into their classroom teaching.

Learner Activation and Humanistic Aspects

The course aims to use optimally the options embodied in the smart FLS, achieve maximum learner involvement, and apply collaborative learning. The various teaching and learning theories and teaching models recommend keeping the learners active during the lessons (Akhtar & Saeed, 2021). Yet, this seems to be the most challenging and unpredictable aspect of a lesson. A lesson that initially progresses as planned, sometimes following a presentation, becomes chaotic once the learners have to take action. For example, once asked to use technological tools for learning purposes, unpredicted difficulties emerge due to learners' different extent of cooperation, ability to concentrate, level of understanding, and learning pace. Using multiple screens for demonstration serves those at different points on the lesson progress axis: One screen presents the lesson outline, the assignment, and the password to enter the tool being learned, while the learned tool interfaces are displayed on other screens. Struggling learners or those whose learning pace is slower can complete the required activity and the parts they missed in their own time and proceed in collaboration with their co-learners.

The humanistic education worldview sees the ultimate purpose of human thinking and actions in promoting human development, well-being, and dignity (Aloni, 2014a, b; Walukow et al., 2023). New education and innovative teaching place the learner at the center and adjust the educational process to individual capabilities and limitations, learner curiosity and specific wishes, and other humanizing aspects (Shmakova et al., 2021). The following paragraphs illustrate how the proposed teaching model articulates polyphonic wisdom. We will show that the proposed model focuses on the learners and adjusts to their capabilities, accommodating the teaching demands to the learners' concentration capacity and progress pace while at the same time using varied illustrative means and promoting peer teaching and collective learning. Moreover, we will show how technology-rich face-to-face and online learning spaces foster collaborative relationships in the spirit of the sociocultural and humanizing education approach.

Activity in a Multiple-Screen Learning Model

The physical and digital means available in an FLS classroom enable advancing various pedagogical aspects. The teacher uses his screen to show the lesson plan on a presentation and give learners instructions. The teacher also uses additional screens to explain the learned educational application. After introducing the application in a presentation projected on the teacher's main screen, the application interface appears on a second screen. While seeing the instructions to enter the application on the main screen, the students can see the application on a second screen. The teaching thus becomes more personalized, adjusting to students whose learning pace is slower, who have concentration difficulties, or who arrive late for class.

While the students learn—often collaboratively in a group—how to use the learned application and what options are available for implementing it in teaching, they move the mobile chairs and gather around other mobile or fixed screens in the FLS for group work. Often, one group member connects to the screen, and the others watch the group products or meet in the application for joint work. The same group screen is used later in the lesson to display the group's products before the whole class. Working in small, intimate groups encourages the students to be more involved in learning (Casquero-Modrego et al., 2022). The available multiple screens enable using varied illustration means, boosting peer teaching and collaborative learning. This links the content, space, and pedagogy, channeling technology in this direction. Combined, these components eventually give rise to polyphonic wisdom.

Schematic Description of the Multiple Screen Learning Model

The model uses simultaneously three screens to illustrate pedagogical uses of technological tools:

(a) A teacher's screen displaying the lesson outline and activity instructions.
(b) A screen of the teacher's interface with the application.
(c) A screen of the students' interface with the application, displaying the learned application.

This model may be applied to different pedagogies and topics, displaying simultaneously parallel processes or several aspects. Its implementation comes particularly handy during learner activation, often the most complex and challenging part of a lesson. If the lesson includes group activity, we recommend using additional group screens.

Model Activity

The presented teaching model uses screens for dynamic student activation. It is flexible and may include up to five stages according to need. It is possible to apply using, for example, stages 1 and 5 or 2 and 5 described below.

Stage 1: Using the Main Screen (Screen 1) to Introduce the Learned Application and the Instructions for Its Use

The teacher introduces the lesson's topic on Screen 1. He or she introduce the learned application and the instructions for its use (for example, how to enter it). If the number of students is high, it may be best to project the presentation on all the classroom screens to ensure that those sitting away from the podium can watch it. The teacher manages the presentation from the podium.

Stage 2: Adding Secondary Screens to Demonstrate the Activity Against the Instructions on Screen 1

At this stage, the teacher activates two secondary screens (Screen 2 and 3), showing the interfaces of the learned application and the activity planned on it. Thus, the activity instructions are on Screen 1, while screens 2 and 3 show the learned activity from the teacher's and students' perspectives, respectively. At this stage, the teacher connects screen 2 to an end device such as a laptop, iPad, smartphone, or any other device installed with the learned application and uses the teacher's interface on screen 2 to demonstrate the activity that uses this application. Screen 3 displays the students' interface with their activity. This arrangement allows more advanced students to progress faster, use their personal devices to enter the application following the instructions on Screen 1, and start exploring it as future teachers and design an activity. Slower students or those who joined the activity later than others can watch the class activity instructions on Screen 1 and advance at their own pace. This way, collaborative group work is possible despite the gaps in the capabilities and pace of the group members. Instead of presenting the components of the learned topic in a row, multiple-screen learning presents them in parallel, expanding the learners' options and flexibility in determining their pace and mode of progress, thus increasing the personalized and humanizing aspects of the learning. Integrated technological means, simultaneous multiple learning channels, and the humanizing flexible learning space promote the polyphonic wisdom paradigm that stands at the center of this book.

Stage 3: Student Group Activity Using the Group Screens

Once the students have read the learned tool's operation instructions on Screen 1, watched the demonstration and usage of the tool on the teacher's interface, and saw on Screen 3 the students' side of performing the learned activity with the tool, they enter the application to experience using it. They form teams that carry out the activity together using each one of the classroom screens. Each team gathers around a screen and connects to it through an end device (laptop, smartphone, tablet, or iPad). While performing the activity on the group screen, they can read the activity instructions in one or several ways: on the main screen, on an instruction sheet, through a

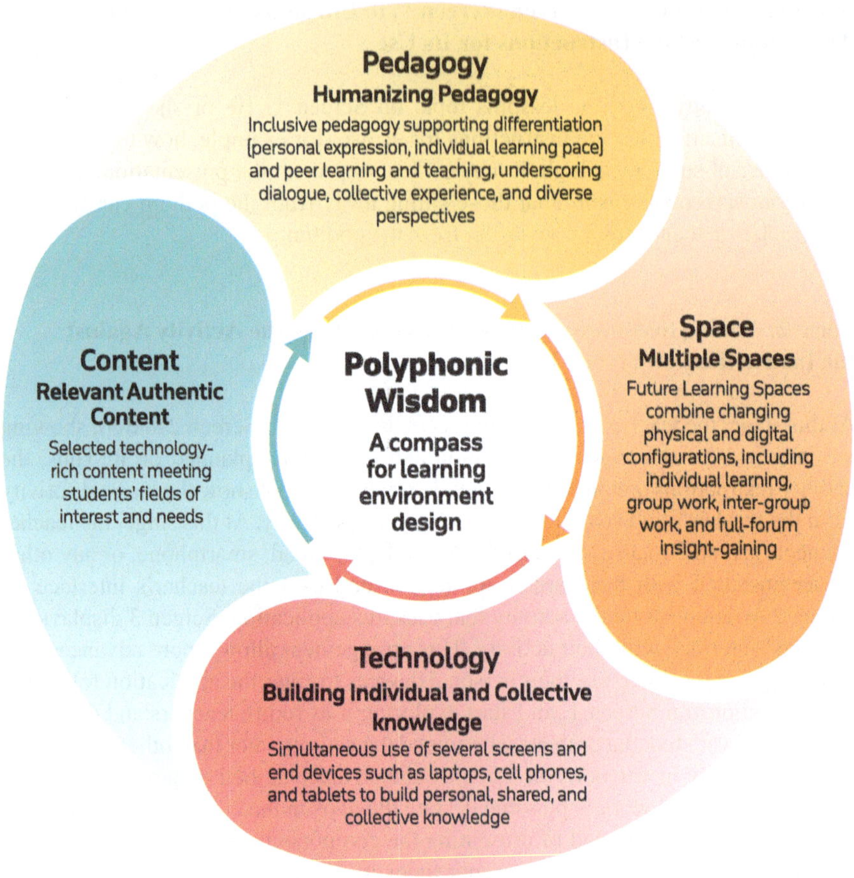

Fig. 1 The polyphonic wisdom model

link sent to each student, or on the course website. If the class comprises many students, it is possible to enlarge the teams. Students who prefer working alone rather than in a group may use their own devices instead of the group screen. While adjusting to the participants' learning pace, this humanizing option also caters to their personalities and preferences in performing the activity. The multiple-screen activity promotes diverse opinions and viewpoints on the learned subject and the humanizing collaborative nature of the learning (Fig. 1).

Stage 4: Activity and Product Presentation on the Team Screens Before the Course Plenum

Once one or all the groups have completed the activity or the activity time has ended, each group presents in its turn the product it created with the learned application before the whole class. The class members switch from their group screen to that of the presenting group and form a half-circle around it. Moving between group screens and hearing different presenters adds interest to the lesson. It refreshes the students' alertness, increasing their interest in the learned content and alleviating monotony and concentration difficulties.

Stage 5: Lesson Summary on the Main Screen

The teacher summarizes the lesson on the main screen from the podium, recapping its content and activity, which is still on display on the groups' screens. The teacher also presents the lesson summary on Screen 1. Screen 2 continues to display the application's teacher interface, where the activity was designed, while screen 3, the learners' interface, shows the students' activity. The group screens dispersed around the classroom display the products of the group activities. Over the summary, the teacher may refer to the different screens, concretizing the abstract summary and assisting learners with diverse learning styles and abstract understanding levels in understanding the studied material. The lesson ends with discussing how the tool supports understanding a learned topic. At the end of this and any other lesson, the teachers may ask the students to briefly summarize in their own words what they learned in the lesson and have the other students complement the missing parts.

We have shown that the multiple-screen model creates a learning experience that encourages learner involvement and dissolves teacher-student hierarchy through movement between their traditional roles and making those roles more flexible. In multiple-screen teaching, the students' products displayed on the group screens stand at the center. Individual and small-group voices are the components creating the whole forum polyphony. Empowering the learners and placing them centerstage are additional values—pedagogical and collaborative—of the multiple-screen display, engendering together a polyphonic model.

Practical Contribution and Insights Gained from Multiple-Screen Use in an FLS Classroom

Teaching in an FLS classroom offers a more varied experience than a regular one. While using such a classroom in the traditional way is possible, sometimes the physical and technological flexibility it offers concretizes the learning and increases the students' involvement. In a traditional classroom, teaching is confined to the conventional means.

The students' learning experience is somewhat challenging as they must overcome technological obstacles and give up the comfort zone of the traditional classroom and individual learning. In most cases, students will not leave their comfort zone and experience another type of learning unless the teachers take specific measures to activate them.

During the teaching of the course Integration of Technological Applications in the Classroom, the students appeared to struggle with the technology but felt great satisfaction once they succeeded. Over the process, technology stands at the center, becoming a significant part of the lesson. By concretizing the learned content, technology, one of the course topics, enhances the learning. This significant contribution of the FLS classroom can also apply to many other courses, allowing the use of technology and expanding the repertoire of uses this physital (combined physical and digital) space offers.

Technology stands ready behind the scenes to allow for a better, more humanizing, personified, and group-oriented pedagogy. However, the insufficient technological skills of teachers and students in the education system are weak points that call for improvement (Alamri et al., 2021).

The complexity and diversity of classroom technology require teaching it formally in a course to ensure that students master it. Yet, it is also possible to simplify classroom technology or give up part of its capabilities. For example, when the FLS classroom first became operative, connecting to any of the room's numerous screens from any mobile device was possible. This task was complicated, requiring specialized software to connect each device to the system. Realizing that teachers and students both struggled with this complexity, a small computer was installed next to each screen, allowing them to function independently and locally as separate workstations. Student groups can consequently work on a particular screen without connecting to the complex classroom network. While narrowing the potential options, this friendly method is simple to operate.

We recommend to organize and impart to the students the knowledge required to use classroom technology. One way to achieve this is by appointing "technology trustees," students who have already experienced using it and can assist those about to delve into it. It is essential to motivate the students to use this technology, as it is much simpler to give it up. While outstanding students will employ technology to improve their classroom activity, struggling students can be motivated by extra points and improved grades for technology use. Once the students master the technology and can benefit from the pedagogy it enables, such as working in groups and illustrating the learned topics to the entire class, the increased activation of students through using FLS technology could reduce the need for a teacher's presence. While a teacher must be present in every lesson, at least to summarize it, examining whether his or her presence is required over the entire lesson is worth investigating.

References

Abdelshiheed, M., Maniktala, M., Barnes, T., & Chi, M. (2023). Assessing competency using metacognition and motivation: The role of time-awareness in preparation for future learning. *arXiv preprint arXiv:2303.14609*.

Akhtar, M., & Saeed, M. (2021). Applying activity based learning (ABL) in improving quality of teaching at secondary school level. *Pakistan Journal of Educational Research and Evaluation (PJERE), 3*(2).

Alamri, H. A., Watson, S., & Watson, W. (2021). Learning technology models that support personalization within blended learning environments in higher education. *TechTrends, 65*, 62–78. https://doi.org/10.1007/s11528-020-00530-3

Aleisa, N. A. A. (2022). Graduate students' use of social media as a learning space. *Cogent Education, 9*(1), 2010486.

Aloni, N. (1999/Revised 2014a). Humanistic education. In M. Peters, T. Besley, A. Gibbons, B. Žarnić, & P. Ghiraldelli (Eds.), *The encyclopedia of educational philosophy and theory.* Retrieved October 18, 2014.

Aloni, N. (2014b). Dialogic education. In M. Peters, T. Besley, A. Gibbons, B. Žarnić, & P. Ghiraldelli (Eds.), *The encyclopaedia of educational philosophy and theory.* Retrieved October 18, 2014.

Ben Farrow, C., & Wetzel, E. M. (2022). Faculty perceptions of interactive learning spaces within construction programs. *Journal of Civil Engineering Education, 148*(2), 04021017.

Bogiannidis, N., Southcott, J., & Gindidis, M. (2022). An exploration of the lived experiences of a visual art teacher in a smart classroom. *Contemporary Educational Technology, 14*(1), ep329.

Casquero-Modrego, N., Núñez-Andrés, M. A., & Iniesto-Alba, M. J. (2022). Effects of small-group learning on the assessment of professional skills through a PBL activity. *Transactions in GIS, 26*, 1735–1753.

Cheung, S. K. S., Kwok, L. F., Phusavat, K., et al. (2021). Shaping the future learning environments with smart elements: Challenges and opportunities. *International Journal of Educational Technology in Higher Education, 18*, 16. https://doi.org/10.1186/s41239-021-00254-1

Dimitriadou, E., & Lanitis, A. (2023). A critical evaluation, challenges, and future perspectives of using artificial intelligence and emerging technologies in smart classrooms. *Smart Learning Environments, 10*(1), 1–26.

Gambo, Y., & Shakir, M. Z. (2023). Evaluating students' experiences in self-regulated smart learning environment. *Education and Information Technologies, 28*(1), 547–580.

Gros, B. (2016). The design of smart educational environments. *Smart Learning Environments, 3*, 15. https://doi.org/10.1186/s40561-016-0039-x

Núñez-Canal, M., de Obesso, M. D. L. M., & Pérez-Rivero, C. A. (2022). New challenges in higher education: A study of the digital competence of educators in Covid times. *Technological Forecasting and Social Change, 174*, 121270.

OECD. (2018). *The future of education and skills education 2030.* OECD Publishing.

Rotary-Saban, M. (2020). *Lemida rav tehumit bemerhav 'yotzrim atid', merhav hadshani uforetz derech beveit hasefer Nir beKiryat Ono* [Multidisciplanry learning in a 'Creating the future' space, an innovative ground breaking space in Nir School, Kyriat Ono]. *Hinuch heterogeni belimudey mada vetechnologic* [Heterogeic education in science and technology studies], *43*, 57–62. (In Hebrew).

Shi, H., Gao, B., & Zhou, Z. (2021, May). A survey on the satisfaction of diversified learning space in Colleges and Universities. In *6th international conference on education reform and modern management (ERMM 2021)* (pp. 267–272). Atlantis Press.

Shmakova, A., Ryzhova, Y., & Suhorukhih, A. (2021). The impact of ICT education on humanistic innovative potential. *Education and Information Technologies, 27*, 1–16.

Shohel, M. M. C., Ashrafuzzaman, M., Azim, F., Naomee, I., Rahman, M. S., & Siddik, M. A. B. (2022). Blended learning space for primary and secondary education: Challenges and opportunities in resource-constrained contexts. In *Designing effective distance and blended learning environments in K-12* (pp. 187–222). IGI Global.

Singh, A. D., & Hassan, M. (2017). In pursuit of smart learning environments for the 21st century. In: *Current and critical issues in curriculum, learning and assessment*, UNESCO International Bureau of Education. UNESCO. Retrieved from https://unesdoc.unesco.org/ark:/48223/pf0000252335.

Spector, J. M. (2014). Conceptualizing the emerging field of smart learning environments. *Smart Learning Environments, 1*, 2. https://doi.org/10.1186/s40561-014-0002-7

Vygotsky, L. (2004). *Lemida beheksher hevrati: Hitpathut hatahalichim hapsychologiim hagvohim* [Mind in society: The development of higher psychological processes]. HaKibbutz Hame'uchad—Sifriat Po'alim. (In Hebrew).

Walukow, D. S., Wesnawa, I. G. A., Kertih, I. W., & Mudana, I. W. (2023). Analysis of the effect of a humanistic approach in online learning on student independent learning and student satisfaction. *MOJEM: Malaysian Online Journal of Educational Management, 11*(2), 50–70.

Part V
Epilogue

Epilogue: Holding Both Ends of the Stick: Humanistic Empowerment and Technological Power in the Service of Education and Learning

Nimrod Aloni

A distinct and well-known characteristic of quality cultural works is the compatibility between form and content, styles and messages. This quality is present in this book starting from its title, through the statement of its intentions in the introductory chapters, to its last words. The book is polyphonic in its contents, approaches, and styles; refuses any simplistic dichotomy and reduction; and insists on the "both and" approach that establishes complex abilities—those that establish the wisdom of observation and judgment regarding the right thing, in the right place, at the right time, to the right extent, and to the right recipients.

I wish to elaborate on and demonstrate this distinct quality by reference to two masterful books published in recent years—by thinkers known as public intellectuals whose skills go beyond content expertise or academic scholarship. The first is Micah Goodman's *Broken Attention: How to Heal a World Fractured by Technology* (2021). As with any technological revolution, Goodman claims, in the digital revolution for all its blessings and achievements, human and social costs are involved. The devotion to the screen culture, let alone addiction to the digital style of living, has led to social distancing, alienation from natural and cultural assets, and an increase in the levels of mental "stress", loneliness, depression and suicide. Basic life skills are damaged, such as: orientation in physical spaces, reading other people's emotions, complex judgments, discernment and diagnosis skills, empathic imagination, social intelligence, sense of proportion, and good taste. At the root of the new disabilities that digital technology has imposed on us—via processes of self-maiming and self-crippling—is the loss of sensitivity, attention, attentiveness, and reflexivity: in our relationships with ourselves, with others, with the natural environment and with the works of culture. This is a process that eradicates our ability to enjoy a life of quality in its fullness, of attentive dialogue, of social cohesion,

N. Aloni (✉)
Kibbutzim College of Education, Technology and Arts, Tel-Aviv, Israel
e-mail: Nimrod.Aloni@smkb.ac.il

Y. Yondler et al. (eds.), *Cultivating Future-Oriented Learners*, Understanding Teaching-Learning Practice, https://doi.org/10.1007/978-3-031-63253-2_15

and of a humanist democracy. The price is both psychological, in the areas of mental emptiness and emotional suffering, as well as in the public space and the political arena: in extremism, polarization and populism that are fueled in social media and threaten to eliminate liberal and pluralist democracy.

The second book that wisely and critically informs us of the hardships and challenges of the twenty-first century is that of the historian Yuval Noah Harari *The History of Tomorrow* (2015). On the one hand, Harari claims, it is quite clear that the most significant growth engine these days is scientific-technological progress. Since the nineteenth century, we have witnessed an acceleration in scientific and technological developments and the rise of knowledge economy. Those who do not keep up to date are left behind and condemn themselves to a decrease in their ability to sustain a quality of life, to a low standard of living and an inability to compete in the global economy. On the other hand, the uninhibited race for economic growth, through technological innovations and neo-liberal capitalist competition to increase profits, could easily bring upon us an ecological holocaust, a class-based and divisive society, and the elimination of democracy in favor of populist and authoritarian regimes. Furthermore, the penetration of digital technology into all areas of life and the latest developments in the field of artificial intelligence pose an immediate and tangible danger to freedom of thought and will and makes more dramatic the treat from thought and behaviour engineering. Therefore, Harari claims, the main task of twenty-first century humanity is to protect itself from its own unleashed scientific and technological powers, and to employ its humanist powers in ethical deliberation and practical wisdom to ensure the sustainability and flourishing of both human culture and the natural environment.

The distinct characteristic of the books by Goodman and Harari and their relevance to this book—which concerns a new educational strategy for addressing and coping with the challenges of the twenty-first century digital revolution—is that they are not tempted to take the easy one-sided path of choosing a dichotomous and simplistic approach. Instead, they seek to hold the stick at both ends and challenge us to develop complex thinking and practical wisdom for the sake of leading a full and sustainable life. In explicit words, both Micah Goodman and Yuval Noah Harari accept the emerging reality of the dominance of digital technology and its contribution to higher standards of living, but at the same time both call us to develop practices of humanization through observation, meditation, ethical deliberation, intimacy and empathy with nature and fellow humans, critical engagement with intellectual traditions, and responsibility for the common good. Precisely in view of the acceleration in the obsessive races for material wealth, social success, speed, efficiency, and technological refinements, in their opinion, a balancing intensive investment is required in the development of intellectual, moral, and spiritual resilience. Such capacities or spiritual foundations are badly needed if we are to succeed in curbing the terrible slide into the crumbling and destructive culture of addictions, loneliness, violence, depression, consumerism, and alienation that are empirically associated with the digital age and the pressing social-environmental crisis.

It is against the background of this wise and responsible strategy of grasping both ends of the stick that the polyphonic approach of this book and the insistence on cooperative-humanistic pedagogy and hybrid learning spaces should be understood.

Comforting yet inadequate solutions are embodied in sticking to the orthodox frontal and subject-centered pedagogy, while ignoring the alienation and boredom it imposes on students, as well as in giving up the assets of liberal education and classroom discussion learning in favor of total dedication to digital technology. The desired and balanced solution, in my opinion and in the spirit of this book, is to harness the multidisciplinary, multivocal, multicultural and the manifold digital learning media to develop complex abilities of feeling, thinking, imagining, and social interaction—including acute caring and responsibility for the common good.

After all, if we have learned anything from the lessons of the ideologies and cultural trends of the twentieth century, it is precisely the lesson of avoiding getting caught up with the "wave"—with any blind conformism and admiration to some absolute truth, ideal, theory or method. As Martin Buber puts it, "The first task of genuine educators" is "to rescue one's real personal self from the fiery jaws of collectivism which devours all selfhood… To keep the pain awake, to waken the desire" for personal agency and full life (1971, p. 492). As educators, we are not interested in raising religious or secular students, left-wing or right-wing children, but rather cultivate and empower individuals endowed with complex mental capacities—emotional, intellectual, and social—which would help them to deal wisely with the predicaments and challenges of the lived reality—for the benefit of their personal development and for the promotion of the shared good.

I would like to offer another conceptualization of the usefulness of the educational strategy presented in this book. I will call this activist pedagogy, evident in three life-spaces: the inner-personal space that focuses on activating personal agency, the social or public space that focuses on activating political agency, and the pedagogical-didactic space that focuses on activating learning agency (Aloni and Veugelers, 2023). It is to the third form of activist pedagogy that we should attend first, because it is directly linked with the innovation this book is introducing in hands-on, holistic and polyphonic teaching-learning strategies: summoning digital technology, manifold learning media, and a host of hybrid didactic features for activating experiential and meaningful learning to classes of students who have been alienated from learning by the traditional and standardized old pedagogy. In other words, a central and valuable feature of this book lies in its exploration of spaces of polyphonic and hybrid didactic formats that open opportunities for diverse forms of independent and group hybrid learning, exploratory learning and project-based learning, place-based learning, and global and multicultural learning.

A second space where hybrid, polyphonic, interdisciplinary, constructivist, and cooperative learning is linked with activist pedagogy focuses on the cultivation and empowerment of self-agency and development of the student's personality; namely, employing these methods in the service of activating and intensifying humanizing processes in the souls and minds of the students towards a more complete humanity. In line with the aims of existentialist, critical, and progressive educational theories, activating the inner-personal space by means of such innovative, diverse, and hybrid forms of learning amounts to combating the vices of inertia, conformity, and submissiveness and celebrating the virtues of personal agency, autonomy, creativity, critical thinking, entrepreneurship, and authentic vitality.

The third space of activist pedagogy that benefits from the innovative, polyphonic, and hybrid pedagogies advanced in this book is the social-political one. It amounts to new possibilities for empowering social engagement, political literacy, and agency towards a more just and humane social order. As argued in the book's Introduction, we live in times of dramatic change, global reality marked by a "permanent and continuous crisis": environmental, democratic, social, and cultural. Global warming and the destruction of the natural environment, political populism and extremism, growing socio-economic gaps, social distancing and rise in mental sickness, the prevalence of "post-truth" and "fake-news" mentality on social media, and the declining respect for broad learning and serious culture—these are all global phenomena that put the new generations at serious risks. From our perspective as educators, overcoming these risks is essential for working towards a flourishing and sustainable future. Hence, one promise of the innovative, hybrid, and polyphonic pedagogy canvased in this book is that it would contribute to WHAT the known demands of us: that educators around the world, as Giroux puts it, would engage themselves in the "struggle for ways in which the pedagogical can be made more political and the political made more pedagogical" (1988, p. 63–64). With its emphasis on polyphonic discourse, the contribution of this book for enhancing social justice and humanist democracy goes even further. As Roger Simon puts it, it "encourages and make possible the realization of a variety of differentiated human capacities" (1987, p. 372) as well as "enabling those who have been silenced to speak", and those "who have been marginalized economically and culturally to claim in both respects a status as full participating members of a community" (1987, p. 374).

What could be more suitable than ending this Epilogue with polyphonic poetry? In an interview conducted by Helit Yeshuron with the poet Yehuda Amichai (2016), she feels baffled by the fact that throughout his long writing career he avoided writing political and controversial poetry, unlike colleagues such as Natan Zach and Dalia Rabikowitz. His straight and simple answer was that he doesn't have to address directly political topics because "my poetry helps those who read it to become non-fascists". He then presents a more complete answer, linking the blessing of polyphony—in the sense of acquainting the readers with multiple, diverse, and complex perspectives and nuances of the human experience—to generating processes of humanization. He demonstrates it in two of his well-known poems. The first, "A Man in his Life", where he states that "Ecclesiastes was wrong to claim" that "there is a time for everything" and that in dealing with life's challenges one must adopt one pattern of behavior at a time and reject the others. "A man in his life has no time to have time for everything," claims Amichai, and it is better to approach each of life's challenges with a broad, rich, and diverse spectrum of sensitivities, insights and perspectives. And in the second poem, titled "What Kind of a Person", Amichai demonstrates through his own personality the blessing of polyphony: " I'm a person with a complex plumbing of the soul, sophisticated instruments of feeling and a system of controlled memory at the end of the twentieth century"—a blessing that keeps us humans from losing our human image and degrading our human dignity by simplistic, light-headed and narrow-minded solutions.

References

Aloni, N., & Veugelers, W. (2023). Ecohumanism, democratic culture and activist pedagogy: Attending to what the known demands of us. *Educational Philosophy and Theory*. https://doi.org/10.1080/00131857.2023.2295216

Amichai, Y. (2016). *A man in his life*. https://onbeing.org/poetry/a-man-in-his-life/

Amichai, Y. (n.d.). *What kind of a person*. https://allpoetry.com/What-Kind-Of-A-Person

Buber, M. (1971). On the education of character. In J. P. Strain (Ed.), *Modern philosophies of education*. Random House.

Giroux, H. A. (1988). Literacy and the pedagogy of voice and political empowerment. *Educational Theory, 38*(1), 61–75.

Goodman, M. (2021). *Broken attention: How to heal a world fractured by technology* (Hebrew). Kinneret, Zamora, Dvir, 2021 [Hebrew]).

Harari, Y. N. (2015). *The history of tomorrow* (Hebrew). Kinneret, Zamora, Dvir.

Simon, R. (1987). Empowerment as a pedagogy of possibility. *Language Arts, 64*(4), 370–383.

Yeshuron, Helit (2016). *How did you do it? Interviews with poets* (Hebrew). Kibbutz Meuhad.

The manufacturer's authorised representative in the EU is Springer Nature Customer Service Centre GmbH, Europaplatz 3, 69115 Heidelberg, Germany. If you have any concerns regarding our products, please contact ProductSafety@springernature.com

Printed and bound by CPI Group (UK) Ltd, Croydon, CR0 4YY
30/09/2026
02225238-0002